The Mindbenders

A Look At Current Cults

JACK SPARKS

THOMAS NELSON PUBLISHERS
Nashville

Ninth Printing

Copyright © 1977, 1979 by Jack N. Sparks

Second Edition

Library of Congress Cataloging in Publication Data

Sparks, Jack.
  The mindbenders.

  Includes bibliographical references.
  1. Cult. I. Title.
BP603.S65   291   77-3564
ISBN 0-8407-5686-0

Preface

Though this book bears my name as author, it is really the joint production of three men. Dick Ballew and Jon Braun labored fully as much as I in bringing this work together. We planned, researched, debated, and wrote together as a unit. The result is a book we believe truly offers vital information on, and refutation of, seven of the most dangerous new cults of our day.

You may legitimately ask why we chose the seven cults we did from among the host of new sects emerging in this country. The answer is simple:

First, we chose from among the groups with which we were most familiar.

Second, we wanted to refute the most dangerous cults and those most likely to be encountered.

Also entering into our decision was the degree to which the seven cults are managing to attract a following.

Admittedly, there are some very dangerous cults we did not include. What we have done with these seven, however, will be found valuable in understanding and dealing with many others. Much of the refutation can be directly applied to similar groups. Most Hindu-type sects have a religious and philosophical base identical to those we have analyzed.

When we came to Berkeley in 1969 and established the Christian World Liberation Front, I faced some of these new cults for the first time. Within a week, I had my first encounter with a follower of Sun Myung Moon. Within six months, we had our first convert from the Hare Krishna sect. That same year there was a harsh brush with part of the core group which became the Children of God. That experience taught us to keep an eye on them and their progress. Always around during these years have been the devotees of Maharishi Mahesh Yogi's Transcendental Meditation. His devious promotional methods have been an education in the power of advertising and organization.

From the early seventies on, we have also occasionally run into the campaign of The Way, International, which inserted itself everywhere the so-called "Jesus Movement" brought significant numbers of young people together. We have also seen and experienced the influence of Witness Lee and his "Local Church" in our midst. In 1972 we watched the spectacular rise of Maharaj Ji, the teenaged guru from India, who subsequently fell from his great heights of popularity and yet maintains a significant following. Along the way we've ministered to many whose lives have been damaged by one cult or another.

This book comes as a result of our conviction that it is time to give a clear picture of what these cults do, and what they believe, in contrast to the Christian Church. We have concentrated especially on the theological differences between Christianity and the seven sects. What people believe about God *is* important and it does affect what they do. Always and forever the historic, orthodox Christian faith has been called upon by God to stand against heresy and the efforts of Satan to destroy human lives. We have taken here the kind of strong stand we believe is required to fight Satan's vicious efforts.

We must not forget the Church of Jesus Christ is meant to be an outpost of the kingdom of God in this world, a priesthood led by the Holy Spirit. In every time and in every way we must be true to our God, reflecting our knowledge of His nature and obeying His commands. Our objective has been to demonstrate how strikingly these cults differ from the Christian Church and how they are bending peoples' minds rather than guiding them under voluntary subjection to the Triune God.

We must acknowledge assistance from many others. Our associates, Ken Berven, Peter Gillquist, Ray Nethery, and Gordon Walker have been of inestimable help. Linda Wallace, Peggy King, and Mary Phillips have typed everything many times without complaint—even with enthusiasm. Marc Dunaway gave unstinting help in proofreading and running errands. From a great host of sources came information which we simply could not have collected on our own.

Among the sources we must not forget to mention are Mr.

and Mrs. J. C. Crampton of Redondo Beach; Alan Wallerstedt, Spiritual Counterfeits Project of Berkeley; and the library of the Graduate Theological Union in Berkeley.

Our efforts here have been put forth in the service of Christ and His kingdom. We trust that the Church will be benefited by these refutations of her enemies.

Jack Sparks
Berkeley, California

Preface to the Second Edition

There is just one reason for this particular revision of *Mindbenders:* The dramatic and sudden climax of the Peoples Temple cult, founded and led by Jim Jones, has raised some issues about the Christian Church, issues not seen in any of the other cults we examined in the first edition. We considered the matter serious enough to undertake an immediate analysis, refutation, and statement.

Of course, in the whole dark and devilish realm of anti-Christian religions, the scene is constantly shifting as the battle of the two kingdoms continues. Those groups we refuted in the first edition of *Mindbenders* are still around and continuing to play an active role in Satan's desperate efforts to overthrow the kingdom of Christ.

As we would have expected, there are changes. A. C. Bhaktivedanta Swami Prabhapada, founder and supreme leader of the Hare Krishna movement, died during 1978, and we have yet to see how this will ultimately affect his cult. Cracks appeared in the apparent solidarity of Witness Lee's "Local Church," as heir-apparent, Max D. Rapoport left—followed by significant numbers of cult-members in Denver, Boston, and Anaheim. Phone calls and correspondence from some of those defectors indicate that *The Mindbenders* has been helpful to them.

PREFACE

Some cults have banded together to offer a stiffer front to opposition. In April, 1978, for example, the Church of Scientology, the Unification Church, and the Children of God announced the formation of the "Alliance for the Preservation of Religious Liberty." Meanwhile, in the strange world of Guru Maharaj Ji, devotees continue oblivious to the world around them. A recent phone call to the Denver headquarters of his Divine Light Mission (concerning activities of the cult) elicited this response from the young woman who answered the phone: "I don't know anything about that. I spend all my time meditating." And so it goes.

In our task of preparing the new chapter on Jim Jones and the Peoples Temple, we had the assistance of so very many people that we cannot possibly give due credit to all. Marc Dunaway and John Finely undertook to gather information in Redwood Valley, Ukiah, and the San Francisco Bay area. They conducted many interviews and dug up invaluable written records. In Indianapolis, Rob Murray, Greg Watts, and others pursued leads and put together materials that made a coherent analysis of Jim Jones possible. Close to home, LuAnne Dunaway, Linda Wallace, and Peggy King went far beyond the call of duty to make sure all was completed on time. Our thanks to them and others who remain unsung.

J. N. S.
January 15, 1979
Isla Vista, California

Contents

PART I

Yardstick for Truth

Yardstick for Truth

You will notice several unique things about the make-up of this book. Though it is factual in its handling of data, it is not written in technical or theological language. It is written so the average reader can grasp what these groups teach, how they operate, and why they are wrong.

Also, I have sought to make it a handy reference work that you can return to again and again. The chapters on individual cults are all organized with the same basic format.

A. An Introduction to the Cult.
B. History and Theology of the Cult.
C. Method of Operation by the Cult.
D. A Refutation of the Cult.
E. A Brief Profile of each Cult.

This format not only facilitates study, but also gives the reader a ready source for accurate data when confronting people from these cults.

Our consideration begins with a brief look at *orthodoxy,* a feature included to aid your understanding. As you would expect, many Scriptures are used to show the errors of the mindbenders. In addition, I have included quotations from the ancient creeds, the famous confessions of Christendom, and comments from great saints of the Church. My purpose here is twofold.

Above all, these cults are "one-man shows." The authority for their authenticity goes back no farther than their founders. All, except Maharishi Mahesh Yogi of Transcendental Meditation, use the Bible extensively and, of course, claim their interpretation of those Scriptures is the only correct one. It is the Church which must answer these heresies and false religions. I have sought to make sure my interpretations are thoroughly in line with the stance of the historic Christian Church.

13

The Christian Church has spoken out boldly against those who twist and pervert the truth of God. Many of the creedal and confessional statements included here still smell of the smoke of battle. They come from God's people when they had their backs against the wall. These statements were put together with great care, some of them when the very existence of the Church was threatened. Their words are battle-tried. They've weathered well. Now they are brought to duty again in these current wars.

Of course, the creeds, confessions, and writings of the saints are not Scripture. They were never even meant to rival Scripture. But they are powerful expressions of the Church's interpretation of Scripture, and I use them here so that it is far more than a matter of my interpretation of the Bible as against that of the heretics.

An appreciation of the greatness and strength of the Christian Church in the past is a second reason I've used the creeds and confessional statements. The people of God have a fantastically rich heritage. People are plenty eager these days to talk about the darker pages of the Church's history, and I'll grant that some of them are pretty grim. But there are many glorious pages, too. Some awesome wars of debate were fought and won, many at great cost. We live today in the fruit of the victories of our fathers. Appreciate those who have so boldly gone before, for they trusted in and had the leadership of the Holy Spirit. Enjoy your roots in the past. The creeds and confessions contain, perhaps, the greatest legacies they have gained for us. Their labor was not in vain in the Lord.

An Issue of Judgment

There is a certain sense in which these cults and false religions are a judgment on a modern Church which has floated adrift from its historic moorings. The Scripture is being fulfilled which says, "With what judgment you judge you shall be judged." The mod-mood of much of the contemporary Church—both liberal and conservative—has been to treat our spiritual forebearers with some degree of theological disdain. Sort of, "They were okay for their time, but our understanding is so much better." So we've pressed ahead, insisting on our right and duty to come up with our own new interpretations and our own new formulations of doctrine.

But even before the ink has dried on our modern works, they are rejected by others who insist on the same right to private judgment apart from us. We have sown a wind, and the whirlwind we are reaping is blowing our children away.

Make no mistake: these cults are growing. Daily they are picking off numbers of people, not only from religiously indifferent backgrounds, but also from staunchly Christian homes. In addition to the seven cults dealt with here, there are dozens of others, not too much different, which get their share, too. It's time to stop this wandering indifference to the ancient landmarks and return to the harbor of the faith of our fathers.

I've Seen It with My Own Eyes

This book does not grow out of theoretical observations. Over the past eight years of living in, and being involved with, a Christian community in Berkeley, I have seen the disciples of these and similar groups come and go. I have dealt with them, argued with them, pled with them, and wept with them—witnessing first-hand the devastation of many people who have been caught in the well-spun web of various of these cults.

A few years ago I performed the wedding of a young couple who had been Christians only a short time. They were eager to grow in their relationship with the Lord. After a few months they returned to the young man's home in a midwestern city. There they encountered the Local Church of Witness Lee. Soon they were followers.

When that cult established a "church" in Berkeley, they returned. No longer did I or any of their former Christian friends here have anything valid to say about the faith. No, that cult had discovered the truth "lost" by the Church for more than 1800 years. Only *it* was right. Only from Witness Lee could they learn how to worship. All other Christians were now regarded with pity.

Discussion was impossible. We were met only with tolerant smiles and the stock "Hallelujah" and "O Lord Jesus" phrases of the cult. A promising young couple disappeared into the wilderness of a mind-capturing heretical cult which sneers at

15

the doctrines of our fathers. They have lost their way, and who knows what the final result will be for them?

This young couple, going here and there under the orders of Witness Lee's cult, are only two of millions captured by these heresies. Lives are being controlled and destroyed on the pretense of offering a way to God.

The Mindbenders

These widely divergent religious movements have one awesome and terrifying thing in common. They are mindbenders. They're not just after converts in the conventional sense. They want your mind, and they want absolute control over it. All too often they succeed. The goal of their mind control is behavior modification; many call it just plain brainwashing.

The particulars vary from cult to cult, but the method is essentially the same. It's a three-step program. Not three steps in sequence, but three steps which go on simultaneously.

Step one is "deprogramming." Your past is all wrong. No matter how sincere your parents or your church may have been, they were wrong. Do you hear? Do you understand? What you always thought was right is wrong, wrong, wrong, wrong! Reject it. It cannot help but hurt you. You must not let it hinder your life any more. It's the cause of your trouble.

Step two demands your will be captured by the cult. The human will does not function apart from the mind. Thus, if the normal function of the mind can be altered, control of the will can be gained. Habitual patterns of behavior and response will be broken and a new program put in its place. All the cults accomplish this trick in basically the same manner. At some point they introduce you to a way to temporarily put your mind out of gear into a kind of "freewheeling." From the *mantra* of Transcendental Meditation to the "pray-reading" of the Local Church, the result is the same. The mind goes into neutral and the will is impaired. And you, the convert, are ready for reprogramming.

Step three is the concentrated reprogramming phase. Intensive teaching or indoctrination is the prime means. Day after day, like the dripping of rain, the old concepts are methodically dug up and the new ones planted in their place. A whole new structure is raised. In all of this the convert is hardly aware anything is taking place.

Though all these mindbending movements are religious (including Transcendental Meditation, which loudly protests it is not), there is absolutely nothing divine about their methods! I believe the mind control these groups practice is every bit as naturalistic as that used by the Communist Chinese with the POWs during the Korean War years ago. And the end result is the same.

The ideologies of these religious systems so saturate the subjects they behave almost as predictably as puppets on strings. Radically and steadily, behavior patterns change to those desired by the cult. Finally, the convert, his will now lame through "mindlessness," dutifully behaves without the conscious exercise of his will. As one ex-participant in The Way explains, "I lost my free will; I was a robot."

Those who have wrestled free from the grip of the mindbenders have had to learn to reassert their wills. The recovery period for these escapees is long in most cases. For few will the scars ever completely disappear. Some will never see their wounded personalities fully healed.

The Yardstick for Truth

"Jesus Christ is not God!" is the bold and blatant calling card of Victor Paul Wierwille, founder of The Way, International. Sun Myung Moon of the Unification Church implies he himself is the Lord of the Second Advent, the one who has come to do what Jesus Christ "failed" to do. And Witness Lee of the Local Church has announced the appointment of what amounts to a fourth member to his "Trinity," the Church. "They are now four in one," he writes.[1]

It seems inconceivable that such claims should be given a second thought by people brought up in the shadow of the Christian Church. But astonishingly, millions of people in modern America are buying these incredible notions. They are being lured into cults and false religions whose teachings echo the same tiresome blasphemies consistently refuted by the Christian Church in the past.

Some are drawn in because of desperation, some because of

rebellion against society and God. Others buy in out of curiosity, or just plain boredom. Who knows all the causes? The result is the same. It's a dead-end trip. And the cost! It is beyond estimation. Those involved have no idea how high the price is for such ventures.

One young man I know—let's call him Mitch—got attracted to Transcendental Meditation. He paid his fee and learned the technique. Being inquisitive, he wanted to learn more of what it was all about. He began reading the Hindu scriptures, and listening to a variety of gurus. When I met him, he had gone through the initiation process of Guru Maharaj Ji. As we talked about Jesus Christ, Mitch kept insisting there had to have been a succession of "spiritual masters" equal to Jesus. Each age had to have a living incarnation of God.

But then, after he had been around a while, he said he wanted to be a Christian. In his mind, however, Mitch could never quite accept Jesus as the only Son of God. The problem forever came up in conversation. He liked what he saw in Christians, but "what about the good people who follow these other leaders?" Finally, he left because we were "so authoritarian about Jesus."

That wasn't the end of our contact with Mitch, though. He kept coming back to talk. Always he harked back to his "god-consciousness" experiences in meditation. Weren't those as valid as Christian worship experience? He was never able to get past that. Our answers weren't satisfactory to Mitch, and eventually he just drifted away. Last I heard, he was following another guru who had helped him "see visions of God." Mitch has become so confused it is doubtful he will ever be able to simply come to the Lord and accept His reign.

In considering what is orthodox theology, we need to define some terms. First, the word "theology," "theo" and "logy" is really two terms. The first part, "theo," comes from a Greek word *theos* which means "God," and "logy" comes from a Greek word *logos* which means "word." So, when we talk about "theology" we mean "words about God" or "god-logy."

Everyone has a theology. Everyone has his own words or views about God. Even atheists have a theology; they don't believe there is a God beyond themselves. Agnostic theology claims to not know if God exists or not. A highly developed theology in which the topics are listed in order is termed a "systematic theology."

Another word we need to define is "orthodox," which also comes into English from two Greek words, *ortho* and *doxa*. *Orthos* means "straight, right, safe, true, or correct." The Greek word *doxa* means "belief." When you refer to that which is "orthodox," you mean "straight, safe, right, true, or correct belief." When you put orthodox and theology together, orthodox theology is straight, right, safe, correct, and true beliefs about God.

Conversely, one other word we need to understand is "heterodox." The Greek word *heteros* means "different." If you are heterodox, you are adopting different, that is, unorthodox beliefs. In Gal. 1:6 Paul says, "I am astonished that you are so quickly deserting him who called you in the grace of Christ and turning to a different gospel."

The word "different" here means a spurious gospel, a false gospel. Those who were coming into Galatia were presenting a gospel which was *heteros;* it was "another" gospel. Paul says of them in verse 9, ". . . If any one is preaching to you a gospel contrary to that which you received, let him be accursed." And so the anathema, or the curse, is placed on heterodox belief.

The word "heretic" comes from a Greek term, *hairetikos* which means someone who is factious, that is, who sets up his own beliefs in opposition to those of the orthodox beliefs. In the Church of Jesus Christ, a heretic is someone who has departed from the accepted norm of belief—from orthodox theology. The ultimate yardstick for both theology and all other matters of faith and life is what God Himself has said. The Christian Church has the true and trustworthy record of the Scriptures which God has given to humanity. Inspired by the Holy Spirit, they are the foundation of all Christian theology. The problem arises when two voices both insist on their adherence to Scripture, yet teach opposite beliefs.

Someone is bound to ask, "All right; Rev. A may call Prof. B a false prophet, while the professor insists the parson himself has departed from the faith. Both have convincing arguments. They both refer to the Scriptures as their authority. How do I know who's right?"

Almost all serious believers in Jesus Christ—and even some

19

nonbelievers—are seeking to stand for the truth. I suppose the great majority of us are fed up with new or novel doctrines. But when we say the Church of Jesus Christ stands for *orthodoxy* or *orthodox theology*, what do we mean?

The safe and correct belief in the Church of Jesus Christ is that which was taught by the twelve apostles. In Acts 2:42, after the day of Pentecost when 3,000 people came to know Christ and came into the Church, we read, "And they devoted themselves to the apostles' teaching and fellowship, to the breaking of bread and the prayers."

The apostles' teaching or the apostles' doctrine is that taught by those twelve men who spent three years with Jesus Christ and were personally taught by Him. They were commissioned by Jesus Christ to give the norm of Church doctrine, that which is orthodox theology. Therefore, any departure from that norm these men taught is *heterodox;* it is a "different" belief from the apostles' doctrine.

Now we come to the twentieth century. What is our concern with orthodox theology? Why should we teach and preach apostolic doctrine? Why must what we teach square with the doctrines taught by the twelve apostles of Jesus Christ?

In John 14:26 Jesus promised His apostles, "But the Counselor, the Holy Spirit, whom the Father will send in my name, he will teach you all things, and bring to your remembrance all that I have said to you." Jesus was saying the Holy Spirit would come after He left and would bring to their recollection everything He said during those three years.

And the promise of the Holy Spirit is for us today as well. We have the Holy Spirit in the twentieth century. Thus, whatever the Holy Spirit teaches us will be in accord (if He indeed has taught it) with apostolic doctrine. That is, it will be orthodox. The Spirit of truth does not teach a different belief!

In John 16:13 it is recorded that Jesus said, "When the Spirit of truth comes, he will guide you into all the truth; for he will not speak on his own authority, but whatever he hears he will speak, and He will declare to you the things that are to come." He will guide you, the twelve apostles, into all the truth.

Again, when He guides *us* into the truth it will be the truth that was taught by those twelve apostles as they received it from Jesus Christ. *That* is why we are concerned about orthodox

20

theology, the kind of theology in keeping with Scripture and the apostolic teachings.

As I have said, we must have the Holy Spirit in order to understand this apostolic doctrine, and all the things of God. Paul made this clear in 1 Cor. 2:14, "The unspiritual man does not receive the gifts of the Spirit of God, for they are folly to him, and he is not able to understand them, because they are spiritually discerned." We cannot *discern* the things of the Spirit unless we are *taught* by the Spirit.

The apostles made it clear that what they taught was in accord with the Scriptures. For example, when Matthew wrote, he often said, "just as it was said in the scriptures." He constantly quotes the Old Testament, showing that Jesus Christ is the fulfillment of these Scriptures. What he gives, then, is the *apostolic interpretation* of the Scriptures. Therefore, we today must base our case on Scripture.

In 2 Tim. 3:16 Paul says, "All scripture is inspired by God and profitable for teaching, for reproof, for correction, and training in righteousness." Okay—all Scripture is inspired by God and is profitable for teaching, that is, for doctrine. Thus we seek not only to depend on the Holy Spirit to teach us what is apostolic doctrine but, secondly, we know that when the Spirit guides, the result will be in accord with the Scriptures.

It is at this very point we face a critical problem with the cults, for all of them depend on a novel, different interpretation of the Scriptures. They are all "other" gospels; they depart from the apostolic orthodox theology. It is here we must oppose the *private interpretation of Scripture.* This means there are no tricky or hidden meanings of Scripture known only to the initiated few, the followers of one particular cult.

In 2 Pet. 2:1 it says, "But false prophets also arose among the people, just as there will be false teachers among you, who will secretly bring in destructive heresies [they will introduce doctrines that depart from the norm of the church, from the norm of apostolic teaching], even denying the Master who bought them, bringing upon themselves swift destruction."

How do they do this? I am not aware of a single heretic in the history of the Christian Church who did not try to base his case on Scripture! Not only do the orthodox base their cases on Scripture, *but so do the heterodox*—you must realize that. Just

21

because someone comes quoting Scripture does not necessarily mean he is teaching the truth, no more so than the fact that I am quoting Scripture means I have the truth.

Remember the question: *how* do people bring in their destructive heresies? Very simple. Peter, in 2 Pet. 1:20-21, explains it: "First of all you must understand this, that no prophecy of scripture is a matter of one's own interpretation, because no prophecy ever came by the impulse of man, but men moved by the Holy Spirit spoke from God."

Peter is saying here that *no Scripture is of any private interpretation.* What do these heretics do? They come in saying they have an "inside track" on the teaching of the Holy Spirit—that it is they who know what is apostolic doctrine, that they alone have the truth. They come in with their own private interpretations of Scripture. We in the Church stand against that.

Now the question comes: "Okay, I buy the need to be orthodox, but who gets to determine what is orthodox and what is not?" This is the crucial issue which confronts us in the twentieth century—especially when we come to dealing with current cults.

It may be helpful to note a few points of orthodox theology on which heterodox theology often differs. Deviations from these apostolic interpretations of Scripture are some of the identification marks of heresy.

One major matter is the unconditional acceptance of all of Scripture (the sixty-six canonical books) as God's revelation. Heresy is inevitable when parts of Scripture are accepted while other parts are denied.

A second vital doctrinal concern is the view of the nature of Christ. Orthodox theology holds He is fully man and fully God at the same time—two natures in one person. The controversy on this issue is not new. Appollinarius, in the fourth century A.D., stressed Christ's divine nature while making His human nature less than complete, which caused problems in relation to salvation. His teachings were condemned by the Council of Constantinople in 381.

Nestorius emphasized Christ's two natures (human and divine) to such an extent that he ended up with two persons. His teachings were condemned by the Council of Ephesus in 431.

Eutyches insisted that after the Incarnation, Christ's two

natures were mixed into one—the divine nature. This view was refuted by the Council of Chalcedon in 451. This same Council went on to define the orthodox view of Christ; it held Christ was "complete in Godhead and complete in manhood, truly God and truly man," having "two natures, without confusion, without change, without division, without separation." This is, and always has been, the orthodox view.

Thirdly, orthodox theology holds to the doctrine of the Trinity: the Father, the Son, and the Holy Spirit. All three are distinct and equal persons, and together they make up *one* God. Early heresies on this issue include Gnosticism, Monarchianism, Arianism, and Macedonianism.

Certain teachers from among the heretical groups, called "Gnostics," considered Christ one of many gods which had emanated down from the one good God. Some followers of a view called Monarchianism taught that Christ was merely a good man, not God. Arius and his followers believed Christ was a created being, subordinate to the Father and of a different essence from the Father. Because of the virtue of His life and His obedience to God's will, Christ was to be considered divine but not deity. Macedonius believed the Holy Spirit was a created being and was on a level with angels. All these ran up against the orthodox interpretation of Scripture and were condemned.

In the great christological debates of the fourth and fifth centuries, the orthodox Church held to a view from which it has never departed. Because of the nature of salvation, involving union and communion with God, Christ must be, as the Scriptures say, fully God and fully man. If He is not fully God, He cannot bring us into union, and if He is not fully man, man cannot be healed.

The fourth area concerns salvation. Orthodox theology holds that men are saved as they accept the atonement of Christ's death on the cross as payment for their sins and come into communion with God through the new birth. Let's look for a moment at Acts 15, where we find an example of deviation from the apostolic interpretation of Scripture on the subject of salvation.

A doctrinal problem had arisen in Antioch. There were some men who began to introduce heterodoxy, that is, they brought in a different belief. It says in Acts 15:1-2, "But some men came down from Judea and were teaching the brethren, 'Unless you are circumcised according to the customs of Moses, you cannot be saved.' And when Paul and Barnabas had no small dissensions and debate with them, Paul and Barnabas and some of the others were appointed to go up to Jerusalem to the apostles and the elders about this question."

Here was an heretical opinion introduced in Antioch. Could Paul and Barnabas solve the problem? No. The thing had gotten out of hand. So the brethren sent them to Jerusalem, to the apostles and elders, to debate the issue there. The debate: are we saved by keeping the law of Moses or are we saved by the grace of Jesus Christ?

They came to a unanimity of opinion. (They did not come to a democratic majority, by the way—that's very important.) They *unanimously* determined what was the true doctrine, and therefore in Acts 15:22 it says, ". . . it seemed good to the apostles and the elders, with the whole church . . ." Acts 15:25 says, "it has seemed good to us . . ." Acts 15:28 records, "For it has seemed good to the Holy Spirit and to us . . ."

What they arrived at there in the Council of Jerusalem was said to be the teaching of the Holy Spirit. They arrived at the correct teaching and withstood the heresy the way heretics have been dealt with throughout Church history—the study of the Scripture in Church councils guided by the Holy Spirit.

In addition to these differences in doctrine, there are a number of practices which are characteristic of heretical cults and which are inconsistent or contrary to Biblical injunctions and the orthodox theology. Among these are:

1. Fixing an exact date for Christ's return.
2. Controlling the minds of the adherents.
   (It is clearly contrary to Scripture and is a mark of all heresies.)
3. Domination of the group by one man who is considered the sole authority and interpreter of God's truth.

Look for these features in each of the seven cults discussed in this book.

This brings us to the twentieth century. We must pay attention to the orthodox councils of the Church, the first of which was Acts 15, because those councils were called together to determine by Scripture and the Holy Spirit what is the norm—what is orthodoxy.

Perhaps the most famous of these councils which the whole Church agrees to is the Council of Nicaea, out of which came the Nicaean Creed. Today, all orthodox Christendom holds to that creed. Anyone who does not, embraces heterodoxy. The whole point made at that council was that they were not formulating new doctrine but rather were passing on to us what the apostles themselves taught. Therefore we pay careful attention to the definitions made by those councils as they studied the Scriptures under the guidance of the Holy Spirit. Christians today must re-learn to establish continuity with the past and with our predecessors in the faith. Only then can we refute these modern cults and heresies.

Yardstick for Truth—Footnotes

1. Lee, *The Practical Expression of the Church*, (Los Angeles: Stream Publishers, 1970), p. 43.

PART II

The "Eastern" or Hindu Cults

An Introduction to
Transcendental Meditation

Bill Smith, 41, had grown up in a midwestern city, the son of a hard-working service station operator. His father and mother considered themselves "good Methodists" and regularly sent their small children to Sunday School, though Bill and his brothers and sisters stopped going in their teen years. Bill had had little contact with church since. He had gone to college, become a schoolteacher, and gotten totally wrapped up in the affairs of just living. He was now divorced, living alone, teaching, and feeling the tensions of life.

Many times on the bulletin boards at the public library or at the school Bill had seen notices issuing an invitation to attend an introductory lecture on Transcendental Meditation. It was a familiar sight, but today as he scanned the board a voice beside him said, "Why don't you try TM?" The person standing there looked vaguely familiar; Bill had seen him around.

"Why?" Bill asked.

"It gives you a calmer, clearer, more relaxed state of mind and being. I know; I practice it," he answered.

"But," Bill had vague remembrances, "Isn't TM some kind of Hindu religious thing?"

"Oh no," was the reply, "TM isn't a religion, though it is developed out of techniques discovered by great teachers in India. Why not go to the introductory lecture? It's free and you don't have anything to lose."

Well why not, Bill thought. He really was uptight these days. School term was over and he hadn't found a summer job yet. So on Wednesday night Bill found himself sitting with about fifteen other people listening to that introductory lesson on TM.

The claims were impressive. The instructor said emphatically that TM is not a religion nor a philosophy. Nor do you have to take up some special diet. It is, according to the instructor, *a scientific technique helping a person achieve a high state of mental relaxation and simultaneously attain his full potential.* These claims and others were backed up by statements from scientific research.

After the second lecture Bill was ready to give it a try. To become a candidate for initiation he had to pay a fee, but he qualified for the student rate because he took night classes, so he could manage that. He was told to bring an offering of six flowers, three pieces of fresh fruit, and a white handkerchief. That sounded hokey—even a little religious—but he had committed himself. . . .

It was strange entering the room where the ceremony was to be held. Incense hung heavily in the air and candles were the only lights. The offering had to be placed on a stand in front of a picture of someone called Guru Dev.

Bill was understandably uncomfortable, yet filled with a tingling anticipation. He was told to stand in front of all this while the teacher in charge of the ceremony sang something called "The Puja." Bill couldn't understand it because it was in Sanskrit. If he could have, this is what he would have heard.

PUJA

Whether pure or impure, whether purity or impurity is permeating everywhere, whoever opens himself to the expanded vision of unbounded awareness gains inner and outer purity.

Invocation

To Lord Narayana, to lotus-born Brahma the Creator, to Vashishta, to Shakti, and to his son, Parashar, to Vyasa, to Shukadava, to the great Gaudapada, to Govinda, ruler among yogies, to his disciple, Shri Trotika and Varttika-Kara, to others, to the tradition of our masters I bow down. To the abode of the wisdom of the Shrutis, Smritis, and Puranas, to the abode of kindness, to the personified glory of the Lord, to Shankara, emancipator of the Lord, I bow down. To Shankaracharya, the redeemer, hailed as Krishna and Badarayana, to the commentator of the Brahma Sutras, I bow down again and again. At whose door the whole galaxy of gods pray for perfection day and night, adorned with immeasurable glory, perceptor of the whole world, having bowed down to him, we gain fulfillment. Skilled in dispelling the cloud of ignorance of the people, the gentle emancipator, Bramananda Saraswati—the supreme teacher, full of brilliance, him I bring to my awareness.

Offering

Offering the invocation to the lotus feet of Shri Guru Dev, I bow down.
Offering a seat to the lotus feet of Shri Guru Dev, I bow down.
Offering an ablution to the lotus feet of Shri Guru Dev, I bow down.
Offering a cloth to the lotus feet of Shri Guru Dev, I bow down.
Offering sandalpaste to the lotus feet of Shri Guru Dev, I bow down.
Offering rice to the lotus feet of Shri Guru Dev, I bow down.
Offering a flower to the lotus feet of Shri Guru Dev, I bow down.
Offering incense to the lotus feet of Shri Guru Dev, I bow down.
Offering light to the lotus feet of Shri Guru Dev, I bow down.
Offering water to the lotus feet of Shri Guru Dev, I bow down.
Offering fruits to the lotus feet of Shri Guru Dev, I bow down.
Offering water to the lotus feet of Shri Guru Dev, I bow down.
Offering betel leaf to the lotus feet of Shri Guru Dev, I bow down.
Offering coconut to the lotus feet of Shri Guru Dev, I bow down.
Offering camphor light.

White as camphor, kindness incarnate, the essence of creation, garlanded with Brahman, ever dwelling in the lotus of my heart, the creative impulse of cosmic life, to that in the form of Guru Dev, I bow down.
Offering camphor light to the lotus feet of Shri Guru Dev, I bow down.
Offering water to the lotus feet of Shri Guru Dev, I bow down.
Offering a handful of flowers.

Guru in the glory of Brahma, guru in the glory of Vishnu, guru in the glory of the great Lord Shiva, guru in the glory of personified transcendental fullness of Brahman, to him Shri Guru Dev, adorned with glory, I bow down. The unbounded, like the endless canopy of the sky, by whom the moving and unmoving universe is pervaded, by whom the sign of That has been revealed, to him to Shri Guru Dev, I bow down. Guru Dev, Shri Brahmananda, bliss of the absolute, transcendental joy, the self-sufficient, the embodiment of pure knowledge, which

is beyond and above the universe like the sky, the goal of "thou art That" and other such expressions which unfold eternal truth, the one, the eternal, the pure, the immovable, to the very being of that which is the witness of all intellects, whose status transcends thought, the transcendent along with the three gunas, the teacher of the truth of the Absolute, to Shri Guru Dev, I bow down. To him by whom the blinding darkness of ignorance has been removed by applying the balm of knowledge; the eye of knowledge has been opened by him and therefore, to him, to Shri Guru Dev, I bow down.
Offering a handful of flowers to the lotus feet of Shri Guru Dev, I bow down.

Bill was getting a lot more "religion" than he had initially bargained for. At the end of the song, he knelt beside the teacher who then pronounced Bill's own personal "mantra," the Sanskrit word by means of which he would do his daily meditation.

Already he had been unknowingly involved in worship and there was more to come.

Bill now began his twenty-minute periods of meditation twice daily. He was to aim for a state of altered consciousness which was somewhere between being awake and being asleep. By now he was grasping the fact that the whole thing was much more a religious matter than he had been told. Actually, he didn't mind. He'd learned this useful technique, and it did make him feel rested. Besides, he was sort of getting into it. It seemed so much more "spiritual" and deep than the Christianity he'd been taught in Sunday School.

It's time to leave Bill and look at the nature of Transcendental Meditation. It is a technique of yogi meditation developed by a man called Maharishi Mahesh Yogi. He studied under a very well-known religious leader in India and thoroughly absorbed his brand of Hindu pantheism. When his teacher died, the Maharishi put his technique together and in 1959 headed for the United States.

Since the technique was designed for popular use, produced noticeable results, and his prices weren't too high, the Maharishi quickly developed a following.

THE HISTORY AND THEOLOGY OF TRANSCENDENTAL MEDITATION

WHO IS MAHARISHI MAHESH YOGI?

In 1959 a bearded guru from India arrived in California and immediately incorporated a non-profit religious organization called the Spiritual Regeneration Foundation. Its stated objective was to offer all persons ". . . spiritual growth, peace and happiness through a system of deep meditation."[1] Very few people seemed interested for several years.

Then all of a sudden Maharishi became a household word. What happened?

Guru Dev

Let's go back into Maharishi's past. In India he was a disciple of a Hindu guru named Swami Brahmananda Saraswati Mahaharaj, more familiarly known as Guru Dev.

Hindu religious sects trace their lineage by successions of gurus. Maharishi is very proud of Guru Dev. In one of the publications of the Spiritual Regeneration Movement there are several pages of praise of his accomplishments. Maharishi says Guru Dev brought a spiritual revival to northern India. He was also worshiped by Rajendra Prasad, the first president of the Indian Union.

Why bother to tell you all this? We want to find out what Maharishi teaches, why it's selling like hotcakes, and what's wrong with it. Guru Dev is the taproot of Maharishi. According to Maharishi, Dr. Prasad's successor as president of the Indian Union called Guru Dev "truth in a human body." He was a very famous man in India.

Maharishi

One day, the man who was to be known as Maharishi Mahesh Yogi went to study under Guru Dev. In Hindu sects, the disciple is supposed to worship and serve his spiritual master. So that's what Maharishi did. He caught Guru Dev's eye and became his favorite pupil. Apparently, Maharishi showed a lot of promise.

33

Just before Guru Dev died, he called for Maharishi and told him to figure out a simple form of meditation. It was to be one which anybody could practice and be able to reach "bliss consciousness of Absolute Being." Hold onto that term for a few pages. What you need to catch here is that Maharishi was to develop a new technique for an old Hindu religious result.

Well, Maharishi headed for a cave and lived there two years. When he came out, he had his new technique which he called "Transcendental Meditation." For some reason people in India didn't seem to get all that excited about it.

Go West, Religious Man

Pretty soon Maharishi was on his way to the West, to market his religious program among people who, as he said, "are in the habit of accepting things quickly." That's why we find him in California in 1959. However, people didn't accept his program all that quickly in America either. He was heard of here and there, but nothing big resulted until one day he ran into George Harrison of the Beatles, who was studying religion.

Boom! The Beatles took up TM. Shirley MacLaine, Mia Farrow, The Rolling Stones, and a whole host of other famous people went for it. Suddenly, Maharishi was big in the West. Hiring advance men, he went on speaking tours. In those days he was asking for a week's pay to teach people Transcendental Meditation. John Lennon could handle it, but Joe Smith, the plumber, gulped when he heard. Outside the famous people there was a lot of excitement, but few takers.

The Beatles and many others lost interest. On an eleven-city U.S. speaking tour, Maharishi lost his shirt. Nobody wanted to hear him. Back to the drawing board. Maharishi revamped his whole program. Vocabulary and methods were worked over; religious terms went out the window and in came scientific and psychological terms.

Back in California Maharishi formed a new organization: Students' International Meditation Society (SIMS). Centers for SIMS were set up near major university campuses. A new campaign to attract students was built. A graduated fee system was set up so students would pay less than adults. Maharishi had hit it just right. In the late 1960s American youth were trying everything different. Hindu philosophy was being "discovered," and his no-religion system was just right.

A brand new emphasis was developed. Maharishi and his aides began to emphasize the material benefits and leave out the spiritual. "It's not a religion; absolutely not," said Maharishi. By 1970, converts had begun to pour in. Soon Maharishi had six thousand teachers and an income of $20 million per year. Pretty good for a technique that came out of a cave! But what's so attractive about TM?

The Promise

One of the most common brochures distributed by TM centers proclaims confidently that TM:[2]
- can be learned easily and enjoyed by everyone
- provides deep rest as a basis for dynamic action
- improves clarity of perception
- develops creative intelligence
- expands awareness
- insures full development of the individual in a natural way

These impressive promises are reinforced by the further statement that very little time and effort are required to attain these goals. "Transcendental Meditation is practiced for a few minutes morning and evening as one sits comfortably with eyes closed." Reports of the results of scientific studies are quoted for reinforcement. That's impressive. It adds spice to the TM invitation, which is sweetened by the hope that even you can be helped. "Students, housewives, businessmen, scientists, pilots, physicians, musicians and others have all reported practical benefits in terms of their own needs and aspirations!"[3]

That's not the traditional flowery language of the typical Hindu sect. The fact is, though, that TM is still a Hindu religious system and Maharishi still has the same aims. Let's look at the nature of his religion.

WHAT MAHARISHI BELIEVES

What is God? god?

When Maharishi first started doing his thing in this country his usual term for his god was "Absolute Being." He doesn't use that term much anymore. It sounded too "religious" for science-minded America. Besides, he wanted to get into public schools and didn't dare sound religious. So he found a more acceptable term: "Creative Intelligence." Sounds scientific, doesn't it? It's supposed to. Don't let it fool you, though. It means whatever "God" means to Maharishi. (I found that out in the textbook used in New Jersey's public schools: *Science of Creative Intelligence for Secondary Education,* First Year Course, "Dawn of the First Year of the Age of Enlightenment.")

Well, then, what is "Absolute Being" or "God" or "Creative Intelligence" to Maharishi? That will take some explanation; the concept is unfamiliar to Americans so it will be hard to take in. Follow carefully. I won't use Absolute Being or Creative Intelligence. I'll use "god" with a small "g," so we don't mix up Maharishi's idea with the Christian God who is far different.

Maharishi's god is everything. I mean, it literally is! It is impersonal and is always there in everything—every object, every being that exists, even every force. It is the universe and yet is more than the universe. Now this god isn't personal, remember. There's no *person* you can pray to who can make things happen. All nature is part of god. Catch the idea?

Now, god is also more than nature. It is everlasting. It has no limits. Some of it is seeable or knowable and some of it isn't. This god (impersonal Absolute Being or Creative Intelligence) is the force of, and the force behind, the whole universe. Like I said, everything is god and god is everything. Rocks, thoughts, bugs, and people are all god.

When Maharishi writes about god, however, he tells us it is absolutely different from evil. Every possible good quality like intelligence, knowledge, bliss, and glory are supposed to belong to god. Nothing bad does. Somehow Maharishi manages to exclude evil from everything. That's quite a contradiction. But contradictions like that don't seem to be the problem in Hindu systems that they are for us.

So Maharishi can come up with statements like "I am That, Thou art That, all this is That, That alone is, and there is nothing else but That."[4] Maybe that statement defines his god best of all.

How Things Exist

Maharishi's system comes out of the Hindu scriptures. He follows a certain line of interpretation. To him the material world comes out of god. It is god formed into mind and matter. He uses the term "expressing" for the act of creation. There isn't any person like our God who creates by "making" something. Creation is supposed to be god "expressed" or somehow becoming mind and matter.

To understand that, we have to learn some terms. One is *prana,* best defined as the disposition of god to create. It's like there is an internal force in god which causes it to create. It can't help it. That's how Maharishi solves the problem of how the world came into existence.

Now, god is impersonal, right? Yes, but . . . Maharishi gives god personal characteristics. It's one of those strange contradictions. The purpose of creation is "the expansion of happiness", he says. Apparently creation is essential to the happiness of god. How an impersonal force can want happiness we aren't told. But *prana* is the characteristic that does it.

So the great variety of life oozes out of god, while god remains the same. In invisible form, it is mind; in visible form, it is matter. Everything exists because it is god's nature for creation to come out and *prana* is causing it.

Maharishi talks about the "Ocean of Being"—the whole "pool" of what god is. Now if *prana* is the disposition for that pool of god to create, something has to cause particular things to form, right? There's a word for it: *karma.*

Karma is *a force acting on that pool.* As a matter of fact, *karma* is *action.* It keeps things moving, causing an endless cycle of things to come into being and to go out of being. A bug is born and dies and a horse is born and dies and a human is born and dies and. . . .*Karma* has a goal: mind. Mind has a goal: *karma.* It's an ongoing cycle. Maharishi says it is like the tree and the seed. Which comes first?

You see, Hinduism (and that's where Maharishi comes from) believes there is an endless cycle of incarnations and reincarnations in the universe—like the bug-horse-human series. If you've been a good bug, you may get to be a horse in the next life. If you've been a super good bug, you might even become a human. But if you're a very bad human and have lived only aware of material things, you could end up being a bug in the next life.

Now what causes beings to move from one thing to another?

37

You guessed it—*karma. Karma* is action, right? So the *karma,* or action, of our past life has brought us to our present state in the cycle of evolution. Mind caused that action. So the cycle goes on and on and on. And notice, god isn't beyond natural law, but is confined by it.

What We Are

According to Maharishi's concept, a human being, or for that matter any life in creation, has three parts: the body, the mind, and the self. The body is just the material shell brought about by *prana* and *karma.* Inside is the mind, invisible, but experiencing and acting. Self is sort of a seed of god (impersonal Absolute Being or Creative Intelligence) which actually shows up in all the visible and knowable aspects of the being.

Creation and uncreation, life and death, keep going on in cycles as god forms and reforms through the action of *karma.* You may have lived as a stink bug and now as a human being. But the big thing is that only when you have been born in a human body do you have the possibility of awareness of god. Stink bugs aren't aware of it.

In the end, the body doesn't count. It comes and goes. What counts is that third part—self—and its awareness. Maharishi would tell us god is always there, but the continuous cycles of life and death produce minds and bodies. We are part of god. Life is Creative Intelligence expressed in creativity, purity, and bliss. Essentially then, life is divine, if you can think of divinity as an all-inclusive "it."

The Purpose of Life

Maharishi sees the real purpose of life as the expansion of happiness, which comes from that personal characteristic he attaches to his impersonal god. The nature of god is to create in order to expand happiness. The endless cycle of life and death is the process through which happiness somehow is expanded. What happens is that when the cycle reaches the highest form—humanity—expansion of happiness is possible. Individual human beings have the possibility of evolving to perfect awareness of god.

How? you may ask. Maharishi has a list of characteristics which he considers superior: intelligence, power, energy, creativity and bliss. (We might note that he doesn't consider love, patience, and faith to be superior.) Expanding happiness, he says, involves expansion or growth of these superior characteristics.

Maharishi believes that the human nervous system is so developed and evolved that we can experience all these superior characteristics in pure form. That, he tells us, is the purpose of *human* life. We're the bridge, somehow, between god and creation. Our duty is to cultivate the superior or divine characteristics and pass them on to the whole creation.

Developing the "Divine Characteristics" Within

Maharishi thinks it is possible for every human being to develop these divine characteristics. If we fail, we disgrace ourselves and fail our source (god) which after all, is inside us. Unfortunately, he says, failure is frequent. By our own failure, our enjoyment of life is limited and we suffer. This suffering doesn't simply come from failing to live up to our full potential—it's something deeper. We're too careless or indifferent to find out how to get to and bring out the divine nature inside us.

There it is: the failure that causes all the problems and suffering of humanity. It's all the fault of indifferent people who don't know how to dive within themselves to reach god. That's why, Maharishi says, we can't see the real purpose of life. It's why we don't realize we're supposed to enjoy life, to create, to serve ourselves and others. Thus, we cause great loss to the whole universe.

What is normal life? Everybody wants to know that. Maharishi has an answer: It's getting body, mind and that inner self operating together to bring about the natural process of evolution. What natural process of evolution? Well, now that you're in the privileged human state, it is getting to a higher state of consciousness. You are to come to the point of enjoying the eternal value of "bliss consciousness" of god. I know what you're asking: What in the world is bliss consciousness? It's getting all wrapped up in that impersonal Absolute Being (god) which is down deep inside you.

Maharishi doesn't say it's wrong to enjoy material things— that's fine. Just don't forget bliss consciousness, because human life is abnormal without it. In fact, as far as he is concerned, all the activities of living and interacting with other people are just side issues. Carrying on this minor business of living must not be allowed to distract us from the main aim. When we reach the state of bliss consciousness, he says, we have attained normal human life.

Being Better than Animals

If you look at just the business of carrying on life, Maharishi says, humanity isn't any better than the animals. What's the difference then? It's our brain! Our brain enables us to have a broader view of life, so we can live according to real values. We can distinguish between right and wrong.

Maharishi believes we're above the animals because we can live in a state of awareness of god. Remember the stink bug? It can't live that way. But if you don't live in that state of awareness, you're in trouble; you'll suffer and be unhappy. You reap what you sow!

This is the way it happens in Maharishi's system. Any wrong word or deed will reverberate through the universe, forever causing trouble, and return to have its effect on you even if it takes a million years. A million years! Won't I be dead? Not according to Maharishi. You'll just be somewhere in another body.

Maharishi believes your soul stays around until it merges into impersonal Absolute Being once and for all. Until then it will exist as an individual in one incarnation or another, experiencing the fruits of its past. Meanwhile there is no way you can escape your sins. It's as if there is no forgiveness.

But what if you've already merged by the time the effect of that sin gets back? It gets passed to your next of kin; if you don't have any, someone else gets it. That's the action of *karma*. (In Maharishi's system you'd better hope your great-grandmother was a good woman!)

You see that god (Creative Intelligence, impersonal Absolute Being) is considered to be in everything *in the whole creation*. Every object, every being, every force is tied together so closely that they influence one another with every move. What you do affects the whole universe. It follows that if you're not properly adjusted to your purpose, you affect the whole world adversely!

Holding that view, Maharishi believes that somehow we need to get things arranged so every person is good, kind, and virtuous, both in thought and action. That way everybody will influence the outcome positively.

How are people going to come into such a virtuous way of life? Well, Maharishi thinks the only way is by gaining that state of god awareness he calls bliss consciousness. He thinks when we reach that state we'll always do the right things because we're in tune with the purpose of god. Now the question is, of course: How can we get there when the effects of our past actions (in this life and others) are always with us, and we aren't able to reach that state of awareness?

Salvation is Within You

Maharishi says it's up to you. We each have to work out our own destiny. We must each find a way to get inside and pick up only those thoughts which are in tune with god. Then we can use those thoughts in saying and doing the right things. It may sound like he's going to drop you right there, but he isn't. He's got a plan to help you.

Ordinarily, Maharishi discloses, we experience only *three* states of consciousness: *waking, dreaming,* and *dreamless sleep.* Okay, so far there's nothing new. But he says there is a *fourth* state: *complete knowledge of the Self alone.* It's a state of consciousness in which everything is cut out except god within. Maharishi says it is the reality behind the first three and calls it the state of "pure awareness." He assures you there's no way to reach it without help.

But even the fourth level is not the top. Maharishi has more for you. The fifth level takes that awareness of Self and adds back *the awareness of the outside world* which you experience in the ordinary waking state of consciousness. Above that level is the *sixth* state of consciousness in which one experiences all the subtle qualities of the world you can experience *with your senses.* You experience the "essence" behind everything. Maharishi calls that "God-consciousness" (small "g" for us, remember).

That's not quite the end of it. Maharishi says there is still a higher state to strive for, but it requires living on the sixth level for a period of time so that perception becomes sharper. Then, he promises, *maybe* you can get to that state of consciousness in which you grasp the subtlest of *the essence of creation,* but also *pure* Absolute Being. This *seventh* or ultimate state is named "Unity" by Maharishi.

What Is It?

By now you're wondering what in the world is a "state of consciousness." Let's tackle it. The *waking state* you already understand. That's when we say we're "conscious." We can feel, see, hear, think, and so on. We're aware of the world. Then there's *dreaming.* Your mind experiences things that aren't real, right? You seem to see and hear, etc., but the objects aren't actually there. Perhaps you could call it a second state of consciousness. *Dreamless sleep* is another thing. I would call that *un*-consciousness.

Now to get to Maharishi's "state of consciousness." About the best phrase I can find to describe the fourth state is *throw your mind out of gear* so it's blank. You're just gone from the world of the senses.

In the fifth state, you apparently experience unreality and reality at the same time. It's like *you're living in two worlds.*

The sixth state appears to be one in which you're *detached,* seeing and feeling but getting hallucinations about it.

That seventh state supposedly is one in which *all the previous experiences are enhanced.*

The fact is, however, that from the fourth state on, *your mind is out of gear and you've turned yourself over to something other than yourself.*

Maharishi says it takes surrender, submission to the Almighty power of nature. That's significant. What can "the Almighty power of nature" be but the god of this world, the devil? Keep that in mind for later; right now we want to follow Maharishi.

Okay, surrender. But it's not as simple, Maharishi tells us. You can't just decide to surrender. As long as you still have any thoughts at all—even a thought of surrender—you are not surrendered. So how is surrender accomplished? Maharishi acknowledges that many methods have been proposed and some may work. He, however, has discovered a simple and direct technique which anyone can use. For a fee, he will teach it to you. You can't just read about it; you have to be instructed by someone who knows how.

Transcendental Meditation

Maharishi's "simple and direct technique" is called transcendental deep meditation, shortened to transcendental meditation, commonly called TM. Now we've got to deal with his meanings of "transcendental" and "meditation."

"Transcending," of course, means going beyond the limits of something. Maharishi intends to get people to experience god, Absolute Being, Creative Intelligence. But god, he tells us, is outside the range of our senses. What we are to "transcend" is our senses. We are to get beyond all seeing, hearing, touching, smelling, and tasting—beyond all thinking and beyond all feeling; that is, to the place where your mind is out of gear.

"Meditation" is the process of concentrating on something, trying to put the mind on it to the exclusion of everything else. It means giving, as much as possible, the entire attention to the object of meditation.

Maharishi says his process of transcendental deep meditation involves the selection of a proper thought and learning how to progressively experience that thought until you arrive at its source. The source? Absolute Being, or god in our terminology.

Now, we've got to deal with an item difficult to understand. What does it mean to "progressively experience a thought"? You take the thought, turn your full attention on it repeatedly, going over and over it. The idea, according to Maharishi, is to progressively experience the thought at deeper levels inside you. He wants you to have the feeling of tracing that thought closer and closer to your inner self. Supposedly, the mind is entranced by this process and eventually goes beyond every sense to god at the deepest level inside.

I can't imagine how you would even know this is true, because, after all, thinking is gone. Maharishi says an important side benefit is that the conscious capacity of the mind is enlarged, but that the real benefit is that the purpose of life is accomplished. Well. . . .

How You Get It

Let's suppose you're crazy enough to decide you want to do this. You pay your fee (you didn't think you could get it free, did you?) and you get your instructions. There's an offering to bring—flowers, fruit, and a white handkerchief. At the appointed time you arrive and are shown into an incense-filled room, where there's an altar. Kneeling (preferably; they will let you stand if you insist), you stare at a picture of Guru Dev, Maharishi's spiritual master, while an initiator sings the Puja, a Sanskrit hymn of worship (see page 30). Since it's in Sanskrit you don't understand a word of it.

The first part of the hymn is a recitation of a long list of legendary and historic names of the line through which the holy knowledge is supposed to have passed. Each person listed is supposed to be a fully realized expression of god. They all got to "Unity." Thus, they are worshiped. The remainder of the hymn concentrates upon offerings to and worship of Guru Dev. This initiation liturgy is central to the concept of transcendental meditation. Most Americans, not understanding the language, have no idea they're worshiping a deity.

Ceremony over, you are given your *mantra,* the Sanskrit word which is the "thought" upon which you're supposed to meditate. We'd better give this *mantra* some attention. It's supposed to be very individual, selected for you personally, with selection based upon your own unique characteristics. You are to tell it to no one. You are warned it won't work for anyone else.

It's really incorrect to call it a "thought." What you are given is a Sanskrit sound which has supposedly been passed down through the holy masters. If it has a meaning, you don't know it, because you don't know the language. Anyway, you don't meditate on the *meaning,* you meditate on the *sound.*

The *mantra,* then, is not a "thought." You concentrate repeatedly on a meaningless sound, supposedly tracing it deeper and deeper into your inner self. Something does happen to people. They do go "out of gear." Some people report demonic experiences. Others just report a time when they went "out."

Surprisingly, you don't have to meditate a lot. Twenty minutes in the morning and twenty minutes in the evening will do it. Maharishi will teach you how to go on—even to "Unity"—if you show aptitude and are disposed to go so far. Of course, it will cost you more money and time.

THE METHOD OF OPERATION OF TRANSCENDENTAL MEDITATION

TM IN ACTION

Transcendental Meditation is probably the most Americanized of all the Hindu religious groups operating in this country. Maharishi runs a tight ship. His highly controlled organizational structure could be the envy of any business corporation. He has established his empire to implement a World Plan with seven ambitious goals:[5]

1) To develop the full potential of the individual
2) To improve governmental achievements
3) To realize the highest idea of education
4) To eliminate the age-old problem of crime and all behavior that brings unhappiness to the family of man
5) To maximize the intelligent use of the environment
6) To bring fulfillment to the economic aspirations of individuals and society
7) To achieve the spiritual goals of mankind in this generation

These aren't just paper goals. Maharishi really goes after them. The activities of the whole TM empire are geared to programs relating to their achievement. His organizations cover the whole range. Check these:

Student International Meditation Society
American Meditation Society
World Plan Executive Council
American Foundation for Creative Intelligence

Maharishi International University
Maharishi European Research University
Institute for Fitness and Athletic Excellence
Affiliated Organizational Conglomerate

Each organization has its special role to play in the fulfillment of the World Plan. Their development has not been haphazard. The Maharishi is very serious about his religion and its world-wide promotion.

Promotion means the wise use of media. Maharishi has a team of experts which operates a huge publishing enterprise, television production, and public relations in all influential areas of American life. Science, medicine, business, and athletics have been given special attention. It's no accident the San Francisco Giants set June 5, 1976, as TM day, with three Philadelphia Phillies giving TM testimonies and Golden State Warrior Charles Dudley being honored as TM athlete of the year.

Science and TM

When Robert Keith Wallace, a TM meditator, did his Ph.D. thesis on the physiological effects of TM,[6] a realm of research possibilities opened up. His report of slowed heartbeat and apparent relaxation appeared in *Science, American Journal of Physiology, Scientific American,* and *New England Journal of Medicine.* Dr. Herbert Benson, his collaborator, wasn't all that impressed with TM and developed a simpler technique of his own which achieved the same result. TM publicity, however, milked the Wallace thesis for everything it could get. The thing is still quoted by them.

A rash of other research reports has since appeared. Most of them are poorly designed, based on poorly controlled experimentation and prove nothing. Still, the fact that somebody did a study of the application of TM to a human problem tends to get people all hyped up. So it gets tried in other places.

TM has been used in programs on alcoholism and drug dependency by the U.S. Army and other agencies. Prisoner rehabilitation has been attempted through the use of TM. Maharishi is thrilled. He promotes it. After all, more and more people are practicing his religion. Meanwhile, nobody really knows how much good or bad is done.

Nor has the business world been neglected. Articles have appeared in business magazines extolling the benefits for executives, with charts from the research of Wallace and others. A TM booklet, "Creative Intelligence for Businessmen," has been widely circulated. Favorable essays on TM assail the eyes of the airline passenger who opens the flight magazine and the patient who leafs through familiar periodicals in the doctor's office. Enthusiastic endorsements have appeared in such prestigious journals as *Harvard Law Record, Yale Alumni Magazine, Today's Health,* and the *Phi Delta Kappan.* The happy meditator becomes an evangelist, assisted by the TM public relations staff.

Schools and Government

Maharishi has aimed high. He has put real effort into getting to educators, lawmakers, and government officials—with results. TM has been endorsed by school systems and state legislatures in several states. School children have been taught to practice meditation in classrooms.

Take New Jersey, for instance. The state department of education funded a TM course for five high schools, paying for the development of a 295-page textbook by Maharishi International University. Would it surprise you to learn that TM trainers have been taught in programs underwritten by National Institute of Mental Health grants?

All that government help has been made possible by Maharishi's repeated claim that TM does not involve any religious beliefs. That way the American constitutional prohibition of the mixing of "church and state" can be avoided.

Apparently Maharishi doesn't mind a little deception in these things. Here's how he puts it:

Whenever and wherever religion dominates the mass consciousness, transcendental deep meditation should be taught in terms of religion. . . . Today, when politics is guiding the destiny of man, the teaching should be primarily based on the field of politics and secondarily on the plane of economics. . . . It seems for the

47

present, that this transcendental deep meditation should be made available to the people through the agencies of government (*The Science of Being and the Art of Living,* Signet Books, New York, New York, 1968. pp. 299, 300).

Maharishi manages to get access to the highest governmental levels—the heads of nations. There the TM sales pitch is that if one percent of the population meditates, they'll affect the rest of the people enough to reduce crime and tranquilize the whole society. He's even got statistics, based on a supposed survey of 240 American cities in which at least one percent of the people practice TM. According to the statistics presented, crime dropped an average of 17 percent.[7]

Who knows whether these claims are true or false? Of course, whether they are or not doesn't have anything to do with the validity of TM. But the publicity value certainly is strong.

Sucking People In

If a movement's going to grow, though, it has to attract people. TM does that in a big way. Again, it is organization and know-how.

Free introductory lectures on TM are held in the 375 city academies operated by TM, and in convenient public places everywhere—libraries, public and private school facilities, and rented halls.[8] These lectures are widely advertised in local newspapers. Posters are placed on public bulletin boards and in other prominent places. The word is also spread by enthusiastic meditators. Frequently there are spot radio and television announcements. No publicity stone is left unturned.

These introductory lectures are sales meetings. Every possible inducement is used to entice people into initiation. Endorsements and supposed benefits are stacked one on the other. Hundreds, perhaps thousands of such lectures are given every week. No matter if only one or two people attend (it's usually much more); a recruit is a recruit, and the number of meditators grows by leaps and bounds. Probably close to a million, maybe more, Americans have been initiated to date.

Then there are personal appearances by Maharishi. He shows up in a lot of noticeable places. When one prominent TV show moderator became an initiate, follow-up was immediate. Soon Maharishi gave an introductory lecture during an episode of the show. It wasn't long before a video tape of the whole thing was a standard tool in the local centers.

You're probably wondering about money, right? How does all this get financed? In the good old-fashioned American way. Fees.

It's enough to make the traditional Hindu guru shudder, but here's the price schedule: $125 for adults, $200 for families, $65 for college students, $55 for high school students, and $35 for youngsters ten through fourteen.[9] Right now there are probably 30,000 or more initiates per month. You figure the take.

What Happens to the New Meditators

After initiation there is a fifteen-minute introductory meditation. Then the new meditator fills out a form asking about that initial experience. That's the beginning of the checking process to make sure meditation gets established.

There are going to be three successive nights of follow-up sessions. Each time there's a questionnaire to check progress. Questions are answered and some further information is given. The questionnaires in particular are designed to reinforce the basic notions and intent of the twice a day practice of meditating on the *mantra*. They seem to sort of guide the meditator, by suggestion, into what is supposed to be experienced.

Meditators don't find out much about what the real aim is until the last follow-up session. That's when most initiates get their first glimpse of the religious nature of TM. The lecturer talks about bliss consciousness and all the other inside goodies. Our new initiate finds he can get more training so he can reach another level of consciousness. Of course it's going to cost more money.

The fact is, there are a lot more training courses available: retreats at $20 to $30 per day; courses in residence at major centers for $500; even a 33-lesson video-taped course on "Science of Creative Intelligence" which costs only $45; and many more. Oh yes, we mustn't forget—each new initiate goes on the mailing list and regularly receives a newsletter advertising more activities and giving special messages from Maharishi.

Meditators who show enthusiasm, promise, and intelligence are likely to end up working somewhere in Maharishi's empire. It takes a lot of teachers, of course, with these 375 or more centers around the country. This, plus all the TM money that has gone into the purchase of facilities and equipment, require a wide variety of help. So recruiting is important.

Nobody gets paid much—$300 a month is probably about average. Some workers only get about $25 a month, plus room and board. Hundreds of people seem ready to volunteer to work for little or nothing for the fulfillment of the World Plan.

Apparently there is no common worship among TM devotees. It's all individual—twenty minutes twice a day. Time is allowed twice a day for workers and students to engage in the expected morning and evening meditation.

A New University

Maharishi International University occupies the former Parsons College campus in Fairfield, Iowa. It is a rigidly-run institution with a carefully controlled curriculum, structured according to TM doctrine. Robert Keith Wallace (remember his Ph.D. thesis?) is president. Under his direction everything is designed to prepare people to propagate TM. Student behavior is at least as tightly managed as at the most conservative Christian college. A sense of purpose is said to pervade the thinking of the 600 or so students. Oh yes, the university also has a community outreach project—getting enough Iowans to meditate to turn Iowa into the first "ideal state."

Moving On

Everything moves in the direction of implementing the fulfilling of the World Plan. Money doesn't seem to be kept on hand. TM purchases property at a fast pace, often old resort facilities. Everything is heavily mortgaged, because spreading the program is all-important. Maharishi has learned well how to combine religion and business.

One thing is strange, though. He goes his way with the money to build his empire, and his converts go their way. Many of them, perhaps most, gradually drop out of meditation without ever knowing that the technique they learned was supposed to develop "God-consciousness."

A REFUTATION OF
TRANSCENDENTAL MEDITATION

Mindlessness and Christianity

Today, many Christians are picking up techniques such as TM for throwing the mind out of gear. At the same time, many people with Christian heritages, who should be turning to the Lord, are dabbling with mindlessness instead. There are even books (written by Christians!) which purport to show how TM can be helpful to Christians. That is *not* true. Maharishi's system won't fit into the Christian scheme of life. We're not concerned with whether his ideas are or are not internally consistent. That is irrelevant. Our main interest is in whether they square with the historic teaching of the Christian Church. They don't, and those who are trying to mix the two are in for trouble.

Who Has the Truth?

Maharishi bases his teaching on the mythical Hindu scriptures. Even these confused and contradictory writings, however, are not the authority for his solution to humanity's problems. No, *he* has discovered the way, and we must follow *him.* He is the authority on which everybody is supposed to depend completely. This *one man* comes along in the twentieth century, goes into a cave, and independently derives the answer. What arrogance!

But wait. Is that really wrong? Isn't one man's opinion as good as another's? What is wrong with a solution devised by one person? Well, there are lots of things wrong with it. First of all, one person's mind is too limited to figure out a solution for the problems of the whole human race. If you're going to solve *everybody's* problems, you'd better have a mind that is all-knowing. Maharishi doesn't have that kind of mind.

In addition, Maharishi, for all the beauty of his words and the efficiency of his technique, hasn't solved humanity's biggest fear or problem. Death. He himself still faces it. Someday Maharishi himself will die. What then of his technique for achieving peace by throwing the mind out of gear?

Reality?

In Maharishi's Hindu view, everything consists of the same nature. He believes that when everything is said and done, there is no difference between God and creatures or between matter and spirit. Absolute Being (god) includes everything in the universe. Thus, everything is divine. What nonsense! That idea eliminates God for all practical purposes. Maharishi's position hinges on the idea that everything has the same nature.

Now, if God's nature is the same as that of the creation, then God's nature is *created* nature. And if God's nature is created, it's useless to talk about God at all. The fact is that the Scriptures teach that God's nature is *uncreated* and all other natures are *created.* Notice I made that plural. The Apostle Paul makes a distinction between the natures of various things.

> But God gives it a body as he has chosen, and to each kind of seed its own body. For not all flesh is alike, but there is one kind for men, another for animals, another for birds, and another for fish. There are celestial bodies and there are terrestrial bodies; but the glory of the celestial is one, and the glory of the terrestrial is another. There is one glory of the sun, and another glory of the moon, and another glory of the stars; for star differs from star in glory (1 Cor. 15:38-41).

Even the creation shows differences among natures. Think how much more the Creator must be distinct from His creation. Consider. A contractor builds a house. No one looks at the house and confuses it with the contractor. No one in his right mind says the contractor and the house are of the same nature. In the same way, only a fool confuses the universe with the One who made it. There is one thing you can't get around—the order and harmony of the universe demonstrate a designer and builder.

> The heavens are telling the glory of God; and the firmament proclaims his handiwork (Ps. 19:1).

If we confuse the universe and its Builder, we deny the Builder's existence. Such a denial reveals the denier as a fool.

> The fool says in his heart, "There is no God" (Ps. 14:1).

Unfortunately, we must say God has judged Maharishi a fool. He looks at the universe and says no difference exists between matter and spirit. Since God is a Spirit, no distinction exists between God and creation. Therefore, God doesn't exist, that is, God as a person. So, Maharishi is an atheist, and atheists are fools because they reject the obvious evidence for a personal Builder of the universe. As the Scripture says:

> Ever since the creation of the World his invisible nature, namely, his eternal power and deity, has been clearly perceived in the things that have been made. So they are without excuse (Rom. 1:20).

Maharishi and those who follow him are blind fools and are totally *without excuse*.

What a difference there is in the Church of the Lord Jesus Christ! That Church, following the Scriptures, has always made a clear distinction between God and creation. The great church father, Athanasius, put that distinction quite well back in the fourth century.

> God is by nature invisible and far beyond our understanding. He is so far above created existence that humanity could very easily have missed knowing Him, because they are made out of nothing while He is unmade. However, because God is so loving and good to mankind and because He cares for the souls He has made, He gave the universe the order it has by His own Word. He did that so that even though He is invisible, by nature, people would be able to know Him at least by His works. Often, even an artist is known by his works, even when he's not around. . . . Look at the circle of heaven and the path of the sun and the moon, and the places and the movements of the stars, all moving in different directions. Who can look at the consistent order they display and resist the conclusion that they didn't get that order by themselves, but were rather put into order by a maker distinct from themselves? (*Against the Heathen,* by Athanasius, Part III, point 35.1,4, a free modern language version)[10]

But Athanasius doesn't stand as a single light, way back there in history, all by himself. Church creeds, such as the Westminster Confession (1647), demonstrate how the Church has always been careful to respect the distinction between God and His creation.

> God has all life, glory, goodness, blessedness, in and of Himself. He is all-sufficient in Himself so He doesn't need any of the creatures which He has made. He doesn't get any glory from them. He just shows His glory in them, on them, by them and to them . . . (a free modern language version of a passage from Chapter II, Point II).[11]

That same creed, in another place, affirms clearly that creation is not part of God.

> God the Father, Son and Holy Spirit, wanted, in order to show the glory of His eternal power, wisdom, and goodness, to, in the beginning create or make out of nothing, the world and everything in it, both visible and invisible (a free modern language version of Chapter IV, Point I).[12]

Maharishi's view is that we (humanity and indeed all creatures) are just god expressed. This view cuts across the current of biblical teaching about our nature. From beginning to end, the actual making of humanity is affirmed.

> Then God said, "Let us make man in our image, after our likeness; and let them have dominion over the fish of the sea, and over the birds of the air, and over the cattle, and over all the earth, and over every creeping thing that creeps upon the earth." So God created man in his own image, and in the image of God he created him; male and female he created them . . . And God saw everything that He had made, and behold, it was very good. And there was evening and there was morning, a sixth day (Gen. 1:26, 27, 31).

What a contrast there is in the dignity given humanity here with the lack of dignity given by Maharishi! He confuses us with the animals over which we are to rule. This Scripture has been demonstrated all through history and even today by the obvious fact that humanity, however badly, does indeed rule over all other creatures. Even having that role, however, we must not think we are God.

> Yet, O Lord, thou art our Father; we are the clay, and thou art our potter; we are all the work of thy hand (Is. 64:8).

How could anyone confuse a potter and the clay he works with? God is just as clearly different from humanity. In the midst of it all, we must remember that He cares for us. And that is a wonder!

> It has been testified somewhere, "What is man that thou art mindful of him, or the son of man, that thou carest for him? Thou didst make him for a little while lower than the angels, thou hast crowned him with glory and honor . . . " (Heb. 2:6-7).

Yes, He does care for us and is concerned about us. And this same passage reminds us of another difference. We're of a different nature from the angels, which are unseen creatures made by God. How clear, then, that we're not of the same nature as God!

No, you can't be a Christian and accept Maharishi's ideas about god and creation. He is inadequate to decide these things. There's too much for one man to handle. Nature shows he is wrong. Scripture says he is wrong. The Church condemns his position. Maharishi is just plain heretical on the nature of God and the nature of man.

The Purpose of Life

Maharishi says the expansion of happiness is the purpose of life. Let us assume for a moment that he is right. After all, God does want us to be happy. The Westminster Shorter Catechism reflects the view of the historic Church when it says the chief purpose of humanity is to obey God and enjoy Him forever.

The expansion of happiness? That has a beautiful ring to it. But Maharishi's god is mindless. You have to imagine, then, that without any cause at all, there's a drive toward happiness in the universe. What an illogical idea!

In his system, humanity is most happy when in a mindless state. Is he right? No, because happiness is not mindlessness.

How can you possibly be happy while out of your mind? That is called *insanity*. Subtracting your mind subtracts from you as a person and makes happiness something totally negative. Your mind is you! Does he mean you are going to be happy without you involved? How absurd. How could anyone possibly be interested in such nonsense and foolishness?

The right way is *not* to remove your mind from an active part in happiness, but to get your mind actively and creatively involved in happiness. Mindlessness is a cop-out, not a solution. Mindlessness leaves you a nothing, a zero with the edges rubbed out. It puts you in the dangerous place of complete emptiness.

Jesus gave a far different idea of happiness in His famous Sermon on the Mount. In Matt. 5:1-11, He used the word "happy" nine times. Every one of those statements on happiness requires the active involvement of your mind. For example:

> Blessed are those who hunger and thirst for righteousness, for they shall be satisfied (Matt. 5:6).

Hungering and thirsting after righteousness is a *mental attitude*. You can't have such an attitude without the active use of your mind. Wanting righteousness involves thinking about what is right. You have to use your mind to do that. Right? Right! People who want righteousness, He says, will get it. No mind, no righteousness, no happiness.

God wants us to be happy, as the Scriptures and the Church teach. God provides for our happiness.

> Bless the Lord, O my soul; and forget not all his benefits (Ps 103:2).

God has given humanity so much. We can know Him. We can be His children. We can learn how to look after His creation properly. It was well put by Irenaeus: (Against Heresies, IV, xiv, 1) in the second century.

> In the beginning God fashioned Adam, not because He had need of man, but that He might have a being on whom to bestow His benefits. . . . Nor did He order us to follow Him because He

56

needed our service, but because He thus conferred on us salvation.[13]

Yes, God gives us so much, most of all salvation in Jesus Christ, which we accept and believe with our minds. What a difference between the empty mindlessness of Maharishi's "happiness" and the fruitful use of the mind in the attainment of the happiness God offers us!

The Problem

Humanity's problem, according to Maharishi, is ignorance. He says the problem is we don't know how to dive inside and unfold the divine glory that is already there. That's not right. The real problem of ignorance is not knowing God. The reason we don't know what's wrong inside us is that we don't know God. This ignorance of God is the most serious ignorance humanity has. As a result, people go dark on the inside. As the Scriptures say:

> They are darkened in their understanding, alienated from the life of God because of the ignorance that is in them, due to their hardness of heart (Eph. 4:18).

> For although they knew God they did not honor him as God or give thanks to him, but they became futile in their thinking and their senseless minds were darkened (Rom. 1:21).

The darkness within people is a result of their separation from God. Maharishi would have us believe our problem is ignorance of how to dive within ourselves. No, it is not the glory within which is cut off from us, but the glory of God. The fact is that *sin* is the problem.

> What then? Are we Jews any better off? No, not at all; for I have already charged that all men, both Jews and Greeks, are under the power of sin . . . since all have sinned and fall short of the glory of God . . . (Rom. 3:9,23).

Yes, sin cuts us off from the glory of God. The Church has recognized full well the source of the problem, as the Heidelberg Catechism (1563) put so clearly:

Did God create man wicked and perverse? No: God created man good and after His own image, so that he could rightly know God, his creator, heartily love Him and live with Him in eternal happiness, to praise and glorify Him. Where did this depraved nature of man come from? It came from the fall and disobedience of our first parents, Adam and Eve, in Paradise. That is how our nature became so corrupt that we are all conceived and born in sin (free modern language version of Part One, Questions 6 and 7).[14]

From the very beginning, humanity has been sinful and thus cut off from our holy God.

Salvation

Sin calls for salvation. We need forgiveness for our sins. But it is not forgiveness that Maharishi offers.

Poor Maharishi! He knows human behavior is important. Everybody is supposed to be perfect in behavior, he tells us. But there is no forgiveness in his system. Karma, the result of action, goes on, you will never escape it. Since what we need (by his definition) is to dive inside and unite with divinity already there, he offers us a method, TM, which is supposed to develop "god-consciousness." That doesn't provide forgiveness from sin. Maharishi doesn't say it does, but he thinks we will be better people if we follow his plan. Better people? With guilt and the results of sin still dogging our footsteps?

Christianity, however, has been built from the first on the provision of God for the sin of mankind.

For I delivered to you as of first importance what I also received, that Christ died for our sins in accordance with the scriptures, that he was buried, that he was raised on the third day in accordance with the scriptures . . . (1 Cor. 15:3-4).

What Paul delivered certainly is of first importance! As the Nicene Creed says:

The Lord Jesus Christ . . . for us men and for our salvation, came down from heaven, and was incarnate by the Holy Ghost of the Virgin Mary, and was made man; and was crucified also for us under Pontius Pilate; he suffered and was buried; and the third day he rose again, according to the Scriptures . . . .

That is the direct provision of God for our sins. *He* did it; *we* can't, as the Scriptures plainly teach,

> . . . without the shedding of blood there is no forgiveness of sins (Heb. 9:22).

> Let it be known to you therefore, brethren, that through this man forgiveness of sins is proclaimed to you (Acts 13:38).

No, Maharishi's "salvation" doesn't work. You can't pick your own salvation anyway. The Scriptures are clear on that.

> For by grace you have been saved through faith; and this is not your own doing, it is the gift of God—not because of works, lest any man should boast. For we are his workmanship, created in Christ Jesus for good works, which God prepared beforehand, that we should walk in them (Eph. 2:8-10).

The Christian Church has always held the same truth concerning the Lord Jesus Christ as that gift of God. We could not possibly find a way to earn forgiveness. But here is the provision made by God which brings us into His kingdom as His children when we accept it and give up our arrogance.

Maharishi's plan does nothing but mess up your mind. His *mantra* and its repeated repetition can only serve as a shot of morphine to the soul, deadening it to its guilt and need. He will leave you in a more wretched condition than he found you. This false messiah, this anti-Christ, must be boldly renounced for what he is!

It may seem a bit bold on our part to say that about Hindu teaching which is so popular at this time among many Americans. The mood of the day is, "If it's helpful, let's use it." But TM is not helpful. It weakens the human will and is devastating to the human personality.

It may even help the sinner to better adjust to his sin (as by that numbing shot of morphine). That is not help. It is like trying to cure a ruptured appendix with pain-killers. It kills the pain, but the patient dies. Those who are flocking to TM do so because they can't seem to get their acts together the way they think they should. But they haven't found the cure. They've found a temporary religious pain-killer.

Like a harmful drug, TM will ultimately kill its patient. Perhaps he gains a painless death, but that doesn't alter the fact that he loses his life. Make no mistake: Maharishi's TM is a religion, a false religion which does indeed have some pain-killing characteristics that can dull the pain of the human soul estranged from God. But it can neither satisfy nor save. The Thirty-Nine Articles of the Church of England have an appropriate confession which strikes at the heart of the matter.

> They also are to be condemned who presume to say, "Every man shall be saved by whatever law or sect he professes, just as long as he diligently lives his life according to that law and the light of nature." Holy Scripture gives us only the Name of Jesus Christ as the means by which men can be saved (free modern language version).[15]

It was true before these English Christians wrote it. It was true when they did. It is still true today.

> And there is salvation in no one else, for there is no other name under heaven given among men by which we must be saved (Acts 4:12).

A BRIEF PROFILE OF TRANSCENDENTAL MEDITATION

1. History
   —Founded by Maharishi Mahesh Yogi in 1959 in California.
   —Maharishi formerly a pupil of Guru Dev, leader of a Hindu sect in India.
   —Slow start in United States but revamped program in late 1960s by eliminating all religious vocabulary and adopting scientific and psychological terms.
   —Claims not to be a religion.
   —By 1976, many converts with 6,000 teachers and an annual income of $20 million.

2. Beliefs
   —God is the impersonal "Creative Intelligence" which includes everything in existence. This god seeks happiness through creating.
   —The purpose of life is happiness sought through an endless cycle of incarnations and reincarnations.
   —This happiness is attained by diving within ourselves to discover this creative intelligence within us, thus ridding ourselves of ignorance of who we are. This discovery is "bliss consciousness."
   —"Bliss consciousness" is only attained through the seven steps of transcendental meditation.
   —The mind is by-passed and these steps are accomplished by a liturgy called the *mantra*.

3. Method Of Operation
   —Has a World Plan to be fulfilled in this generation through TM's technique of meditation.
   —All areas of society systematically reached through television, newspapers, and magazines.
   —Seeks government endorsement and incorporation into classrooms.
   —Free introductory lectures offered but courses cost a substantial amount. Has established a university in Fairfield, Iowa, and buys much property, especially old resort facilities.
   —Many low-paid volunteers help spread TM.

4. Refutation
   —TM hasn't solved man's greatest problem—the fear of death itself.
   —God is not everything; rather, He has a nature totally distinct from His creatures.
   —Happiness is not mindlessness; it involves the mind by which one knows God and willingly obeys Him.
   —Ignorance of ourselves is not our problem; rather it is ignorance of the true and living God.
   —TM offers no forgiveness for sins.

TRANSCENDENTAL MEDITATION—FOOTNOTES

1. Paragraph 1, Article Second, Certificate of Incorporation of the Spiritual Regeneration Movement, filed with Office of the Secretary of State of the State of California, July 7, 1959.
2. "Transcendental Meditation as Taught by Maharishi Mahesh Yogi," SIMS-IMS National Center, 1015 Gayley Avenue, Los Angeles, California, 1973, p. 1.
3. *Ibid*, p. 2.
4. Maharishi Mahesh Yogi, *The Science of Being and Art of Living* (George Allen and Unwin Limited: London, 1963), p. 33.
5. Article Second, Certificate of Incorporation of the Students International Meditation Society, filed with Office of the Secretary of State of the State of California, as amended October 7, 1974.
6. Wallace, Robert Keith, "The Physiological Effects of TM," Ph.D. Thesis, University of California at Los Angeles, 1970.
7. Maharishi, *The Science of Being and Art of Living,* pp. 299,300.
8. Meyer, Eugene L., "The TM Empire," second of a four-part series, *Washington Post,* 1975.
9. *Ibid*, first of four-part series.
10. Schaff, *A Select Library,* Volume IV, pp. 22-23.
11. Schaff, *Creeds Of Christendom,* p. 607.
12. *Ibid*, p. 611.
13. *Irenaeus,* pp. 66-67.
14. Schaff, *Creeds Of Christendom,* pp. 309-310.
15. *Ibid*, p. 499.

An Introduction to Divine Light Mission

Bob Filmer, social services worker for the family welfare department in Mountain City, was having lunch with an old college classmate. Somehow, their reunion wasn't as comfortable as he had anticipated. Bill was into some new religion.

"No kidding," Bill insisted, "this is different. Guru Maharaj Ji is beautiful. He's changed my life!"

Bob laughed nervously. "Oh come on. Don't hand me that bull. I've heard about that young fraud."

Bill protested. "What you've heard isn't true! I received Knowledge from him and I know. All my anxiety and unhappiness has been replaced by such peace and love that I'm a new man. I want you to have the same thing."

"I can't imagine you talking that way," Bob was amazed. "You were never religious."

"I've never experienced anything like this. He has put me in direct contact with the whole energy of the universe," Bill replied seriously.

"That's unbelieveable."

"But it's true. Why don't you come to the ashram tonight? He's here and you can hear him in person."

Bob was inclined to be indulgent. Anyway, it should be interesting. "Okay, okay. What time?"

Walking up the steps to the large, solidly built house that was the ashram, Bob felt out of place. Inside, he wondered why he had agreed to come, but there was Bill, smiling happily to greet him. What had happened to that guy anyway? He hadn't been so affectionate and bubbly back in college. Sure was strange.

The music wasn't bad, though the words seemed a bit much with their obvious adoration of the guru. But Bob was handling it. He didn't even flinch much at the overdone devotion to Maharaj Ji and his wife when they came in.

When things settled down and the guru began to speak, Bob expected to find out what the whole thing was all about. Frankly, however, it didn't make much sense to him. Everything seemed disconnected, and the guru mostly told a bunch of stories which were supposed to mean something. Most of the people laughed and nodded but the meaning did not get through to Bob. Why couldn't he understand this stuff? Was he thick? Or were all these people crazy?

When the meeting was over and people were milling around, Bill asked, "Well, what did you think? Did it make sense to you?"

"I don't get it at all," Bob answered flatly.

"Well, how about talking to someone who can explain everything, then? One of Guru Maharaj Ji's helpers."

Bob got impatient. "Oh what the hell, Bill! You've got your thing. Why push it on me?"

"Look, Bob, I love you. Guru Maharaj Ji loves you. Please listen. When you get the Knowledge, you'll know what I mean."

So Bob listened to a mahatma. The man sat across from him and looked him directly in the eye. He seemed so honest and direct that Bob went away thinking it could be that these sincere people were right and maybe he didn't know anything. He promised to come back the next evening.

As the days and meetings went by, Bob began to soften. He took time off from his job. He listened and listened to those confusing little parables till he knew he didn't know anything anymore. He was ready to take Knowledge. On initiation night he threw himself face down before the altar decorated with pictures of Guru Maharaj Ji and became a premie. He felt the vibration inside and was convinced that the door to the kingdom of heaven had been opened for him.

They said, "Quit your job and come live in the ashram. There's work to be done."

He quit the job. Friends said he was crazy. But somehow all he wanted to do was serve Guru Maharaj Ji.

THE HISTORY AND THEOLOGY OF
DIVINE LIGHT MISSION

Among the multitudinous Hindu sects in India, the Divine Light Mission might never have made much of a splash. Its program in that country was not unusual. The teaching is one of many variations of the school of yoga called Siddha Yoga. All you need to know is that the guru is all-important. He's the means to "enlightenment." The idea is, if you're completely devoted to the guru and serve him with abandon, he'll lead you to all the answers. Each guru passes on his role to a successor when he dies.

Maharaj Ji's father was a famous guru in India, Paran Sant Satgurudev Shri Hans Ji Maharaj. Wealthy and highly respected, he served a large group of followers for some forty years. He formed an organization called Divine Light Mission. Nobody in the West heard about him, but that would change in the next generation. His youngest son showed a lot of promise. Divine Light literature claims Hans Ji always thought the boy would be a great spiritual master.

It seems there was good reason to think so.

A Boy Guru

Born in 1957, Maharaj Ji gave his first "discourses" to his family at the tender age of two. Soon he was speaking publicly. His first English language speech was given when he was six.

Then, suddenly, when Maharaj Ji was eight, his whole world changed. His father died. Everybody was very sad. The great Spiritual Master had died. Who could replace him? The young guru says an inner voice kept telling him he was the one. He didn't want to be Spiritual Master, but the voice persisted.

So, at his father's funeral, the eight-year-old Maharaj Ji stood up and said, "Don't be sad, here I am." Everybody fell prostrate to receive his blessings. His family, Divine Light leaders, everybody present. There it all began. A precocious youngster stepped into his father's shoes, with the help of his mother and three older brothers. It wasn't very long until he announced he was going to take the "Knowledge" he had inherited to the whole world. All of a sudden the Divine Light

Mission became unusual. The whole world! A boy leader! Wow! His disciples were impressed.

Significantly, Hans Ji Maharaj had left behind an efficient organization and millions of disciples. The movement functioned smoothly and apparently grew. In 1969 Maharaj Ji sent his first representative to the West. Mahatma Guru Charanand, one of his leaders, went to England to get things ready. A year later Maharaj Ji dropped out of school. At the end of a huge parade, on the outskirts of Delhi, he dropped his "Peace Bomb." He, the great Spiritual Master, was going to establish peace in this world.

In June, 1971, the Western world got its first public view of Maharaj Ji. At a pop festival in England, the gutsy little guru drove boldly up in a white Rolls Royce. Stepping up to the microphone, he spoke for five minutes before anyone thought to pull the plug.[1] England buzzed.

Meanwhile, in the United States there was a small but growing group of disciples. A few people who had traveled to India searching for meaning in life had run across Maharaj Ji. They became disciples (called "premies" by the Divine Light Mission) and formed a budding organization. They called for the guru, and he said he was coming. Somehow, distributing flyers, this enthusiastic dozen or so pumped up publicity. *Newsweek* picked up the story. Hundreds of curious people came to the airport. "The Lord has come!" proclaimed the flyers. Maharaj Ji was here. It was July, 1971.

The boy guru was an instant success. His first Guru Puja festival in Colorado in the summer of 1972 brought an estimated 2,000 converts. The bandwagon was moving. For two years he was the hottest thing on the guru circuit.

Maybe it was the efficiency of his father's organization and the guidance of his mother and brothers that enabled the Divine Light Mission to capitalize on this sudden growth. The young Maharaj Ji himself, after all, was only fourteen years old. Remarkably, there were Divine Light centers (called ashrams) springing up all over America by the fall of 1972.

In the midst of this sudden spurt, the American counterculture was shocked by the conversion of arch-radical Rennie Davis. Soon Davis was traveling around as an ardent, evangelistic devotee of Maharaj Ji. Disillusioned youth flocked for a peek at the guru who could capture such a noted symbol.

By the time spring, 1973 rolled around, DLM was reporting 480 centers around the world.[2] In the United States there were supposed to be 35,000 members. The wheels began to roll at the U.S. headquarters in Denver. Almost every kind of enterprise seems to have been set up, from repair shops to thrift shops. At the headquarters itself there arose a record company, a motion picture company, a newspaper, a magazine and the Divine United Organization. Guru Maharaj Ji was making it big.

Up ahead in November, 1973 was an event advertised as the most important occasion in the history of the world—Millennium 1973, to be held at the Houston Astrodome. Great things were expected and there was to be a huge crowd, estimated hopefully at somewhere between 80,000 and 200,000. Hundreds of thousands of dollars were spent to make sure that everything was just right.

The day came and disappointment ruled. Less than 20,000 people showed, including a number of "troublesome" Christians whose presence and literature was disturbing to the "powers that be." Bills from the event brought financial embarrassment. When it was all sorted out two months later, the Mission owed $600,000 more than it had.

So began a turn in fortune for the youngest guru in America. He was, after all, still an adolescent, and his practical jokes and childish behavior had up until now been dismissed as "God-play" by his indulgent family and followers. Now in the midst of financial crisis, his expensive cars and irresponsible carryings-on were less comical. Still, he was the Spiritual Master and you adore the Spiritual Master. He does no wrong.

In May, 1974, Maharaj Ji married a devotee who had served as his secretary. Eight years older than her teenaged husband, Marolyn Lois Johnson got a Hindu name: Durja Ji. The marriage did not sit too well with his family. A new emphasis developed to pay the bills: give 10 percent of your income. It was to be a bad year for the movement and its master in spite of the joy of wedded bliss.

The hassle between the young guru and his family grew.

They griped about his lifestyle—nightclubs, dancing, drinking, and most horrible of all, meat-eating.

Either he hustled them off to India or they split in order to consolidate their forces, but they went. Back home, his mother, Mataji, said Maharaj Ji was out as God and his oldest brother Bal Bagwan Ji was in. Maharaj Ji flew to India. His family, he said, thought they ruled by divine right. Wrong. His kingdom was not of this world.

Did they think they could throw the Lord of the universe out of office? How ridiculous! On went the controversy, but in the end Maharaj Ji remained in control, at least of the major part of his movement. and especially in the west.

Back in the United States he and Durja Ji had a baby, Premlata. Things picked up. Old bills got paid. In the summer of 1975, *Divine Times* claimed 201 communities in the United States and hundreds more in 66 countries.[3] Premies (devotees) were evangelizing by doing a house-to-house survey on meditation. Large crowds appeared at festivals.

Still, the problems were not over. Enthusiasm for DLM was eroding and there were thousands of dropouts. In early 1976, DLM admitted that active U.S. membership was no more than 10,000. Another plan of organization was instituted with a renewed emphasis on the establishment of stable communities. With new momentum, Maharaj Ji will continue to be heard. Let's take a closer look at his teachings and this "Knowledge" which holds the loyalty of so many followers.

WHAT THE DIVINE LIGHT MISSION BELIEVES

Who is God?

God, to the devotees of Guru Maharaj Ji, is the ever-existing source of everything. Sometimes God is spoken of in personal terms; other times He is described as an impersonal force. He is described as creating everything and as being in everything. Thus, God is the force behind all things and He is the divine Light in all beginnings.

Also, He has come bodily in human form time after time throughout human history. Among these incarnations were Vishnu, Ram, Krishna, Jesus Christ, and Buddha. There has, in fact, been a succession of Satgurus (a Hindu term meaning Perfect Masters), but only one for each age. These Perfect Masters are supposed to be incarnations of God, actually being fully God in human form.

It's a real mishmash. This movement comes out of Hinduism, believing in an impersonal god which is everything. They know that the Western mind won't buy that without change. So they've made some big adjustments. In the West, with its Christian tradition, we think of God in personal terms. So they use personal terms within a Hindu context. It's all designed to confuse and to convince.

Now you see how DLM can call God "He" and then say "He is pure energy" and "He is self-existent in all beings at all places and at all times." If you substitute the word "it" for "He," you'll have a better picture of their god. It's a great way to slip Hinduism in under the door. Besides, the DLM system requires that the guru be worshiped. Using familiar language gives the impression he's something like Jesus Christ.

Replacing Jesus

In countries where there's a Christian tradition, DLM also has to get rid of the uniqueness of Jesus. Get rid of that uniqueness and you can dismiss Christianity. They've got a way of doing that, too. DLM literature quotes John 5:39-40, for example:

> You search the scriptures, because you think that in them you have eternal life; and it is they that bear witness to me; yet you refuse to come to me that you may have life.

Emphasizing the word "think," they come up with a novel interpretation. Jesus, we are told, was saying everyone needs a *living* Master. Then picking up on Jesus' statement that "the kingdom of God is within you," (Luke 17:21), they imply that *every person in the world* has God inside. Taking John 9:5, "As long as I am in the world, I am the light of the world," they say, see, He was the Light only as long as He was here. Jesus was the living Master of His time, we are told, and He helped people get in touch with the divinity within. But we need a *living* Master today—Guru Maharaj Ji.

69

Maharaj Ji knows, though, that people who know the Bible and Christian teaching won't give up the uniqueness of Jesus easily. That's why he and his helpers center their attack on the interpretation of John 1:1, "In the beginning was the Word and the Word was with God, and the Word was God."

Now follow along carefully, because they're really slippery and tricky here. A DLM statement puts it this way. "You say the Word is Jesus Christ. Let's substitute 'Jesus Christ' for 'the Word.' Then it reads, 'In the beginning was Jesus Christ and Jesus Christ was the Father, and Jesus Christ was God.' How can the Son be born before the Father? Fathers come before sons. That can't be right. The Word is something else."[4]

What nonsense! We're going to deal with this in detail when we refute DLM theology. Right now I want you just to notice how the blasphemer has twisted the sentence.

But let's go on. Having so effectively (they think) disposed of the notion that Jesus is the Word, DLM continues. Maharaj Ji says this Word really is the source of everything and, in fact, is everything. It is pure and perfect energy which has no creation and no destruction. As a matter of fact, he tells us, this Word is God, and He is inside us.

In another place a DLM writer puts it differently. "In the beginning was the Word," he says, means that in the beginning was the "cosmic vibration," because after all, words are vibrations when spoken. So here's what it is, he proclaims, "Out of that cosmic vibration have come all of ourselves, our soul, which is part and parcel of it."[5]

God in a Human Body Today

Thinking it has disposed of Jesus Christ, DLM gets on with its business. You've guessed, or know, by now that Maharaj Ji is supposed to be today's Perfect Master. All the tricky business of impersonal god and personal God all mixed up comes into play now. Guru Maharaj Ji is proclaimed God with a human body, possessing all of divine Light and Knowledge. He is the fullness of divine Love. DLM is big on love.

All the inconsistency and slipperiness in DLM god-talk can leave your head spinning. God is the force and energy of the universe and is present in all living beings. Still, in every age there has been someone, they say, who is God in a human body and reveals god within. Apparently they don't want to give a straight picture of what god is like to them.

Creation

Maharaj Ji says "the Word" is literally everything. It is the universe. Atoms and molecules, cells and beings, planets and galaxies, are this Word in material form. Actually, these things are temporary shells, really illusions, which come and go as the Word takes on various forms.

Life is the highest material form and humanity is the highest form of life, we are told. You see, at the very centers of our beings are the seeds of divinity. Your body is only a container for that seed of divinity—your spirit or soul. It is not the real you.

Reincarnation is a big thing in all this. Suppose you just lived for your own self-interest or ignored god when you were a human. Okay, you'll be born as an insect or an animal in your next life to work out the results of that. As far as DLM is concerned, if you don't get "enlightened" during your human life, you're certain to be reborn as some kind of animal. "Better" people do come back as "higher" or more attractive animals, though. If you miss enlightenment but are a good kid maybe you'll get to be an elephant.

Human Advantage

Human life, Maharaj Ji believes, is the ultimate life form. You were given human life so you'd have a chance to experience the oneness with god which is the goal of the soul. You, he says (pointing to you), must realize you are divine. God is already in you. Your soul contains the whole of the energy that sustains the universe.

Don't think he believes everything is good. Evil does exist in the world, and Maharaj Ji implies god created it. But good is also created to counterbalance evil. Somehow or other, god isn't responsible for the action of this evil. Inconsistencies like this abound in DLM writings.

What's the Goal?

DLM tells us the basic goal of human life is to come into union with god. Hold it! That doesn't mean a union or relationship with a being who is a person. No way. It's a merging with the god, the divine within us. We were created to be pure: to have pure thoughts and pure behavior. We'll never make it, though, until we know love. And we can't know love until we have the "god-realization" which comes from the merging of our souls with the divine.

Maharaj Ji wants to unify all humanity. Human life is supposed to be knit together in a common bond, he says. That's what god wants, and it can only come if we all merge with the divine. How it's going to work, he doesn't say.

The Problem

Unfortunately most of humanity is ignorant of its purpose for existing. DLM people make it simple: our problem is basically *ignorance*. We're all too wrapped up in this material world. It's only an illusion, they say, but our senses get bombarded with it constantly. So our inner self is frustrated. We see things, we hear noises, we smell smells, we touch things, we taste things. Our inner being doesn't have a chance. Maharaj Ji insists this frustration is why there's so much trouble among human beings. Our minds are just too busy with all the input we get from our senses.

Deep down inside, though, he says, our souls really want union with god. The continuing ignorance of our minds prevents it. The fight goes on between the desire of our souls and the ignorance of our minds. We're in darkness because ignorance wins. That's very bad, according to DLM theology, because human life is the only living state in which we can attain salvation through "god-realization." If we don't get it during our human existence, who knows when we'll get another chance? How would you like to pass through a thousand years of life as, say, grasshoppers and spiders?

There's something important that goes along with that. They believe we experience in human life the results of lack of devotion to god in previous incarnations. However, DLM does not believe we got human life because we earned it. It is by grace that god gave it. Now this is important: They say we got this human life so we can escape from delusion and realize our true selves. In human life, and *only* in human life, we can *rid ourselves of the illusion that we are separate individual identities and immerse ourselves in the creator.* Read that over and get it down. It's DLM's basic position on what we need.

DLM really sneers at all the divisions in the name of religion. Christianity especially comes under attack. "Read Ephesians 4:4-6," DLM leaders say. " 'There is one body and one Spirit, one Lord, one faith, one baptism, one God and Father of all, who is above all, and through all, and in you all.' Now look at you. Christianity is split into hundreds and hundreds of splinter groups, all basing their separate beliefs on the *Bible.* You can't unite the world."

What is needed, we are told, is for all of us to unite under their guru. He is called "God-personified," offering love and salvation. After all, they ask, isn't religion supposed to give us bliss and perfect peace? All right, then, remember your true nature. Stop identifying with matter. Realize the god within. Unite with god and all humanity through Guru Maharaj Ji. Then all humanity will be gathered to the goal of eternal happiness and salvation.

Quite a line, isn't it?

Salvation

DLM defines salvation as the state in which the soul attains unity and tranquility by regular meditation. This is the essence of Divine Light teaching. Of course you have to get there, and Maharaj Ji is the *only* one who brings the revelation to make it all possible. He alone, they claim, can as Perfect Master unite us with God.

Can you prove it, we ask?

Sure, they say, here's something Guru Maharaj Ji will do for you. There are spiritual senses of sight, hearing, taste, and feeling. These can be opened up so you can experience divine light, celestial music, divine nectar, and the Word. You can't experience them without a Perfect Master as a guide. All of them are offered by Maharaj Ji as direct benefits of receiving Knowledge from him. I won't teach you a religion, he says; I'll bring you direct experience of God.[6]

Maharaj Ji repeatedly tells us the "True Knowledge" he brings is not at all like the "inferior knowledge" you get from reading Scriptures or listening to teaching. That's important. He defines "Knowledge" in a way foreign to us. His "Knowl-

73

edge" is not a matter of learning. It doesn't have anything to do with the mind. It bypasses the mind.

Just to show you how far they reach to justify by-passing the mind, here is a funny little illustration out of DLM literature. There is a small organ deep in the brain called the pineal gland. Not much is known about its function, but DLM people say they've got it figured out. They say we've got a third eye by which we see the true light when we meditate like Maharaj Ji says. The pineal gland is that third eye, according to their theory, and it actually controls our bodies and their functions. If we really meditate right, we are in control of our third eye and can control our bodies. Now that's really reaching!

Well, back to theology. How do people get this "Knowledge" that bypasses the mind? Basic to everything DLM teaches is the idea that God has come in the form of Guru Maharaj Ji. He's here for one reason—to give practical "Knowledge" of himself and his light. (Remember "Knowledge" isn't knowledge).

Let's suppose you believe and you want Knowledge. Okay, here's what you do. You submit yourself completely in worshipful devotion to Maharaj Ji. Then he extends grace and gives you the secrets of the "Knowledge." Once you've got those secrets, you're supposed to be on your way to "realization of God."

When people decide to submit to Maharaj Ji, they are first screened to see if they're really ready. If they are, they gather in a darkened room (with pictures of the guru all around) to hear a lecture on the inner divine light. After the lecture, a representative of Maharaj Ji (called a "mahatma") guides each person to the secret means for seeing divine light, hearing celestial music, and tasting divine nectar.[7]

This part would be truly comical if it weren't so terribly serious. Here's what happens. The initiator has you press the side of your forehead with the thumb and middle finger of your right hand, while pressing on the lower center of your forehead with your index finger. Presto! You see divine light! I guess you see light!

Then he presses his fingers into your ears. You hear sound. That noise has been described in many ways, but DLM calls it celestial harmony.

Third, the initiator shows you how to curl your tongue back to the point at which it seems you will almost swallow it. There you taste with the tip of your tongue what they call divine nectar. Ugh! Post-nasal drip. Can you imagine they call this "nectar," placed there for your sustenance before birth? They actually claim this is what Jesus lived on during His forty days in the wilderness.

But these three experiences are just the preliminary proofs to prepare you for the ultimate experience. You now learn that there's an inner vibration inside all of us which is the Word. Remember when we discussed TM we said they gave a Sanskrit word as a *mantra,* and you were to meditate on its sound? Well, the *mantra* DLM gives you is the sound of your own breath! It is the "vibration inside all of us!" By this meditation on your own breath, you get the "Knowledge" promised by Maharaj Ji. If you get it right, you're supposed to "bliss out," which is the ultimate experience for DLM people. They say it's an experience of indescribable inner peace. It's advertised as the true experience of divinity, transcending time and space. They also call it experiencing infinity with your body. What happens is your mind gets bent.

Devotees are supposed to meditate for an hour in the morning and an hour in the evening. From now on, the new devotee must give unswerving devotion, submission and service to Guru Maharaj Ji. He's supposed to fall in love with the guru, and give himself over completely.

The goal of DLM is to unite the whole world in this experience. They say it is the connecting ladder between man and god, but they don't mean personal God, they mean an impersonal, "everything" god.

DLM says four blessings have been given to every human being. First, being born in a human body. Second, the scriptures of all religions. Third, god coming to earth as Spiritual Master. Fourth, the individual's own effort.[8] Salvation results when all four are applied in self-denying devotion to Guru Maharaj Ji.

THE METHOD OF OPERATION OF
DIVINE LIGHT MISSION

Divine Light Mission in Action

"Why don't you come and hear the satsang tonight?" "Guru Maharaj Ji himself is talking tonight. Come hear him." DLM devotees (called "premies") are enthusiastic recruiters. They go after their friends, and mostly want them to hear *satsang*. Now, satsangs (holy discourses) are the lectures which are the "main events" in DLM evangelism.

Guru Maharaj Ji came to the West prepared to give up Hindu terminology in favor of plain American language. A few technical terms hang on and *satsang* is one of them. Satsang can be a lot of things. Discourses to the faithful. Informal religious instruction. Evangelistic sermons. Held for the public, satsang is intended to convince people Maharaj Ji is the answer to all their needs, the god they must know.

Held in Divine Light centers, university classrooms, and hired halls, these lectures are widely advertised. In the early days most of them were given by members of the guru's family. But when the rift occurred over how he was living, Maharaj Ji got a whole new set of teachers. He calls them *mahatmas* (another hangover from Hindu terminology) and they serve as instructors and initiators. There are probably a dozen or so traveling around the world. Usually they give the lectures, but others can. When Maharaj Ji is in town, you can bet he'll talk often. So will his wife, Durja Ji.

These teachers are adept in out-of-context quotation of the Bible and books of pagan religions. They glibly twist meanings to point to Maharaj Ji, as in the ways we've already shown. They pretend great respect for all the religious writings of the world, including the Bible. They've read a lot, too, and they've always got a reference at tongue-tip. In question sessions they're good; any quotation can be turned to point to Maharaj Ji. They want Americans to think the "Knowledge" is compatible with Christianity. Mahatmas are sharp, slippery and persuasive.

Backing up these frequent and regular lectures is a schedule of large festivals. Most of them are called Guru Puja Festivals. DLM holds them all over the world now. In keeping with the change of language, the Guru Puja in the United States was to be called the "North American Convention" beginning in 1976. These festivals serve not only to keep the premies excited and busy, but they also attract curious people who become potential converts.

Premies

Behind it all is the grass roots work of the premies. They're programmed to carry out personal evangelism with zeal. They love their guru. They'd better. He says to, and he's god! For their guidance, DLM puts out a *Propagation Handbook*. There they get detailed instructions on how to present the message. Contents cover inner experience, collective consciousness, community, satsang, talking about the "Knowledge," gearing to twentieth century people, and careful presentation of the meditation.

There are other helpful books for them to use, too, such as *People Who Look for Peace Get It, Meditation: The Missing Peace,* and *Changing the World by Changing People's Hearts.* Personal evangelism is not left to chance.

Films and Periodicals

DLM has made many movies, too. All feature Maharaj Ji and his teaching. To give you a notion of what's used, here are four titles: "Soul Rush," "Who Is Guru Maharaj Ji?", "The Perfect Logic," and "Satguru Has Come."

There's a newspaper—*Divine Times* (a new name was being sought in mid-1976). It gives news of the movement, reports of the guru's messages, mahatmas' messages, and lots of pictures—mostly of the guru. .Longer articles with heavier content appear in the slick quarterly magazine, *And It Is Divine.*

Getting Converts

When somebody shows interest, indoctrination begins in earnest. With a prospect who is very receptive, the process may take only a few hours. It has been known to take fifteen hours or more. One former premie claims he was subjected to indoctrination of up to twelve hours a day for a week. He and others who got out say this preparatory instruction is made up mostly of parables which confuse the victim. He ends up feeling inferior, inadequate, and worthless. Ex-premies call this process "brainwashing." It is compared with the negative selling of some encyclopedia salesmen and the mental games described by some former prisoners of war. Some ex-premies swear they were hypnotized.

Initiation

When the prospect is suitably conditioned, the elaborate initiation ceremony follows. (See page 74.)

Now the new premie is ready for instructions on how to live as a devoted follower of Guru Maharaj Ji. First there is a set of written rules:[9]

1) Never put off till tomorrow what you can do today.
2) Never delay in attending satsang.
3) Always have faith in God.
4) Constantly meditate and remember the name.
5) Never have any doubt in your mind.

Former premies say there is also an unwritten code:

1) Stay away from movies and general entertainment.
2) Never swear.
3) Surrender all worldly possessions to the Divine Light Mission. (There seem to be premies who haven't followed this one.)
4) Be celibate. (This one apparently applies to single people. Certainly the guru himself is not.)

To each new initiate goes the premie guidebook, *Life with Knowledge,* intended to be an at-hand reminder of how to continue and to grow in the faith.

Living Together

From the beginning DLM has made a big thing of having its premies live communally. They're supposed to live in ashrams (communal centers) established by DLM. When converts were streaming in, though, that wasn't always possible. Premies were encouraged to set up their own groups, but that didn't work too well. There has apparently been a rather sharp turnover. It's still the program, however, because living in community keeps people centered on the guru. Some ex-premies say living in the ashram kept them absolutely dependent on DLM for every personal need. It tended to keep them enslaved.

Living in the ashrams does seem to keep people hooked on this false religion. Luckily, however, overall organization hasn't been good enough to keep up with all the converts.

Scattered people who weren't under the watchful eye of mahatmas have dropped out with great frequency. By 1976, community and organization were being stressed in a bigger way by the guru. DLM was tightening up. Plans for setting up businesses to support premies were developed. In Denver, the headquarters, premies started the Premrose Hotel.

Love Your Guru

Given the extreme devotion to the guru as god, DLM has to be a personality cult. In the first place, that's the nature of this particular kind of Hindu sect. Maybe the kind of adoration they give Maharaj Ji is beyond your imagination, but everything centers on him. Premies are expected to always desire to see the Master. That's why, when you check out the DLM mail order catalogue, you find more pictures of the guru for sale than anything else. After all, Maharaj Ji is the Lord of the universe to his premies. Everything possible is done to reinforce that idea.

Music is important in worship, isn't it? There have been several "Bliss Bands" formed among premies. The Winter, 1976, DLM catalogue listed "Songs of Love" tapes by some of these groups. The titles of the songs show how this music is used to help build and maintain faith, love, and devotion to the guru: "Oh Perfect Lord," "Shining Grace," "Lord of the Universe," "Hey, Hey, the Father's Come," "Spread the Knowledge," and others like them. You get the picture, don't you? Guru is God, so he's worshiped as God. All devotion is given to him.

Cassette tapes offered through the catalogue also keep people tied in. *All* are satsangs by Maharaj Ji, and the most recent include addresses by his wife, Durja Ji. Most contain songs as well. Also in the catalogues are gold and silver photo medallions, photo buttons, bumper stickers and more of the same kind of stuff. Guru is the focus of everything.

What Happens?

Guru Maharaj Ji's followers have experienced something deep inside. Call it hypnosis, self-induced trance, demonic possession, or whatever; they are enthusiastic about him and what he has given them. Some ex-premies charge the whole

79

trip is hypnotism. One says he was hypnotized into believing for some days that he breathed through the top of his head.

"Extra-sensory perception" (ESP) hypnotism is what is going on, according to one theory. And the existence of families in which gurus appear repeatedly is explained by the hypothesis that the ability to perform ESP hypnotism is hereditary. The idea is, there are people who can hypnotize you even without looking at you. It's their brain to your brain. Though this is speculation, we do know these people are captivated. Sometimes the guru may not be very good at keeping them that way, but he intends to.

Maharaj Ji instructs his disciples: "So whatever extra you have got, give it to me. And the extra thing you have got is your mind. Give it to me. I am ready to receive it. Because your mind troubles you, give it to me. It won't trouble me! Just give it. And give your egos to me because egos trouble you, but they don't trouble me. Give them to me. So whatever extra you have in your mind, or your mind itself even, give it to me. I can bear it. . . . So just try to be holy and try to be a good devotee, a perfect devotee of that Guru who is Himself perfect, who is really perfect."[10] Maharaj Ji is the authority, to be obeyed in all things, to be worshiped, to be served. And the premies do it.

A REFUTATION OF THE DIVINE LIGHT MISSION

Divine Light Mission theology is very much like that of Transcendental Meditation. Therefore, it will be well for you to review the "Refutation" section under TM, because most of it applies to this cult as well.

What's an Incarnation of God?

The nature of God is basically the same to Maharaj Ji as to Maharishi Mahesh Yogi. There are, however, a few twists which we ought to look at. DLM sees god in everything, the same as TM. But, there is this thing in their theology about god having appeared on earth in various bodily forms (incarnations) including Vishnu, Krishna, Jesus Christ, and many others. We've seen they think Maharaj Ji is the current incarnation.

That brings up an interesting question. How can an impersonal god become incarnate? How can mindlessness "decide" to take on a particular human form? There is no answer. That dilemma is all part of the inconsistency of DLM. And the confusion is further complicated when the DLM people throw around personal pronouns such as "He" and "Him" in reference to their god. That is mostly done, as we noted earlier, to suck in people who are familiar with Christianity.

In order to get by with calling Maharaj Ji "God in a human body" in this country; DLM knows that it must get rid of the uniqueness of Jesus. These people know something of how Christianity regards Him. To review for a moment, the initial attack centers on John 1:1;

> In the beginning was the Word and the Word was with God, and the Word was God.

With their own tricky interpretation, they tell us the Word is pure and perfect energy. It is everything; it is God; it is the cosmic vibration. It is, they conclude, the vibration which is inside all of us, demonstrated by the sound of our own breath.

There! They think they have explained the Word and rid themselves of Jesus Christ. Well, they haven't. Because they have no idea of the depth of teaching in the orthodox Church about Jesus Christ, who is the Word. They have no idea how strongly the Church has fought for that truth against all manner of heresies!

There is a consistent interpretation of John 1:1 which has come down through every generation of the Church. The Word is Jesus Christ. Lots of heretics have said, "No, the Word is this or that." All have been rejected.

There are probably no stronger writers on this subject than two men who lived in the fourth century, Athanasius of Alexandria and Hilary of Poitiers. Both gave their whole lives to the work of maintaining the truth of the deity of Jesus Christ, who is the Word. Read first Athanasius, who describes the nature of the Word:

> For if the movement of creation was irrational, and the universe went along without a plan, it would be fair not to believe me. But if

81

it demonstrates reason, wisdom and skill, and if it is ordered completely, then it follows that He who is over it and has ordered it, is none other than the reason or Word of God. But by Word I don't mean that which is involved in and inherent in all created things. No, I don't mean the thing which is called the seed principle by some people. That principle doesn't have any soul or power of reason or thought. It works by the skill of someone acting on it. Nor do I mean a word such as the words that people speak, consisting of syllables pushed by the breath. What I mean is the living and powerful Word of the good God, the God of the universe, the very Word which is God. This Word Who is different from things that are made, and all Creation, is the One own Word of the good Father. This Word is the One Who by His own providence put together and gives light to this Universe. Because, being the good Word of the good Father, he ordered all things, putting all kinds of different things together, making one harmonious order (modern language version of Part III, point 40.3-5, *Against the Heathen*).[11]

That very careful statement clearly denies that DLM's cunningly devised interpretation is anything like the definition the Church has always given to the Word. To go with it there is the statement of Hilary which simply recognizes Jesus Christ as the Word:

Thus we have all these different assurances of the Divinity of our Lord Jesus Christ:—His name, His birth, His nature, His power, His own assertion. As to the name, no doubt is possible. It is written, In the beginning was the Word, and the Word was with God, and the Word was God. What reason can there be for suspecting that He is not what His name indicates? And does not this name clearly describe His nature? If a statement is to be contradicted, it must be for some reason. What reason, I demand, is there in this instance for denying that He is God? The name is given Him, plainly and distinctly, and unqualified by any incongruous addition which might raise a doubt. The Word, we read, which was made flesh, was none other than God. There is no loophole for any such conjecture as that He has received this name as a favor or taken it upon Himself, so possessing a titular Godhead which is not His by nature[12] (*On the Trinity*, Book VII, point 9).

The people of God have taken this stance for nearly twenty centuries. Jesus Christ is the Word, and that means Jesus

Christ is God. Now, as to incarnations of God, the Scriptures also speak.

> For in him the whole fullness of deity dwells bodily . . . (Col. 2:9).

> And the Word became flesh and dwelt among us, full of grace and truth; we have beheld His glory, glory as of the only Son from the Father (John 1:14).

The Christian Church has always said those Scriptures, and many others, mean Jesus Christ is the one who took on a bodily form and was God in a human body. We could turn to many creeds to show that fact. Here is the statement of the Third Ecumenical Council, held at Ephesus in 431 AD:

> We ought to follow these words and decrees, considering what is meant by the Word of God being incarnate and made man. We are not saying that the nature of the Word was changed and become flesh, or that it was converted into just a man consisting of soul and body. No, we are saying that the Word, having personally united Himself with a body animated by a rational soul, became man in some unknowable and inconceivable manner. He was called the Son of Man, not just because He wanted to be called that, or just because he took on a human body, but because the two natures were brought together in a true union. That union is made up of both one Christ and one Son, because the difference of the two natures was not taken away by the union. The divinity and the humanity make perfect for us the one Lord Jesus Christ by their unknowable and inexpressable union . . . (free modern language version of a letter by Cyril of Alexandria to Nestorius which letter was adopted in full by the Council).[13]

DLM's Lord vs the One Lord Jesus Christ

Now we can look at DLM's claim that Guru Maharaj Ji is an incarnation of God. Christianity holds the uniqueness of Jesus Christ in such high regard that this particular theological curve must not be passed by. The Scriptures are very specific about who He is, and the Church has always kept His person uppermost in its confessions. When the creed says, ". . . one Lord Jesus Christ, the only begotten Son of God . . . ," it means *one*. Look at the testimony of Scripture:

83

Eight days later, his disciples were again in the house, and Thomas was with them. The doors were shut, but Jesus came and stood among them, and said, "Peace be with you." Then he said to Thomas, "Put your finger here, and see my hands; and put out your hand, and place it in my side; do not be faithless, but believing." Thomas answered him, "My Lord and my God!" Jesus said to 'him, "Have you believed because you have seen me? Blessed are those who have not seen and yet believe" (John 20:26-29).

On his robe and on his thigh he has a name inscribed, King of kings and Lord of lords (Rev. 19:16).

That confession by Thomas has been the confession of millions of Christians for more than nineteen centuries.

Yet for us there is one God, the Father, from whom are all things and for whom we exist, and one Lord, Jesus Christ, through whom are all things and through whom we exist (1 Cor. 8:6).

We, the Church of Jesus Christ, have always said, and will always say, what the Fifth Ecumenical Council, held in Constantinople in 553 A.D. set forth:

If anyone does not confess that our Lord Jesus Christ who was crucified in the flesh is true God and the Lord of Glory and one of the Holy Trinity: let him be anathema (Article X).[14]

Jesus Christ, the ONE, the only begotten Son of God is *alone* the Savior of mankind. In that we simply affirm what the Scriptures teach:

Be it known to you all, and to all the people of Israel, that by the name of Jesus Christ of Nazareth, whom you crucified, whom God raised from the dead, by him this man is standing before you well. This is the stone which was rejected by you builders, but which has become the head of the corner. And there is salvation in no one else, for there is no other name under heaven given among men by which we must be saved (Acts 4:10-12).

Can it be clearer? There is no other name—certainly not Guru Maharaj Ji! *Only* Jesus Christ is the acceptable Savior, as so beautifully put by Martin Luther in his Small Catechism:

I believe that Jesus Christ, true God, begotten of the Father from eternity, and also true man, born of the Virgin Mary, is my Lord: who has redeemed me, a lost and condemned man, secured and delivered me even from all sins, from death, and from the power of the devil, not with gold or silver, but with his holy, precious blood; in order that I might be his own, live under him in his kingdom, and serve him in everlasting righteousness, innocence, and blessedness, even as he is risen from the dead, and lives and reigns forever. This is most certainly true.[15]

Now, what more is there to say? We reject Vishnu, Ram, Krishna, Buddha, Maharaj Ji, and all others who claim to bring "salvation" to mankind. There is a word which the Church applies to all who make such claims.

Children, it is the last hour; and as you have heard that antichrist is coming, so now many antichrists have come; therefore we know that it is the last hour. They went out from us, but they were not of us; for if they had been of us, they would have continued with us; but they went out, that it might be plain that they all are not of us. . . . Who is the liar but he who denies that Jesus is the Christ? This is the antichrist, he who denies the Father and the Son. No one who denies the Son has the Father. He who confesses the Son has the Father also (1 John 2:18-19, 22-23).

Anti-Christ is the word. Many, many people have come to the Church speaking against Jesus Christ. Our Church has always called them "anti-Christs." When Athanasius wrote against one such group of enemies of Christ, the followers of Arius, he said:

There have been many heresies before them, which, going further than they ought, have fallen into folly. But these men, trying in all their arguments to overthrow the Divinity of the Word, have come nearer than anybody else to Anti-Christ. Therefore, they have been excommunicated and condemned by the Church. We who are Christians must turn away from all who speak or think anything against Christ. They are enemies of God and destroyers of souls. As the Apostle John has told us, we shouldn't even 'bid such God-speed,' lest we take part in their sins (free modern language version, *The Deposition of Arius*).[16]

85

On the authority of the Scriptures and their impact in the Church, Majaraj Ji and all who follow him are anti-Christs!

DLM's Goal of Life vs the Kingdom of God

When Majaraj Ji says the goal of human life is to come into oneness with God, it sounds good. His meaning, of course, is for us to get down inside ourselves, contact the seed of divinity there, and dwell upon it. Then, when we die, perhaps we will merge blissfully into god.

The fact is, this is not the goal of human life at all. It is perhaps here that all these cultic groups depart most from Christianity.

The goal of human life is to enter the kingdom of God. That is the theme of the whole New Testament. Consider these passages from the Scriptures:

> So there will be richly provided for you an entrance into the eternal kingdom of our Lord and savior Jesus Christ (2 Pet. 1:11).

> Listen, my beloved brethren. Has not God chosen those who are poor in the world to be rich in faith and heirs of the kingdom which he has promised to those who love him (James 2:5)?

> He has delivered us from the dominion of darkness and transferred us to the kingdom of his beloved Son (Col. 1:13).

> Thy Kingdom come. Thy will be done, on earth as it is in heaven (Matt. 6:10).

> The Lord will rescue me from every evil and save me for His heavenly kingdom. To him be the glory for ever and ever. Amen (2 Tim. 4:18).

Jesus spoke constantly of the kingdom of God. Guru Maharaj Ji also speaks of the kingdom of God. He says humanity must be united and hints the human unity which he plans to bring about is the fulfillment of the kingdom of God.

Consider, however, the nature of the kingdom of God as seen in Christian teaching. Consider, also, the present relation of the Church to that kingdom. The Nicene Creed, speaking of the Lord Jesus Christ, says, ". . . whose kingdom shall have no end," and adds, ". . . one Holy Catholic and Apostolic Church. I acknowledge one Baptism for the remission of sins; and I look for the resurrection of the dead, and the life of the world to come."[17]

Justin Martyr, writing about 150 A.D., expressed the interpretation of the Scriptures which has consistently been held by the Christian Church:

> When you hear that we look for a kingdom, you rashly suppose that we mean something merely human. But we speak of a Kingdom with God, as is clear from our confessing Christ when you bring us to trial, though we know that death is the penalty for this confession. For if we looked for a human kingdom, we would deny it in order to save our lives, and would try to remain in hiding in order to obtain the things we look for. But since we do not place our hopes on the present, we are not troubled by being put to death, since we will have to die somehow in any case.[18]

Historically, the Church has sought to live under the reign of Christ, guiding the people as He commands in this age so they are protected and prepared for that kingdom which will last forever. This modern day anti-Christ, Guru Maharaj Ji, wants to set up an earthly kingdom, with him at its head. He stands condemned by God and His Church for his blasphemy!

A BRIEF PROFILE OF THE DIVINE LIGHT MISSION

1. History
   —Founded by Maharaj Ji's father in India and brought to U.S. in 1971, with headquarters in Denver, Colorado.
   —By fall of 1972, DLM centers called ashrams were springing up all over America.
   —In May, 1974, Ji at the age of 17 married a devotee eight years older than he. Ji's marriage and life-style (craze for expensive cars, dancing, drinking, and meat-eating) caused rift in his family back home in India.
   —By summer of 1975, DLM claimed 201 communities in the United States and hundreds more in 66 countries.
   —Thousands dropped out, and in 1976 the active U.S. membership was only 10,000.

2. Beliefs
   —God is sometimes personal and sometimes impersonal, and has appeared throughout history by many incarnations, the latest of whom is Ji.
   —Maharaj Ji has replaced Jesus Christ as "the Word made flesh" in John 1.
   —Ji is god with a human body, possessing all of divine light and knowledge. He is the fullness of divine love.
   —The goal of human life is unity, accomplished by bypassing the mind and merging with the divine within us. Failure is due to ignorance.
   —This goal is attained by the help of Ji and DLM's system of meditation.

3. Method Of Operation
   —Devotees are called premies, who enthusiastically recruit their friends to hear satsangs (holy discourses).
   —Mahatmas serve as teachers and initiators and are adept at out-of-context quotations of the Bible and books of other religions.
   —The cult is propagated by the personal evangelism of the premies, films, a newspaper, and a magazine.
   —New converts undergo a thorough brainwashing with intense indoctrination.
   —The premies live together communally and give extreme devotion to Ji.

4. Refutation
   —An impersonal god cannot become incarnate nor can mindlessness "decide" to do anything.
   —For 2,000 years the Church has consistently said the Word is Jesus Christ, the eternal Son of God, and has rejected all heresies.
   —Only the second person of the Trinity, the Son of God, has become incarnate in human flesh.
   —Jesus Christ is the only Lord and Savior of humanity.
   —The goal of humanity is not to contact the seed of divinity within us, but to enter the kingdom of God with Christ, not Ji, as King.

DIVINE LIGHT MISSION—FOOTNOTES

1. Kelley, Ken, "Blissed out with the Perfect Master," *Ramparts*, July 1973, p. 53.
2. Cameron, Charles, editor, *Who Is Guru Maharaj Ji?* (Bantam Books: New York, 1973), p. 37
3. *Divine Times*, August, 1975.
4. *Who Is Guru Maharaj Ji?*, p. 267.
5. *Who Is Guru Maharaj Ji?*, p. 265.
6. *Who is Guru Maharaj Ji?*, p. 18, 19.
7. A former premie, "Warning: Meditation Is Dangerous," Citizens Freedom Foundation, Chula Vista, California.
8. *Who Is Guru Maharaj Ji?*, p. 285, 286.
9. Kelley, pp. 54, 55.
10. Maharaj Ji, "You Are Disciples Now," Satsang at Hampstead Town Hall, England, October 31, 1971.
11. Schaff, *A Select Library,* Vol. IV, p. 25.
12. Hilary, pp. 232-233.
13. Schaff, *A Select Library,* Vol. XIV, pp. 197-198.
14. *Ibid,* p. 314.
15. Schaff, *The Creeds of Christendom,* Vol. II (New York: Harper & Brothers, 1877), p. 79.
16. Schaff, *A Select Library,* Vol. IV, p. 71.
17. Schaff, *A Select Library,* Vol. XIV, p. 163.
18. Justin, p. 247.

An Introduction to Hare Krishna

Ellen Ellman was weary. It was hot in the park and there were so many people. She had come here to think and work out where she was going, but not in such a crowd. Dull despair flooded her mind.

When she had dropped out of school, everything had looked so good. She could get a job somewhere and do the things she wanted to do. But it hadn't happened that way. Those past months were a jumble now, and it was hard to even sort through the order of events. She was sick of drugs, sick of the relationship she had with Tom, sick of living if it came down to that.

Her thoughts were jarred by a soft voice next to her ear, "Hare Krishna." Turning, she saw a tall, thin young woman next to her wearing a yellow cotton sari. "You look troubled; would you like some incense?"

"No," mumbled Ellen, "I guess not."

"Why don't you chant Hare Krishna?" asked her companion sympathetically.

"What's that got to do with anything?"

"It makes your troubles go away," was the reply.

Ellen wasn't impressed. "How on earth can a dumb chant do that?"

"Krishna is the same as His Holy name. You taste Him when you chant."

"Sounds crazy," Ellen laughed. "What's your name?"

"Yasoda. What's yours?"

"Ellen."

"Well, Ellen, why don't you come over and join us in our chanting?" Yasoda asked.

"Why should I?"

"You need to give up your anxieties and learn about Lord Krishna."

For companionship, for curiosity, for whatever, Ellen did go along and make some half-hearted efforts to chant. She felt almost hypnotized by the joyful dancing and chanting of the saffron-robed group of Hare Krishna devotees.

Soon she was dancing and chanting with them. It *did* make her forget her troubles, and it was kind of fun.

Later, when she was invited to the temple for a free meal, she went. A tall, thin man evidently in authority sat beside her and talked for a long time about Lord Krishna and the delights of devotion to Him. A few days later, when she was invited, Ellen dropped everything she was doing and moved into the temple.

Thus began a totally new form of life for Ellen: disciplined for one thing; religious for another—something she had never been. Rising early for offering, worship, chant, and prayers, she no longer had to decide what to do with her day. She worked in the temple, attended classes, read the prescribed lessons, walked the streets with companions selling incense and books, and slept little.

With no drugs, with a purpose of sorts, with changed food habits (she didn't much mind the enforced vegetarian diet because she was eating better than in a long time), and a sense of surrender through her chants of the mantra, Ellen felt secure. During the chant before the deities she felt drawn out of her own body; surely she was achieving true devotion to Lord Krishna.

THE HISTORY AND THEOLOGY OF HARE KRISHNA

Krishna Comes to America

In 1965, a Hindu monk in his late sixties arrived on the streets of New York City. He had a mission: to fulfill the instructions his spiritual master had given him thirty years before.

Way back then the man, now known as Abhay Charan De Bhaktivedanta Swami Prabhupada, had been told to preach his message in English and to the West. But he had been a businessman for those thirty years. All he had done during that time about "the message" was to print an English-language magazine called *Back to Godhead*.

What message?

Prabhupada comes from one of the many Hindu sects which say they worship one God. He is a Krishna worshiper. The sect originated when a man named Chaitanya taught that the best way to bypass the effects of living in this material world and get "bliss" is through love and devotion to Krishna. Hindus have always had a hangup about the material world. Krishna is one of the many gods in Hindu myths. Prabhupada claims to be in the direct line of teachers from Lord Chaitanya.

Other gurus from India were adapting to Western customs, some even (horror of horrors!) eating meat. Prabhupada would have none of it. He stuck stubbornly to his Hindu customs and Indian dress. He taught that Krishna is *the* way, and compromised with nobody. He was a strict Hindu fundamentalist.

Help Comes

Prabhupada's American beginnings, in a small storefront on the lower east side, didn't carry much promise. All alone he posted on his dingy plate glass window a small notice announcing lectures. Then he waited for people to come. In his saffron monk's robes he must have been a very strange sight to the local residents. Still, he gave those lectures on the *Bhagavad-gita* to the occasional listeners who appeared. Eventually a few disciples stuck. It was 1966 when he first attracted public notice. The following year, remember, was to be the heyday of the flower children in California. Prabhupada had come at a most opportune time to attract searching young Americans.

Greenwich Village caught the action first. The aging monk lost no time in starting public chants. First he went to Washington Square Park and then to Tompkins Square Park, where he got more attention. Staring eyes and gaping mouths proved he was noticed. Poet Allen Ginsberg and other members of New York's avante garde joined in an early chanting demonstration. That helped attract an article in the *East Village Other*. Prabhupada was becoming famous.

Throughout the hippie world Hindu philosophy was making headway along with hallucinatory drugs. In that well-prepared atmosphere, news about the new Swami spread. Suddenly, he was one of the hottest items on the hippie scene. Maybe his new religion was what they were searching for. Anyway, it was worth looking into.

Moving Out

With this kind of help, Prabhupada soon had a temple going in New York City. Some of his devotees were very intelligent and surprisingly well-educated. In 1968 he opened a print shop. The magazine, *Back to Godhead,* which he had been publishing almost singlehandedly since 1944, had a new lease on life. He had plenty of back content to put in new issues. Shrewdly noting what was attracting the interest of the young, he also designed leaflets. A great mass of literature now spread his influence even further.

Fame and Fortune

A new Hare Krishna temple in San Francisco caused a sensation in the Haight-Ashbury area. George Harrison of the Beatles (a heavy Krishna contributor) wrote a song about Krishna entitled, "My Sweet Lord," and it hit the top. Krishna centers opened in American cities all across the continent—and in Europe. The International Society for Krishna Consciousness (from here on referred to as ISKCON) was firmly established.

Maybe it was the very strangeness and unbending strictness of this new religion that attracted the youth of what had become a novelty-oriented culture. Maybe the philosophical climate was just right. Who knows? But it is a fact that American males in noticeable numbers were shaving their heads (leaving a pigtail so Krishna could lift them to heaven). Young American women were applying a strange religious facial make-up and donning dress common to another culture. They entered Hare Krishna temples to live as devotees of a strange God. There they embraced dietary and sexual codes bewildering to their parents. It won't last long, people said; they'll come out of this one fast. But lots of them stuck.

Income picked up. Mainly it was through the enthusiastic

street begging of devotees. A few large contributors like George Harrison helped a lot. Harrison helped in other ways. He produced more Krishna music: "Govenda," composed of temple songs. His album, "This Material World," continued in the same vein. People were not to have a chance to forget the existence of the Hare Krishna sect.

Prabhupada, though quite old, continued to maintain a fast pace, as if driven. He was: by the devil. He constantly worked on getting the Hindu scriptures translated into English. He is an able scholar, and he knows what he wants to say. His interpretations and commentaries consistently point to the worship of Krishna. That, by the way, is different from the usual commentaries on the Hindu religious books. Most of the others push the "all is one" position.

The writings of Prabhupada are devoured by his devotees. He is their guide to "God." Some of his disciples have built a vast knowledge of his system. The publications of Prabhupada are the heart of the Hare Krishna movement.

WHAT THE HARE KRISHNA PEOPLE BELIEVE

What God is Like

In a number of ways ISKCON is unusual among the Hindu religious groups making headway in America. The unusual thing is that they worship god as a person! This god is Krishna. They call him the Supreme Absolute Truth, from which everything proceeds.

Where do they get it? The *Bhagavad-gita,* one of Hindu scriptures, is the major source of information about Krishna. Prabhupada's interpretation and commentary on that book is ISKCON's "Bible." He claims the first incarnation of Krishna was 5,000 years ago. At least twenty-five incarnations of the godhead have occurred since. None of *them* were completely god, though. No, Krishna alone is the only 100 percent god. Prabhupada calls him the Supreme Personality of Godhead Himself.

It isn't that there is only one god. Prabhupada recognizes many demigods (those are part-gods or lesser gods). Krishna is worshiped as supreme, god of gods, the creator. Actually, the Krishna worshipers speak in a derogatory manner of the common Hindu philosophy that All is One—like we saw in TM and Divine Light Mission. They do believe in a personal god, but what is that god like?

The Playful God

In the *Bhagavad-gita*, Krishna is portrayed as a fun-loving god who frolics with his friends. One story tells of his having 16,108 wives, each provided with a beautiful palace. Each wife had ten children, and each of these children had many other children. This myth demonstrates their god, Krishna, as sort of a playful superman! He is pictured as eternally youthful, perfect, and beautiful. You get the impression he is somewhat mischievous and frivolous. In Prabhupada's *Nectar of Devotion*, he lists and describes sixty-four "transcendental qualities" of Krishna, ranging from beautiful features, to gentleness, to absolute attractiveness to all women.

But Krishna isn't just a superman. Prabhupada says Krishna is not different from his word. Now, Krishna is supposed to have dictated the *Bhagavad-gita* and the *Shrimad Bhagavatam*. So, whether they are written or spoken, the words of those books are considered actual incarnations of Krishna. Not all of him, you understand, but as much as can be packed into words. These words are thus to be worshiped and treated as sacred.

In the course of world history, there have been several incarnations or revelations of Krishna in a human body. They haven't been called Krishna, but they are partial incarnations of him. Prabhupada believes that Krishna is the same as the God of Judaism, the God of Buddhism, the God of Christianity and the God of Islam. Unfortunately, these believers in other religions just don't recognize his true name, Krishna.

Prabhupada has several beliefs outside the mainstream of Hinduism. For instance, he holds that the so-called Hindu trinity (Brahma, Vishnu, and Siva) are simply incarnations of Krishna. These three, by the way, are the names of figures who show up in the fantastic Hindu mythology. We'll run across two of them later. Prabhupada believes these three are all lesser expressions of Krishna. Each of them has a particular role in creation and the ruling of the world. Lord Krishna is held to be supreme, unborn, and unlike the material world. Let's work with these expressions.

Supreme means he is better than everything else and rules it all. *Unborn* means he came into being on his own. *Unlike the material world* means he doesn't consist of matter. He alone, of all the universe, is without cause.

Krishna is Everything

Krishnaites tell us he exists in three aspects: (1) "Localized Supersoul," (2) the shining impersonal brilliance which is the force of the universe, and (3) the Supreme Person. Still, he is held to be one nondual being. We'd better explain all that.

Krishna as localized Supersoul lives in the souls of all people. Everybody's soul is part of Krishna. He is also the force which makes up the universe. He is also the person who made everything and runs it. But all this doesn't mean Krishna is all divided up. Everything is Krishna.

Prabhupada says Krishna is everything, so he can be present in anything. That's how he justifies the construction of wooden and metal forms of various deities to be worshiped by the Krishnaites. You see, since Krishna is present in everything, he can make himself present in these "deities." Thus, a true believer can contact him through them.

Now don't think, the Krishna worshippers say, that just because Krishna has become everything, he has lost anything. Oh no, he is so perfect that even after everything is subtracted from him, his whole being is still there. So the Krishna followers claim to adore him alone as *the supreme One,* eternal, full of joy, bliss, and knowledge. They say believers of other religions really do worship god, because Krishna accepts worship of minor deities as worship of himself. It's just too bad that people aren't intelligent enough to worship him directly. In other words, if you don't worship Krishna you're really stupid.

Prabhupada calls Krishna the light of the world—its cause, center, source, spirit, and energy. He says humans should be humbled and joyful that Krishna, with such perfection and glory, engages in relationships with people who truly worship him.

What is Creation?

All the creation myths and fantasies of the Hindu scriptures are accepted as literally true by Prabhupada. Vishnu is considered to be the very first incarnation of Krishna, being *almost* 100 percent perfect. According to Krishnaites, this Vishnu is the source of creation, the Supersoul of the universe. Now this takes imagination to grasp, but here's how they picture creation.

At the outer boundary of matter lies the Causal Ocean, and on it floats Vishnu, creating by looking, breathing, and sweating. That's an important creation myth to them, showing where things, creatures, and people, come from. Somehow or other it isn't considered contradictory to the myth that out of the very pores of the body of Krishna there are supposed to be innumerable universes coming and going. It's wild.

Lord Brahma is pictured as the first living being in *this* universe. He has about three-fourths of Krishna's qualities. According to the myth, Brahma took on a female form, was impregnated by Krishna, and thus created the universe which includes human beings. As a result, *we* also have about three-fourths of Krishna's qualities. Don't get too proud about that, though. We only have these qualities in very small quantities because of our limited capacity.

In the *Bhagavad-gita* Krishna claims to be the father of all forms and species of life. Vishnu, as a Supersoul, is said by the Krishnaites to live in the hearts of all created beings. An individual soul has no beginning and no end; it exists forever. (We'll get into some implications of *that* later.) Being part and parcel of god, every soul has some share of eternal life and is as full of knowledge as its small size will allow.

What a Human Being Is

Prabhupada says there's a special reason why man, though an animal, can think. It's so we can deal with the questions of why we suffer. You see, he thinks it's the nature of humanity to suffer in this material body. That's in spite of the fact that the *real person* is pure soul, permanent, and not material. Now, that last statement is very important in Krishna thinking. The real, *inner you* is eternal. It's part of Krishna. Your body is made of matter and it is temporary. It causes you suffering.

Krishnaites say we have spiritual bodies which we got from Krishna. Those bodies are like him but different, in the same sense that parent and child are alike and different. This is a point they hit big when they argue against other Hindus who claim to be completely "one with God."

We've talked about reincarnation in connection with other Hindu groups. Prabhupada believes in it too. He thinks all souls live on and on, being born and living in whatever life form Krishna selects, dying, being reborn in other bodies, and on and on forever. What that means is that Krishna philosophy makes us brothers and sisters of trees and ants. Our bodies are considered less real than our souls. After all, we shed our bodies every now and then to get a new one. Prabhupada teaches that our bodies are degrading to us and make us fools. The main thing is that your identity is your soul. That is who you are. You are not this body. It is foolish to think of yourself as a piece of matter when you'll soon be living in a different body.

The Purpose of Life

Krishna consciousness is the main purpose of life. That's what Prabhupada says, and you probably wonder what on earth "Krishna consciousness" is. Basically, it means to understand Krishna and to rebuild the forgotten relationship with him. What you are to do is focus your whole attention on Krishna and love and serve him devotedly. You're supposed to desire to be united with him. You'll understand the idea better as we show how they go about it.

Anyway, Prabhupada says if we don't get Krishna consciousness in this life, we will be tossed back into the whirlpool of birth and death. Then it's up for grabs. We may emerge in the form of any one of the 8,400,000 species of plants, insects, birds, and animals. If you want peace and happiness in this life, and in the next, there's only one way. Enter into the service of God (Krishna).

The Krishna worshipers believe if we develop Krishna consciousness, we will at least be assured of a human body in the next life. The ideal is for our "pure spirit souls" (that's the inner you) to be occupied in blissful, fully-conscious, loving service of Krishna. It is also the goal for all those myriads of beings cyclically evolving through the various species of life. Those souls living in squirrel bodies, dog bodies and fish bodies have the same goal you do. Being in a human body right now, you can get there faster.

Actually, Krishnaites believe our souls are joyful because they are part and parcel of God. That seems a little strange because people aren't aware of that joy, but suppose it's true. Then what's the problem? It would seem that if our souls are joyful, everything is fine. Right? Wrong. We haven't *realized* our relationship with God (Krishna). Until we acknowledge our Father (Krishna), Prabhupada's followers insist, we cannot possibly experience fulfillment, joy, brotherhood, or humanity. That's the first thing. Your life is a mess until you turn your attention on Krishna.

Down with the Body

Secondly, there's this terrible body of ours. It's the cause of our sufferings because it is made of matter. That's a big point to Prabhupada. Remember, he says, it's an illusion to believe we *are* this body. Oh, the body exists, but you're just living in it temporarily. It's just a material shell in which we live for a while. So Prabhupada teaches our goal must be to get out of this material body and into our spiritual one. Until that happens we, individually and collectively, are going to suffer.

Let's go back over it. Basically, our sin is that we have forgotten our relationship with Krishna. So the *main human problem is ignorance,* according to Prabhupada. What kind of relationship is meant? Krishna theology rejects the father-son picture of that relationship. (A father-son relationship, claim the Krishnaites, is one in which the son is always expecting something from the father, always asking.) They mean a frolicking, pseudo-sensual relationship.

Harking back to the myths in the *Bhagavad-gita,* they dig up stories of the adventures of Krishna and his friends. There, they say, we can see that our relationship with him must be of a far greater devotion than a son could ever have for his father. Then, if you've read the *Bhagavad-gita,* your mind goes back to the story of the six-month-long night when Krishna made love to 100 women without their husbands knowing it. You wonder, how does all this fit? It doesn't bother the Krishnaites.

They're ecstatic about the joys and bliss of the intimate relationship rising out of Krishna consciousness and service. What their fantasies are I don't know. . . .

We Are Pure Soul

To most practical people, it would seem that living in this body would make escape from the material world impossible. Not true, we learn from Prabhupada. We *can* come to realize we are not this body, that we are pure soul. It will take some effort. Senses and desires must be denied rather than followed. We must learn, he says, to keep in mind the fact that the material concept of life is an illusion. That is, the matter you live in and around doesn't really count. It's here today and gone tomorrow. Your soul will be here a million years from now.

Happily, we are assured, we have been born into human life. Thus, we are the most intelligent of living beings. We can think. We must realize, the teaching goes on, that this ability to reason doesn't have to be used just to carry on the animal activities of eating, sleeping, and mating. We can use it to get free to God.

Sin and Suffering

Are you upset by your tendency toward sinful activities? Are you suffering? Krishnaites believe these common human ailments are problems we cannot solve on our own. (True enough!) However, they tell us, if you really have faith in god and in a true guru who will teach you Krishna consciousness, you can make it.

According to Prabhupada, your behavior in your past life was such that you have been rewarded by being born into the privileged human form. You have earned it. Don't be proud, though. You are still a fool; that's proven by the fact that you're still in any material body at all. We'll go into it more later, but souls who get completely beyond foolishness get to go live with Krishna.

Human life in general is considered by Krishna devotees to show the foolishness of our nature. Prabhupada repeatedly points to the ills of society and the suffering everywhere as evidence that all people are born fools. He is convinced that

101

any society which doesn't have a class of Krishna-conscious people is doomed. He is trying to create such a class.

As a Hindu, he believes in the four-caste system of that tradition. Those four are; 1) laborers, 2) farmers and merchants, 3) rulers and warriors, and 4) religious philosophers. Religious philosophers are the top dogs. Now, he's not calling for the hereditary caste system of India. What he wants is for the most intelligent people to be trained to the highest degree in Krishna consciousness. In that way they will become the most purified persons in society, and will ultimately save it. The message comes out like this: Perhaps you could be one of these most privileged intellectual spiritual giants. It's worth a try. Besides, even if you can't reach that pinnacle, you have no chance for fulfillment in life unless you (1) give up your material illusions, (2) follow the principles of the Vedas (Hindu moral rules), and (3) strive for Krishna consciousness.

Salvation

Krishnaites believe, as we have said, that God has appeared in many forms. They accept the legitimate worshipers of all these forms as believers. Nevertheless, devotees of Krishna are at the top of the list. Since they worship Krishna, they are his favorites. But how does one become a true devotee?

It starts with finding someone who can guide you. Prabhupada teaches that there is a succession of disciples from Krishna down through gurus to the present time. First, give up and accept the fact that you are subordinate both to material nature and to God. Then you have to go to a true guru, a devotee of Krishna who qualifies and is in the line of succession. When you find him, submit yourself to him as if he were Krishna. Serve him and learn by asking questions of him.

Prabhupada claims to be such a guru. He is accepted as such by his followers. His plan for salvation is very simple. You chant the Hare Krishna *mantra*:

Hare Krishna, Hare Krishna, Krishna, Krishna, Hare Hare
Hare Rama, Hare Rama, Rama Rama, Hare Hare

You don't have to understand the words. That isn't important to the effect. Anyone can make this start, and the result is supposed to be automatic—Krishna consciousness. You begin a personal relationship with him. The chanting, we are told, serves a dual purpose: You are offering and eating spiritual food (called *prasadam*). That is because *Krishna is the same as his name.* Thus, Prabhupada assures us, when you chant you are offering to him and you are also tasting him. It is important to note that *you don't have to understand anything in order for these benefits to take place.* Nevertheless, this is just the beginning. Prabhupada assures us there is much more to be experienced.

Chanting in faith is supposed to have more virtue *and* a higher degree of virtue than ignorant chanting. But now we find that it isn't as simple as Prabhupada promised. If you want to reach the highest levels of Krishna consciousness, it's going to cost you.

Prabhupada calls people to the *service* of Krishna. If you're going to do that, you have to give up some things. You give up meat-eating. You give up alcohol, drugs, anything "intoxicating." You give up "speculation," thinking about anything but Krishna. You give up "illicit sex," any sexual activity except that between husband and wife specifically designed for procreation. (Sex for procreation is defined rather tightly to mean once a month on the wife's most fertile night. That event can only take place after the couple has chanted fifty rounds of the *mantra* on their long chain of beads, which ordinarily takes five to six hours. One wonders if it's worth it!)

There's no chance for purification unless you meet these requirements. Without purification you can't develop much of a relationship with Krishna. Acceptance of these rules is a must for anyone who wants to go into a Krishna temple. And you have to be in the temple to really get anywhere with Krishna.

Cleanse Your Heart

If you're accepted for entrance into the temple, you then learn chanting and dancing before the deities and offering "spiritual food." (Every day special food is prepared to be offered to the deities in the temple. This food is then eaten by the devotees. They're supposed to eat it with great joy because it is endowed with Krishna himself. Therefore, the partaker is eating Krishna when eating this offered food.)

There is a regular prescribed schedule of worshipful activities. Krishnaites believe that undivided attention to these activities is the way to greater and greater Krishna consciousness. Follow this regime, they say, and you will begin to get out of this material body. That means being in an "otherworldly" ecstatic state where you don't even experience the senses. It's yet another method of bending your mind, throwing it out of gear.

It is a maxim among the Krishnaites that the chanting of their *mantra* is the most appropriate method of killing the "false idea of the self as the body." That's the beginning of the process, they say, in which the soul gets into those mysterious blissful and eternal activities which are the essence of knowledgeable service of Krishna. Prabhupada claims that certain "transcendental vibrations" are set up which cleanse the heart of all "wrong ideas." Confidence in this method is shown, for example, by the bumper stickers often seen on Hare Krishna vehicles: "Cleanse Your Heart, Chant Hare Krishna."

Most Krishna devotees experience an ecstacy from chanting which they see as evidence of this "cleansing." The sound vibration of the *mantra,* they think, by-passes all the lower states of consciousness, such as sensual, mental, and intellectual. Again we see the idea is to get out of your mind. Three words, *Krishna, Rama,* and *Hare* appear in the *mantra.* These words have special spiritual value in themselves, according to Krishna theology. Krishna and Rama are both names attributed to the Supreme Deity, and Hare is the energy of the Supreme Deity. Thus, the chant calls upon God (Krishna) and his energy or force. So, we are told, the over and over repetition of the chant attunes the devotee to the supreme energy of Krishna. As a result, the devotee becomes a "realized soul." That is, he is in contact with Krishna.

Prabhupada gives us some idea of what happens when Krishna worshipers go into their "ecstatic" states. Eight things happen, though not all of them happen all the time, at least at first. There's (1) being stopped as though dumb, (2) perspiration, (3) standing up of hairs on the body, (4) dislocation of the voice, (5) trembling, (6) fading of the body, (7) crying in ecstasy, and (8) trance.[1] As we said, the mind gets bent.

Once you're in, there's more and more you can do to be a

better devotee of Krishna. Prabhupada prescribes sixty-four items of devotional service. Of course the new initiate doesn't have to get into all of them right off. There are, however, stages of liberation and classes of devotees. You work your way up. Above all, you'll never make it with an "unrealized" leader who isn't in the direct line of gurus. That's the only way you can be sure you are following the disciplines necessary for Krishna consciousness. You have to submit to a truly inspired channel of the teachings, such as Prabhupada, and it seems he is the only one around.

THE METHOD OF OPERATION OF HARE KRISHNA

Serving Krishna

Prabhupada has built his movement by convincing young people to come live in his temples. There are now about thirty such temples in the United States and another thirty-five or so in other countries. Growth seems to be slow but steady with temples closing and others opening regularly.

When people enter the temple, they come into bondage. Devotees live under a strict ascetic Hindu cultural code. Because the code is anti-materialistic, temple members live communally, with the fewest possible personal articles. Comfort is no consideration. Anybody who complains about the cold or the heat or poor beds is "thinking about the body." That is bad. You're supposed to realize you're not this body. Thinking about the body is detrimental to Krishna consciousness.

All worldly goods are supposed to be donated to ISKCON. You give everything to Krishna. Men shave their heads as an indication of devotion. Every member gets a new Sanskrit "spiritual name" when initiated. All devotees adopt the distinctive dress, which is a kind of Hare Krishna adaptation of the native dress of India. Long, flowing robes cover both men and women. All follow Prabhupada's instructions in every aspect of life. He *is* the authority for everything, from the details of daily life to the interpretation of any scripture. Devotees mostly study only his writings. There is, though, some material by younger disciples which is approved. Prabhupada is the representative of God to his followers. There are hints he may someday be recognized as an incarnation of Krishna.

We've already seen that people who enter the temple have to agree to a set of rules. But there's more. Prabhupada gives instructions on bodily hygiene, dressing, sleeping, and thinking. Some people have called this movement the ultimate dropout because the rest of the society is regarded with pity and disdain. The fact is, devotees drop *into* absolute domination.

Temple Life

Life in the temple follows a rigid and busy schedule. Nine items of ritual are considered essential: (1) hearing about Krishna, (2) chanting, (3) remembering, (4) serving, (5) worshiping, (6) praying, (7) obeying, (8) maintaining friendship with Krishna, and (9) surrending everything.[2] Temple life reflects all these requirements. The daily schedule is built around them.

Sleeping too much is bad. It's considered detrimental to devotion. Ordinarily temple residents sleep only about six hours a night, from 10:00 P.M. to 4:00 A.M. They arise and dress quickly. Then there's a ceremony of awakening the "deities." A very elaborate ceremony is made of uncovering the wooden and metal idols in the temple.

After the ceremony, devotees individually chant by beads, a full *mantra* for each bead on the chain around the neck. That takes an hour or more. The deities are dressed in new clothes for the day, and devotees prostrate themselves full-length before them.

Next, there's an hour of rote study of material prepared under the direction of Prabhupada. The temple president or another leader gives a short sermon. Everybody scatters to do cleaning assignments. It is now 9:00 A.M. and time for a breakfast of food offered to Krishna. After breakfast the work day begins in earnest.[3]

Most days the average devotee goes out on the streets to do begging and peddling. Often the schedule includes public chanting and dancing. You may have seen them in shopping centers, parks, airports, or college campuses. They choose places where there are a lot of people around. Visibility is important. Prabhupada wants people to see and hear his converts in action. It attracts potential devotees.

Married couples have separate quarters, usually outside the temple. Of course sexual intercourse is limited to once a month, and both man and woman have the same heavy schedule as other devotees, but there is some little private life together. Children seldom grow up with their parents. ISKCON has a school in Texas where the children go to learn a life of Krishna consciousness, often as young as four. One wonders what they will be like when grown, having been deprived of the normal love and care of father and mother, subjected to this terrible religious bondage from infancy.

Begging

But the lifeblood of the movement is in street begging and peddling. The money collected there keeps things going. Usually this begging is done wearing the distinctive Krishna dress. In spite of Prabhupada's rigid adherence to his native customs, however, the need for money sometimes dictates changes. Americans don't always react well to the strange dress. For a long time women in the movement have often gone out "disguised" in ordinary clothes. Lately the men have taken to going out with wigs and street clothes. In late 1976 there were even rumors of relaxation of the whole dress code. Apparently there are limits to Krishna disdain for material things! Principles *can* be compromised if the motivation to "keep those cards and letters coming" is strong enough.

When you encounter Krishna devotees on their begging missions, they approach politely, asking if you'd like some incense or a magazine. They'll press the matter if you're reluctant. You can be certain they will ask for money. Aggressiveness in begging is considered to be of great merit. Since money is so important, begging is high service to Krishna. Not only do most of the funds for the movement come from such activities, so do many converts. Anybody who shows any interest at all is attacked with great enthusiasm.

Among the items peddled on the streets (or "given" in return for a donation) is the magazine of the movement, *Back to Godhead.* Approximately 500,000 copies of each issue are printed. There is great effort to get these into people's hands.

Back to Godhead is published by the arm called Bhaktivedanta Book Trust, which puts out a wide variety of literature. Of course, there's a long list of Prabhupada's books.

But there is also the *Hare Krishna Cookbook* and two children's books, *The Krishna Consciousness Coloring Book* and *Pralad Picture and Story Book.* An increasingly large set of cassette tapes is also marketed.

Eating Spiritual Food

Food, its treatment and its consumption is a big deal in the temple. Every bit of the food eaten in the temple is offered to Krishna. Six times a day there is an elaborate ceremony in which food is sacrificed. Only certain kinds of food will do. Krishna philosophy follows principles derived from the *Bhagavad-gita.* Food, like the rest of the material world and behavior in it, is considered to fall into four categories: ignorance, passion, goodness, and pure goodness. Meat, fish, eggs, liquor, along with any food which has been cooked more than three hours before being eaten, falls into the bottom and most unacceptable category, "ignorance." Krishna devotees don't eat them.

Extremely rich foods, very spicy dishes, and heavily flavored foods fall under the definition of "passion," being prepared to satisfy the senses. These are avoided too. Vegetables, fruits, sugar, grains, and milk are categorized in the "goodness" mode as purifying, strengthening, and health-giving. Devotees will eat them if they can't get sacrificed food. "Pure goodness" results when such foods are prepared according to ritual and offered to Krishna. This sacrificed food is supposed to take on the qualities of Krishna, and the eater actually partakes of him.

Consumption is Worship

Each meal is communion with Krishna. Krishnaites believe eating the transformed food takes away the results of sin and protects the eater from future contamination. When sacrificed food is passed out to people in parks and on the streets, it is intended to awaken Krishna consciousness in them.

Festivals

Certain festivals selected from Hindu mythology are publicly celebrated. Extensive advertisement often brings enthusiastic crowds. Of course, popular places are picked by temple leadership, so something of an audience is assured. Elaborately constructed temples on crude wooden wheels lumber through the streets, attracting sightseers to their bright paint and strange forms. Meanwhile, robed Krishnaites dance ecstatically before the deities. Others move through the crowd peddling magazines and other items. Trays of sacrificed food are carried about the crowd and pressed upon unaware bystanders.

Krishnaites aggressively urge people to chant with them. That's a little strange in view of the statement by Prabhupada against chanting by non-devotees. He says "milk touched by the lips of a serpent has poisonous effects." It's one of those curious compromises. Well, money and converts are expected to result from the festival, and it happens.

Temple Evangelism

Temples usually have other activities open to the public. One brochure of the Berkeley, California, temple advertised, "open, seven days a week lectures on Prabhupada's works at 7:30 A.M., 8:45 A.M. and 7:30 P.M." Sunday was publicized as a special day of "love feast," with activities beginning at 4:00 P.M. This meeting featured group singing and dancing, lectures, drama, an Indian vegetarian feast, and movies. Visitors were requested to bring flowers, fruits, or *uncooked* vegetables to "offer to the Lord." People are thus drawn into the worship of Krishna.

Climbing Higher

For those who enter the temple, the daily rigid schedule and hard work can be wearing, but there are incentives. Hardworking, talented, and intelligent devotees who show enthusiastic advancement in the teachings of Prabhupada can go up. Males can become teachers, temple treasurers, and temple presidents. The ultimate in devotion is to renounce wife and family to take the highest monastic vows. A man who has reached that level becomes one of the holy traveling teachers and evangelists of the movement.

Women, though considered hampered in devotion by their female bodies, can become temple singers, head deity-workers, artistic specialists, and respected devotees. Devotees who aren't smart or talented are simply destined to serve the holy ones.

A REFUTATION OF HARE KRISHNA

One-Man Leadership

ISKCON is another of the growing number of religious movements based on the authority and leadership of one man. ISKCON depends entirely upon the interpretation and comment which Prabhupada has made on the Hindu scriptures. Sure, he claims to be in a tradition of Krishna disciples dating from the sixteenth century. We have only his word for that. But it is *his* teaching solely which is followed. He is his own authority.

This is in direct contrast to the way God designed His Church, in which the Holy Spirit guides and teaches. Any member can hear from God, but there are checks and balances. Such a policy was established in the very earliest days of the Church.

> But some men came down from Judea and were teaching the brethren, "Unless you are circumcised according to the custom of Moses, you cannot be saved." And when Paul and Barnabus had no small dissension and debate with them, Paul and Barnabus and some of the others were appointed to go up to Jerusalem to the apostles and the elders about this question. . . . The apostles and the elders were gathered together to consider this matter (Acts 15:1-2,6).

Those who had a claim of revelation were heard. The matter was hotly debated, and a decision was made. In the Church, there can be no freedom for one person to teach whatever he or she pleases or thinks is right.

All teaching in the Church must maintain continuity with the past. The truth must be passed on just as it was delivered.

So then, brethren, stand firm and hold to the traditions which you were taught by us, either by word of mouth or by letter (2 Thess. 2:15).

No single leader can claim sole authority to state doctrine or to command behavior. That is what the Church of Jesus Christ has *always* taught.

An excerpt from the creed of the Fourth Ecumenical Council, held at Chalcedon in 451 A.D., bears out the care of the Church to stick to the same teachings century after century, "Following the holy Fathers, we teach . . . ."[4] They did not dare depart from that teaching. Whatever else may be said about Prabhupada and his Hare Krishna movement, it must be said that its base for authority is far different from that of the historic Church of Jesus Christ.

The Playful God

Prabhupada has a "personal" god, Krishna. Everything is Krishna, but Krishna is more than everything, he tells us. Krishna keeps on putting out universes (he's still creating), which are part of himself, while he remains the same. Prabhupada's Krishna is a person, sort of. Yet, somehow or other many different mythical and real people (gurus like Prabhupada) have been *partial* incarnations of Krishna. If you like consistency, it's an impossible can of worms!

Such a god is radically different from the true God as we have seen Him revealed in the Bible and recognized by the creeds of the Church. Creation is accomplished with deliberate intent by God, who is separate from it. Once it was completed, He did not desert it nor look in upon it casually. No, creation and humanity are looked after with tender love by God. He has purity and dignity in their most ultimate form. Within the body of the Westminster Confession, there is a statement on the nature of God which clearly sums up how the Church sees God.

There is but one only living and true God, who is infinite in being and perfection, a most pure spirit, invisible, without body, parts, or passions, immutable, immense, eternal, incomprehensible, almighty, most wise, most holy, most free, most absolute, working all things according to the counsel of His own immutable and most righteous will, for his own glory; most loving, gracious, merciful, long-suffering, abundant in goodness and truth, forgiving iniquity, transgression, and sin; the rewarder of them that diligently seek him. . . .[5]

Look how sharply God stands out in contrast to the frivolous, mischievious Krishna, who has 16,108 wives! Krishna is a playful and adulterous superman, and no God. Science fiction-like, the fantasies of Krishna's adventures defy the imagination. This Krishna, so the stories go, played cruel tricks on his "friends," fooling them for his own amusement. Women were the objects of his sexual pleasure, while their unknowing husbands slept.

Compare him to Jesus Christ, the true incarnation of God. As the second person of the Trinity, He became a human being. He was fully God and fully man in one person, the one Son of God. While on earth He looked tenderly after His people, treating them with respect and dignity. He healed the sick, cured the lame, and died for us all.

How can anyone who desires holiness prefer the immorality of Krishna to the purity and loving care of Jesus Christ? Look how the Scriptures are careful to record His holiness:

> For it was fitting that we should have such a high priest, holy, blameless, unstained, separated from sinners, exalted above the heavens (Heb. 7:26).

"Holy," "innocent," "undefiled." After hearing the shocking stories of the adventures of Krishna, could we use such words of him? No. He does not measure up to the requirements for a savior. Jesus Christ, and He alone, does.

Reincarnation

We have seen how Prabhupada dwells on the Hindu creation myths which leave neither the creation in general nor humanity in particular any dignity. The material body is an illusion—here today, gone tomorrow.

On the other hand, the poor soul has no beginning and no

end, going endlessly through cycles of life and death in bugs and animals and humans until, hopefully, it earns its way to Krishna. As if that were even possible!

How despairing, how degrading, how unlike the truth! Like a ball in a roulette wheel, the destiny of the human soul is in the fickle hand of chance. The Scriptures show such myths to be lies. We come into being as humans and have but one life on this earth.

> Do not marvel at this; for the hour is coming when all who are in the tombs will hear his voice and come forth, those who have done good, to the resurrection of life, and those who have done evil, to the resurrection of judgment (John 5:28-29).

This is not the first time the Church has encountered such manufactured fables. At one time, for example, a set of ideas similar to Prabhupada's Hindu concoctions were proposed (in the second century) by a man named Origen. They went the rounds for more than two centuries. Then came the day when the Fifth Ecumenical Council (553 A.D.) met to condemn these wicked lies.

> If anyone asserts the fabulous pre-existence of souls, and shall assert the monstrous restoration which follows from it; let him be anathema (Anathema I).

> If anyone shall say that the reasonable creatures in whom the divine love had grown cold have been hidden in gross bodies such as ours, and have been called men, while those who have attained the lowest degree of wickedness have shared cold and obscure bodies and are become and called demons and evil spirits: let him be anathema (Anathama IV).

> If anyone shall say that the future judgment signifies the destruction of the body and that the end of the story will be an immaterial nature, and that therefore there will no longer be any matter, but only spirit: let him be anathema (Anathema XI).[6]

Does not this Hindu fantasy, so glibly promoted by Prabhupada, fall under that condemnation?

Solution

The development of Prabhupada's system leads eventually to a "solution" to the supposed endless round of birth and death and birth. He proposes chanting a *mantra*. That is familiar. We've seen it in TM and the Divine Light Mission. This, of course, can bend your mind and throw you into a fit, but it can't save you.

On top of the chanting, he piles on requirements which add more and more oppression. We must, he claims, only eat certain foods. Sexual intercourse must be only for producing children, once a month, under circumstances which frustrate and degrade.

Finding that chanting plus rules don't free them from guilt, devotees want to go higher. They accept the additional burdens of Prabhupada. Their minds get further bent. Perhaps the conscience is numbed and guilt is no longer felt. But Prabhupada's rules only draw his devotees further and further away from the true God.

As the Scriptures teach, God knows what we are like. He does not pile rules on us which we must obey to be freed from guilt and made right with Him. No, He says, "trust Me, accept my mercy."

> He saved us, not because of deeds done by us in righteousness, but in virtue of his own mercy, by the washing of regeneration and renewal in the Holy Spirit (Titus 3:5).

That mercy is very important to us human beings, but systems like Prabhupada's hide it from us, making us think we are earning salvation. In confession after confession, the Christian Church has kept its people aware of the source of salvation. In the Augsburg Confession (1530) that source is strongly affirmed:

> The churches also teach that people cannot obtain forgiveness of sins and righteousness before God by any power or merit they have or by any works they do. That forgiveness and righteousness is given freely by grace for Christ's sake through faith. It comes to people who believe that they are received into God's favor and forgiven because of Christ, who paid for our sins by His death.

Because of this faith, God accepts us as righteous before Him. Romans 3 and 5 (free modern language version of Article IV).[7]

Oh, wretched followers of Prabhupada. Instead of salvation now and eternally, he offers them only bondage and the way of death! Look what is ahead for those who reject the mercy of God:

> Then I saw a great white throne and Him who sat upon it; from his presence earth and sky fled away, and no place was found for them. And I saw the dead, great and small, standing before the throne, and books were opened. Also another book was opened, which is the book of life. And the dead were judged by what was written in the books, by what they had done. And the sea gave up the dead in it, Death and Hades gave up the dead in them, and all were judged by what they had done. Then Death and Hades were thrown into the lake of fire. This is the second death, the lake of fire; and if any one's name was not found written in the book of life, he was thrown into the lake of fire (Rev. 20:11-15).

Prabhupada and his followers should fear that judgment!

A Dangerous Ritual

Chanting the Hare Krishna *mantra* is worship. It is *not* just the repetition of a harmless rhythmic phrase. The chanter is supposed to be offering to Krishna and also eating Krishna, if you can grasp that.

The words are Krishna, so goes the claim. You offer to him and you eat him. Besides, the *mantra* calls on the "energy" of Krishna. It's a very serious and dangerous ritual. These people offer their words to a false god and the endless repetition of the sounds throws them into a trance. Is it self-hypnotism? Are they opened to demonic possession? Probably both. We can only speculate.

There are effects, however. Personalities change. The outward display of emotions disappears. Human relationships take on mere form; devotees are no longer interested in each other as human beings. As interest in the ritual and devotion to Krishna increase, interest in everything else decreases.

All this is compounded by the ritual of the sacrifice of food. Once offered, it "becomes Krishna." Eating Krishna is supposed to increase the devotee's "consciousness" of him. It is literally true that devotees eat, sleep, and drink Krishna. As the change in their minds progresses, they become ready to do anything commanded in his name.

A former devotee says he had heard it said around the temple that a devotee could do the most abominable things and remain pure. That same person said he left the temple when he found that Prabhupada was not translating the *Vedas* (Hindu scriptures) correctly. What they really describe in the sacrifices, he said he discovered, is human sacrifices. It is true that in the Vedas there are fantastic descriptions of human sacrifice surrounded by wild sexual orgies. Prabhupada's commentaries have played down these and "spiritualized" everything.

But what happens when the next generation of Krishna leaders, reading and understanding Sanskrit, sees what is actually commanded? How will these thorough-going devotees, programmed to literally obey these writings, behave? Might they not follow to the letter the instructions for human sacrifice? We don't know.

Who, after all, leads the Krishna movement? Is this just a power trip of an eighty-year-old Hindu holy man, or the device of a higher power? This movement, unlike TM, has not drawn older, more settled adults, but eager young enthusiasts. What drives them? Are they being drawn by satanic influence into a cult which will one day burst out of quiet, puritanical ritual into a frenzy of bloodletting and sexual license? The Hindu scriptures allow it. They are being conditioned to absolute obedience to those scriptures. Their inner frustrations are being built to the bursting point.

We need speculate no further, but the Church of the living God must regard this movement as a fearful cult, to be denounced with the clearest possible emphasis. There is nothing godly about it.

A BRIEF PROFILE OF HARE KRISHNA

1. History
   —Founded by Swami Prabhupada in New York in 1965, but originated in India by a man named Chaitanya.

—The cult caught on in Greenwich Village by public chant-
ings.

—His magazine, *Back To Godhead,* gained new life and his
influence spread to Haight-Ashbury in San Francisco.

—Krishna centers spread to Europe and the International
Society for Krishna Consciousness (ISKCON) was established.

—The many writings of Prabhupada are devoured by his
followers and form the heart of the movement.

2. Beliefs

—Krishna is a personal god who is everything, so he can be
present in anything.

—The real person of a human being is his pure soul, with
the body being a culprit. Reincarnation is a big deal.

—The main purpose of life is Krishna consciousness, which
is to understand Krishna and rebuild the forgotten relationship with him; therefore, the main problem is ignorance of Krishna.

—This purpose is attained by chanting the Hare Krishna
mantra with the mind being bypassed.

—Eight things happen when the worshiper reaches the
cleansed state through chanting the mantra. Sixty-four
rules of devotional service can then be engaged in.

3. Method Of Operation

—Devotees live in temples under a strict Hindu cultural
code with nine items of ritual followed. About thirty
temples in the United States and thirty-five in other
countries in 1976.

—Sexual relations between married couples is limited to
once a month and the children are seldom raised by their
parents.

—Prabhupada is the authority for everything and is Krishna's representative. The devotees are under his total
domination.

—Money is raised through street begging and peddling,
especially *Back To Godhead.* Tapes and books are also
available.

—Public festivals are celebrated, and temple lectures and worship services are conducted to attract new converts.

4. Refutation
—The Church of Jesus Christ is not led by one man, but operates out of council led by the Holy Spirit.
—The true God is distinct from His creation, but sustains it with love and dignity. The doctrine of reincarnation is evil.
—Jesus Christ is holy, sinless, and a worthy Savior, but Krishna is frivolous, mischievous, and an adulterous superman.
—Salvation is by the grace and mercy of God and not by the useless works system of Hare Krishna.
—Chanting the mantra is a dangerous ritual that turns worshipers into plastic personalities.

HARE KRISHNA—FOOTNOTES

1. A. C. Bhaktivedanta Swami Prabhupada, *The Nectar of Devotion* (The Bhaktivedanta Book Trust: New York, 1970), pp. 230-236.
2. *The Nectar of Devotion,* pp. 118, 119.
3. Levine, Faye, *The Strange World of the Hare Krishnas* (Fawcett Publications: Greenwich, Conn., 1974), pp. 72-80.
4. Schaff, *A Select Library,* Volume XIV, p. 264.
5. Schaff, *Creeds of Christendom,* p. 606.
6. Schaff, *A Select Library,* Volume XIV, pp. 318-319.
7. Schaff, *Creeds Of Christendom,* p. 10.

PART III

The "Western" or "Christian" Cults

An Introduction to The Unification Church

Howie Engsberg, student at State U., was heading across campus at 12:30, making his daily noontime journey to the chem lab. Along the south side of the quad, among the variety of tables set up by what he privately labeled "kooky" groups, was one he had seen before and noticed especially because of the smiling, friendly faces. A large sign, "Creative Community Project," stood to one side. A young woman of student age sitting at the table looked directly at him, smiled, and said, "Hi." Howie stopped.

State U. had not been a particularly happy experience for Howie, who hailed from a small midwestern city where his father was an electrical contractor. Religion had never been a part of the Engsberg family life. He vaguely knew that his grandmother was a Lutheran, whatever they believed. Summer weekends for his family had been spent at the cabin on the lake, about an hour's drive from home. Sunday was a day Howie and his father enjoyed watching pro football on television in the fall and winter. At State he was a dorm student with no close friends.

So when Suzie greeted him, Howie was eager to talk. She was enthusiastic about the communal life at the "house" where she lived. The invitation she extended to him for dinner was most welcome.

When he showed up that evening, Suzie was on hand at the door to greet him. The sign "Unification Church" outside the door was vaguely distasteful, but its presence was far overshadowed by the reception inside. Everyone was bright and friendly. Howie felt wanted. There was a family atmosphere; they spoke of being "The Unified Family." After dinner his new friends invited him to a "retreat" they were having the next weekend. Well, why not? He didn't really have anything else going—and who else on campus had ever given him such attention?

During the weekend the speaker talked about the aims and the philosophy of the group. Howie learned more about the Bible than he had ever known. He found these people revered and followed a very religious Korean man named Sun Myung Moon. This man was the founder of a church much better than the traditional ones. And these, his followers, were disgusted with the other churches because of their disputes and divisions, and also because of illogical doctrines. That struck a responsive note in Howie.

Talking with one of the men later in the day, Howie asked what they believed about God.

"God is the all-holy and ultimate being who created everything," came the answer.

"What about Jesus?" Howie asked. "Don't the Christian churches all teach something about Jesus being God's Son?"

"That's right," replied Harold, his companion. "Jesus is God's only beloved Son, the second Adam, the spiritual Savior of the world."

"What does that mean?" Howie wondered. (The "Savior" thing had always puzzled him.)

Harold explained that in the beginning God had created a perfect couple, Adam and Eve. Satan had tempted them to disobey God and eat of the tree of the knowledge of good and evil and they had fallen, corrupting the whole human race.

"But what was their 'fall'?"

The gist of Harold's reply was that Adam and Eve committed adultery; all their descendants were then corrupted by sexual sin. The human race therefore needed a savior. Jesus was sent by God to redeem them from that. He was the second Adam, or the second perfect Man.

Howie was intrigued. "Don't the Christian churches teach that Jesus' death on the cross brought this 'redemption'?"

It seemed, according to Harold, that this was not entirely correct. What Jesus was sent to do was to establish a new and sinless line of humanity. Unfortunately, He died physically on the cross. This meant that only *spiritual* grafting into Jesus was possible and thus He only accomplished *spiritual* salvation. Humanity was still *physically* fallen. There had to be a new savior in order to bring people back to the original state of total perfection.

"How is that to be done?" Howie asked.

Harold's answer was long and involved. There had been a prophet some years ago in Korea. A new savior had been born. That one was Rev. Moon. Jesus, having failed in his total mission, was no longer one of the Trinity. A new church with a new founder was necessary. That founder was the Rev. Sun Myung Moon, the messiah of the second advent, a living god.

That last statement was hard for Howie to swallow on such short notice. Why hadn't he heard before? But he was hearing now, Harold told him, and the mission of the Unification Church was to unify world Christianity around Rev. Moon. They had a calling and a destiny.

Howie was greatly impressed with their dedication, their warmth, and their apparent love for him. They seemed so sure. Was some great new thing happening in the world that he was being given the opportunity to be a part of on the ground floor level?

THE HISTORY AND THEOLOGY OF THE UNIFICATION CHURCH

> With all nations put together,
> they will be one people in God.
> With all these people in coopera-
> tion with each other, we are going
> to build God's kingdom on earth.

> —Sun Myung Moon

A standard brochure distributed by the Unification Church proclaims:

The Unification Church was founded in 1954 in Korea by Sun Myung Moon. Over a long course of prayer and study, Rev. Moon discovered a series of principles which yielded great insight into the deep questions of human life and faith: the nature of God, the origin of suffering, the purpose of creation and life. As a Christian, he explored many of the puzzling problems of Bible interpretation and found a pattern in the Bible according to which God has been

123

conducting His providence through history and even in the present-day world. In the light of these principles, the deeper meanings of the parables and symbols of the Bible could be clearly seen, as well as the purpose of all religions.[1]

This Sun Myung Moon is the same man who has said (*Time,* September 30, 1974): "God is now throwing Christianity away and is now establishing a new religion, and this new religion is Unification Church." Backing up his bold assertion is the claim of the Unification Church that it has spread throughout the world and is now established and thriving in over forty countries, with three-fourths of a million members in Korea, two million worldwide, and ten thousand supporters in the United States.[2]

Out of the East

Sun Myung Moon was born in Korea on January 6, 1920. He came from a Presbyterian-related family which sent him to Waseda College in Japan to study electrical engineering.

He claims an event occurred in 1936 which changed the whole course of his life. On a lonely Korean mountainside, he says, he received a vision of Jesus Christ. In that vision Moon was supposedly told by Jesus to "carry out my undone task."[3] Those words are important because Moon's whole theology is based on the idea that Jesus failed.

Moon married, fathered a son, and got a successful business going. Living in North Korea following World War II, he associated with pentecostal Christians in Pyongyang's underground church. Among them there came a prophecy of a Korean Messiah. Moon made that prophecy part of his developing self-concept. His preaching was dynamic and he began to amass a group of followers. He started work on a theological system which he soon called "Divine Principle." In 1948 he was excommunicated by the Presbyterian Church.

An interruption in his activities occurred, however, when he was arrested by Communists and was imprisoned for three years. The reasons are obscure. He claims it was because he was anti-Communist. Others say it was for adultery and immorality. In June of 1950 he escaped during a bombardment by U.S. forces.

Settling in South Korea, Moon kept working on his "Divine

Principle." Again he built a following, not neglecting his business interests which today are massive. In May, 1954, he was ready to move. He announced the establishment of his Holy Spirit Association for the Unification of World Christianity, called the Tong-il Church in Korea.

His first wife left him. He says it was because she didn't understand his mission. (It is possible, though that his fathering of a child by another woman may have had some bearing on the matter. Korean Christians claim he has slept with, lived with, and married several women.) For doctrinal reasons which we will get to shortly, it was important for Moon to be married to a woman who understood his mission. In 1960 he married a very young Korean woman named Hak-Ja Han who was quite devoted to him and his mission. They now have four sons and three daughters.

Branching Out

Moon missionaries had covered most of South Korea by 1957. He began getting significant opposition from the Christian churches, which declared his church non-Christian. He continued branching out, and by 1958 he established beachheads in Japan and the United States. During the 1960s, Moon centers were established in various European countries. His greatest success has always been in South Korea, where he reportedly has about a million followers. There may be 50,000 or more members in Japan.

Success wasn't immediate in the United States, in spite of aggressive efforts by Moon missionaries. In 1964, however, he had people scattered all across the United States. By 1970 there were a few hundred converts, and the push was on. When he moved his headquarters to the States in 1973, things began to move. Today he travels all over the United States and the world promoting his religion.

MOON'S THEOLOGICAL SYSTEM

Who is God?

Maybe we ought to ask "What is God?" because Moon does *not* believe in the Christian view of God as Trinity. He flatly tells us Jesus is not God. And we don't learn where the Holy Spirit came from. All we learn is that it is a female spirit thrown in when Jesus accidentally gets crucified.

In Moon's system God is single, not triune. It's sort of complicated, though, for Moon digs up out of an old Oriental book of philosophy, *The Book of Changes (I Ching)*, something called "dualism." Now stay with me. You have to catch something here in order to see what Moon is up to.

God, says Moon, is composed of pairs. Within His singleness there is the original of all pairs and contrasts in the universe. That means male and female, positivity and negativity, etc., are all to be found in that single original Being. You wouldn't believe the complex structure which results when Moon puts it all together.

Anyway, all these dual characteristics are supposed to enter into give and take action, blending into a single whole! As a result this "God" automatically has a characteristic called "creativity," which is why anything else exists.

Inside God are supposed to exist all the individual images out of which eventually come all the individual beings in the universe. It's hard to figure out, but it seems like you and everybody else always existed within God.

But Who is Christ?

If Christ didn't always exist with the Father as the Son, where did He come from? Moon has an answer. Jesus was a man who perfectly understood what God wanted, and did it. Moon wants to capture Christians, so he says Jesus attained the purpose of creation and became one body with God. So you can call him God, but He really isn't. How about that for a run-around?

Moon quotes a lot of Scripture like 1 Tim. 2:5, "For there is one God and one mediator between God and men, the man Christ Jesus," to prove that Jesus is just a man. Then he wiggles on the Scriptures about Jesus' deity by saying a man who fulfills the purpose of creation really has the whole universe wrapped up in him. So you can call Him the Creator, though he isn't the Creator Himself. Another run-around.

In the end, though, Jesus failed. Yes, that's what Moon says, and we'll pick it up later. We'll also find out where the Holy

Spirit entered the picture. First though, we have to consider creation.

Where Do We Come In?

The world and humanity weren't created. Not in the sense of being made, exterior to God, by Him. Moon's followers believe we were projected out of God. The whole thing is a projection of God in a material form. Everything except man is some sort of symbolic incarnation of God.

Man, though, is something different, something better. Now catch this because everything hinges on it! Man is a direct incarnation of God. God put all His energy and all of Himself into man, so that man became the very life of God. That's going to make some later things in Moon's system hard to swallow, but hang on to it. He tells us God put everything together so when it all comes out, the whole creation bears the image and likeness of man.

Dual Man and How He Grows

Remember the pairs in God? Well, guess what? Man's the same way. Everything about humanity is dual: male and female, physical and spiritual, mind and body, and so forth. Moon brings the *I Ching* into everything.

Man was created male and female. There they were in the garden, Adam and Eve. They were supposed to unite around God, have children, and all would be one happy family. Moon calls it the Family Four Position Foundation. Everything was in order for a great big kingdom of Heaven with give and take around God producing billions of perfect children.

Oh, but wait. Man isn't just automatically perfect like he's supposed to be. There are stages of maturity. (Does it seem complicated? You're right!) Moon gives us three stages of maturity for everything—formation, growth, and perfection. Humanity ran into trouble in the middle stage—growth.

A High Angel Blows It

Somewhere back along the line, God had created angels to be His messengers and servants. As Moon sees it, one of the most highly placed, named Lucifer (Satan), got insanely jealous when Adam and Eve were created. He decided that the

127

existence of this pair meant God loved him (Lucifer) less. How to get even?

Well, Moon says, Satan figured it out. This Eve was a very beautiful girl. So he went into the garden, got her alone, sweet-talked her, seduced her, and there it was. She, poor girl, in her immature state, couldn't resist. After Satan and Eve had sexual intercourse, the fat was in the fire.

Eve was ruined. She was infected with the taint of Satan's sin, and there was her future husband running around, still pure and growing toward perfection. So what does she do? You've already guessed Moon's answer. She went right out and had intercourse with Adam, and a whole new ballgame started.

Ruined!

Now there existed an evil Family Four Position Foundation centering around Satan rather than God. Mankind had fallen, and evil embodied in selfishness had entered into the world. God had a problem to solve.

You see Moon holds that the Tree of Life in the garden represented perfected manhood, which Adam should have attained. The Tree of the Knowledge of Good and Evil represented womanhood, or Eve. It seems God's command not to eat of that tree meant that Adam and Eve were not yet to have sexual intercourse. Who could buy a trip like that? Well, people are.

See how it is. Immature Eve unfortunately partook of that tree by her adulterous intercourse with Satan and then dragged Adam into it. It's a great disaster, and as you can see, Moon puts the blame on Eve rather than Adam. The poor guy never had a chance.

Mankind is in a hole. Instead of one master there are two, God and Satan! And, Moon says, from that point every person lives with a constant internal battle, the original self fighting with the fallen self over good and evil. Mankind had fallen spiritually by not keeping faith with God and physically by yielding to the seduction of Satan.

Humanity thus fell into a great pit of ignorance. Yes, says Moon, man doesn't know where he came from, what his purpose is, whether God exists, or the nature of good and evil.

Meanwhile, God has a new task in this world. Mankind must

be restored to his original goodness. And Moon has a plan of history worked out to show how God has worked against evil to bring about that restoration.

Dividing Up History

History, according to Moon's scheme, is divided into separate stages, with a different divinely ordered plan for each stage. If you're a Bible scholar, you know this sort of plan is called dispensationalism. The term doesn't matter, but the idea is all-important to Moon.

He believes there are literally 6,000 years of human history. There are three stages in the progress of mankind. First there comes the "providential age for the foundation of restoration," running from Adam through Noah to the departure of Abraham for Egypt, covering 1,000 years. Along the way Noah was designated by God to restore the race, but it didn't work because his family failed him.

God's next choice, Moon maintains, was Abraham, but he blew it too. However, he and his descendants, Isaac and Jacob, accomplished enough for a new age to start—"the providential age of restoration," lasting 1,930 years. This age is made up of 400 years of Israel's slavery in Egypt, 400 years of the period of the Judges, 120 years of the United Kingdom, 400 years of the divided kingdom of North and South, 210 years of the Jewish captivity and return, and 400 years of preparation for the coming of the Messiah.

That's quite a sweep, isn't it? And in it, if you can believe this, Moon holds there was a series of men who were each supposed to *do* something to make up for that original sin of Eve's and restore humanity to perfection. Moses was next and he did pretty well, but in the end he failed too. Every failure meant there had to be a waiting period. And after every major failure the people of Israel had to go through a period of especially severe hardship in order to make up for it. That's why numbers of years mean a lot to Moon—especially 12, 21, and 40 multiplied by 10.

The Messiah Comes, or Does He?

Now comes the historical event which is vitally important to Christians, but which, according to Moon, didn't work out to be all that big a deal. The next age on his chart is 1,930 years following the death of Jesus—"the providential age of the prolongation of restoration." This age has 400 years of persecution under the Roman Empire, 400 years of Christian churches under the patriarchal system, 120 years of the Christian kingdom, 400 years of the divided kingdom of East and West, 210 years of papal captivity and return, and 400 years for the preparation for the Second Coming of the Messiah.

What happened to Jesus? Doesn't He count? Oh yes, says Moon, in all of that 6,000 years only Jesus lived up to God's ideal of perfected humanity. He came to be the Messiah to restore fallen humanity. Remember that Moon does not allow the Christian concept of Jesus as perfect man and perfect God. He was just a man, though He knew what was needed to accomplish that restoration. Unfortunately, something interfered.

John the Baptist: Supreme Failure

John the Baptist, Moon tells us, caused Jesus' mission to fail. It goes something like this. John the Baptist was supposed to clear up all obstacles left by the failure of the great men who had gone before him. He knew Jesus had come as the Messiah, but he lost faith. He finally gave up on the whole thing. The result? Jesus had to do John's job before He could do His own.

Well, He got going on it, but it was uphill all the way. As Moon sees it, when John the Baptist betrayed Jesus, people were led astray. They quit believing Jesus could be the Messiah.

That posed a big problem. According to Moon, salvation had to be both spiritual and physical, because man is both spiritual and physical. The job of the Messiah was to set up the kingdom of God on earth. That means a kingdom in which people can't sin, so human bodies had to be freed from the possibility of sin. So the Messiah had to marry a perfected woman, have perfect children and adopt people into the perfect family. How about that?

The Cross: Tragedy Not Triumph

Because of the unbelief of the people, Jesus was crucified while He was still doing the work of John the Baptist. Oh yes, that's what Moon would have us believe. Jesus never got to do the work of the Messiah. God never intended for Him to die on the cross, but the people of Israel, not understanding His mission, killed him. To top it off, Moon says, at the point of death Satan invaded Jesus' body.

That is a very significant point in Moon's theology. Just think what that means. It means that physical redemption was impossible through Jesus. That's why we're all sinners. All children are still born stained with Eve's original sin. But wait! It didn't all go to waste.

Partial Salvation

Fortunately, God exercised His maximum power and brought Jesus back to life. Unfortunately, as Moon puts it, His body was not now a physical body but a spiritual one. Still, he could accomplish *spiritual* salvation. How? Well, just as Adam had his counterpart in Eve, Jesus had His spiritually in the Holy Spirit, who was also sent by God. Jesus became the spiritual True Father of mankind, representing the Tree of Life. The Holy Spirit became the spiritual True Mother of mankind, representing the Tree of the Knowledge of Good and Evil.

Get it? The second Adam and the second Eve. Through the give and take action of these two we can be born again when we believe in Jesus as Savior through the inspiration of the Holy Spirit. Moon maintains that. After all, he does want to suck Christians into his movement. So there is such a thing as being born again, and it does do some good. But remember, this is only "spiritual rebirth." We are missing physical rebirth.

By the way, if Moon is right, those of us who are Christians don't go to heaven when we die. We go to an intermediate place called "Paradise." That's because the kingdom of God on earth hasn't been set up yet, so there's no kingdom in heaven to go to. We have to wait for the coming of the Lord of the Second Advent.

Behold, He Cometh

Messiahs come in pairs, too. Moon tells us God does not use the same man twice for the same mission. Jesus is not going to return. Never fear, though; all through this age God has been looking for just one man who will be completely one with Him.

Moon believes Charlemagne could have been the one, but he failed. There may also have been others, but the time periods have to work out just right. If you'll look at Moon's stages of history, you'll see that the period from Abraham to Jesus works out with exactly the same time categories as from Jesus' time to today.

Wonder why that is? Well, think about this. Moon goes to great pains to show us that not only the Bible, but many of the world's religions predict a Messiah to come. We learn that Korea in particular has an ancient book of prophecy, called "Chung Gam Nok," which predicts the coming of the King of Righteousness who will bring about the perfect reign in Korea and be proclaimed all over the world.

In Moon's theology book, *Divine Principle,* we find Korea described as the Third Israel, from which will come the Lord of the Second Advent. Hmm, you say, Mr. Moon is from Korea. I wonder if that is just a coincidence? Well, hang on a bit.

This man we're looking for must, of course, be one who has sacrificed himself completely to accomplish God's purpose on earth. And it has been so long. Mr. Moon feels so sorry for God. You see, God is sad because in all of this time He has not been able to find His perfected Adam. A man is required who will be single-minded in his mission to be the mediator between God and man. This man will give himself, God will be pleased and grateful, and that man will be designated as the Lord of the Second Advent.

A Volunteer

Who will it be? Well, let's see. *Divine Principle* says the Messiah should have been born just after World War I. How interesting that Mr. Moon was born in 1920.

Now I've talked with people in the Unification Church and people who have been in and left. Here is a plain fact: Though Moon never quite claims it in public, his followers believe he is the Lord of the Second Advent. Also, it is quite clear he wants them to believe that.

When Moon enters a room in which his followers are

gathered, they bow in a worshipful manner. Want more? How about this: Moon is called "Father," and his wife is called "Mother," and together they are called the "True Parents."

The Divine Parents

Do you remember that Moon teaches that what is needed for the ultimate, complete *physical* redemption of mankind is a perfected couple to take the place of Adam and Eve? That means the Lord of the Second Advent must be married to a perfected woman, with their marriage centered on God. When that union results in children, the godly Family Four Position Foundation (remember it?) will be established. This couple will be the True Father and the True Mother of mankind.

How do we get in? Adoption! We get adopted into the True Family. Then comes the long-expected kingdom of God on earth. Can you guess the identity of this illustrious family?

Check this statement by Choi-Syn-duk in *The New Religions of Korea:* "Their marriage is called the feast of the lamb by the people of the Tong-il Church, and it has a very significant religious meaning. After the marriage ceremony, the bride was to be called the mother of the universe, or the true mother, and was given the right to receive the deep bows from believers. Up to this time only Mr. Moon had the right to receive the deep bows. After some time the holy mother delivered a daughter . . . and a son . . . these two children are regarded as sinless children by the *church* members."[4]

Do things begin to drop into place? If you have any doubts, how about this? Moon describes the marriage of the Lord of the Second Advent and his bride as the marriage supper of the Lamb, pictured in Revelation. You're right. It wouldn't be very judicious for him to go around saying it in public, but Moon and his Unification Church believe he and his wife are the True Parents come to save us.

The Right Social Order

You may have noticed that Moon's group engages in a lot of anti-Communist activities. That's because he believes God brought about democracy to provide a Christian-like social order. That way people would be free to follow the Lord of the Second Advent.

Satan brought in communism to oppose God. He doesn't want the Lord of the Second Advent to succeed, of course. As Moon sees it, the Lord of the Second Advent will be persecuted and have a very bad time of it, but he won't get killed like Jesus did. Just to make sure, the Unification Church fights communism. Meantime Moon goes about gathering children.

Salvation: Get It Fast

The True Parents are gathering around them the first 144,000 who believe, serve and follow the Second Messiah. There's a big advantage in getting in fast. Moon tells us these people will be the first who experience restoration to original sinless self. They will also have the privilege of assisting all the rest of mankind to achieve salvation. These converts must work, though. Constant driving work for Moon is the price of their salvation. And they also learn they have to work for the salvation of their ancestors, not to mention their descendants.

Salvation: Everybody Gets It

"Salvation of all mankind" is a very literal phrase for Moon. All humanity will be saved. Those people of the Old Testament age who faithfully served God while they were living, returned to earth as spirits at the time of the crucifixion of Jesus (Matt. 27:52). By helping the believers during the present age, they have earned their way into that temporary place called Paradise that we mentioned earlier.

People during the Christian era who have believed, died, and gone to Paradise will come back to earth as spirits and serve the Lord of the Second Advent. I suspect Moon's followers believe they are already here. That activity will pay their way into the kingdom of Heaven. You see by now, don't you, that everybody has to earn his or her way in?

But we're not yet finished with Moon's idea of salvation. What about those people who believed in other religions when they were alive on earth? They, too, will come back in spirit form. They will go to the people of the religion they believed in and help them cooperate with the Lord of the Second Advent in bringing about restoration. That's how they earn their way into the kingdom.

Then there's all those reasonably good people who didn't

believe in any religion when they lived on earth. They'll come back, too, and help people like themselves follow the Second Messiah. That pays their way in.

Some people, however, have been just plain evil on earth. Is there any hope for them? As you would guess by now, of course there is. Moon has set up a complicated system by which such evil spirit people can torment sinful people now living on earth, thereby ultimately earning salvation for both. When all this is accomplished, God will abolish Hell.

One Big Happy Family

So there it is. Moon's fantastic program of redemption which is supposed to bring the ultimate unification of all mankind. All Christians will be united, and they will be joined to all people of all other religions and by all non-religious people.

Oh how glorious! Everybody who ever lived—good, bad, and indifferent—will participate in that great unified family formed around the central focus of Moon, his wife, and his children. Then indeed the whole world will be one people, speaking one language. What malarkey! This is one of the most amazing schemes a human being has ever devised to deceive people and to bring them under oppressive domination.

Who Says?

You may wonder where Moon got all of this. Part of it, of course, he takes from the Bible, usually ignoring orthodox interpretation. Part of it he gets from that book of oriental philosophy we mentioned at the beginning, *The Book of Changes (I Ching).* But the big deal is the revelation he says he got directly from Jesus and God. In the end, if you accept this whole scheme, you accept it because Sun Myung Moon says so.

METHOD OF OPERATION IN THE UNIFICATION CHURCH

Doing It

We have seen that Moon has a goal: unification of the whole world under him. He calls his organization the Unification

Church but he has been accused of forming not a church but a political movement. That's understandable, in light of his methods. His movement, however, does indeed have, as we have shown, a very complex theological and philosophical underpinning. It's a religion, all right.

Moon's ambition certainly isn't to be your run-of-the-mill political dictator. He intends to be the direct representative of God ruling the human race. He says he wants to build God's kingdom on earth. He's certainly busy building something.

The Empire

It's difficult to pin down the extent of Moon's empire, because its arms are often hard to recognize. He doesn't always show his hand. Often concealing the connection with his church, he has set up such a wide variety of special purpose organizations that people get confused.

First, there's the Unification Church, sometimes called the Unified Family, but look what we have to add:[5]

International Re-education Foundation	One World Crusade
High School International Family Association	Professor's Academy for World Peace
Holy Spirit Association for the Unification of World Christianity	Project Unity
International Cultural Foundation	Educational Redevelopment
DC Striders Track Club	Creative Community Project
International Federation for Victory over Communism	Collegiate Association for the Research of Principles
World Freedom Institute	American Youth for a Just Peace
The Little Angels of Korea	New Ideal City Ranch

I have no confidence that this defines the extent of the Moon front groups. He's very prolific in organization.

Then there are business firms owned by Moon and his church:

Il Wha Pharmaceutical Company
Shine Stone Works Company
Tae Han Rutile Company
Tong Il Industry Company
Tong Wat Titanium Company

It all adds up to Mr. Moon being a very busy and very wealthy man.

Moon People

But we mustn't forget that underpinning the whole structure are those people who have been drawn into his Unification Church. It probably has a membership of 300,000 to 500,000 around the world, but most of these are in Korea and Japan. In the United States they say they've got a core membership of about 7,000 with another 30,000 loosely adhering to the church. These core members are the ones who count because they work themselves to death working for Moon. After all, he's their savior. Sometimes they're called "Moon People" or "Moonies" because he's the big thing in their lives.

Sold on Moon as the Lord of the Second Advent, these core members live a hectic communal life. Moon supposedly has centers in 40 countries and 120 cities of the United States. He keeps the Moonies moving around and they seldom get well-settled anywhere. They are pawns in his hands, their daily lives consisting of incessant activity in promoting the various Moon organizations. Sleeping little, they are regularly on the streets peddling flowers, peanuts, candles, or whatever is being pushed at the moment, requesting donations and recruiting.

One thing you find out in a hurry. Moon demands and gets a high degree of commitment. Rigid rules for behavior are tied to salvation and you can bet they are obediently and fearfully followed. Devotion to "the advancement of Principle" occupies the whole life of Moonies, whose jobs are often as church-connected as their religious activities.

In one city I found there was a janitorial company owned by the church, to which Moonies "donated" their labor. In another place the members worked as volunteer help at an organization-owned delicatessen. The driving pace leaves little room for sleep, rest, or recreation—or thinking, for that matter—which may be to Moon's advantage. Some former members say they often didn't get more than four hours of sleep a night. Given that kind of pace, you're going to follow like a zombie until you burn out.

Sex

Relationships between single men and women are carefully monitored. You'd better not get on intimate terms with a member of the opposite sex. That's a no-no. Moon doesn't want his followers to even think about who they might want to marry. Partly, this is supposed to prevent the sin which Moon considers the worst possible—adultery and fornication. That, of course, is the "original" sin he says Eve and Satan, and Eve and Adam committed in the garden. He really hits that one hard. Unification Church members are told that if they commit the "fallen act" in love, it cannot be forgiven. They poison themselves and kill their descendants. To prevent any hanky-panky, single men and single women are never to be alone together.

Marriage partners are arranged—by Moon. Often he sets up a huge group of marriages at one time. He's been known to perform over a thousand marriages at once. Nobody knows who the mate will be until just before the wedding. The last time it happened, in Korea, there were several people from America involved.

Marriage is a special blessing by the Master (Moon) so it's a big deal to have him choose you. By and large marriages are not arranged until people have been in the church for at least three years and have "grown" in their fervor and belief in Moon. It's all connected to the idea of being joined to the True Parents, the Perfect Family, and having perfect children. (I often wonder what these people think when they find out what their children are like.) I'm not quite sure what Moon means when he says that even after being blessed in marriage they must have three years of separation. I do know that married couples are supposed to take a period of time apart in order to give their time to the work of promoting Moon's program.

The Master Speaks

Moon is called "Master" by his followers. Ask Unification Church leaders what that means, and you'll get a run-around. Neil Salonen, U.S. president of the Unification Church, has said it's because Moon is one of the most universal people in the world today, having found the way to unite people. Ex-Moonies claim, however, that the title is given because he is supposed to be the Lord of the Second Advent, who must be served by his followers. We already know that Mr. and Mrs. Moon are considered by followers as the True Parents of mankind.

When Moon speaks, his followers listen and obey. The Unification Church is no democracy. Their leader is looked up to with great reverence. There is worship, and it is worship of the True Parents. Prayer is in the name of the True Parents. The messages always deal with some aspect of Moon's *Divine Principle*.

Since Moon says God has dropped the Christian Church in favor of him, his followers do not think they're coming into the Christian Church. Consequently, they don't practice baptism and the Eucharist. Why should they? They think they're serving the Lord of the Second Advent. Baptism and the Lord's Supper have to do with Jesus, and He failed anyway according to their theology. What meaning has the body and blood of Jesus to someone who thinks Jesus accomplished only spiritual salvation, when they're following Moon who claims to have accomplished both spiritual and physical salvation?

Besides, they've got their own "sacrifices" to bring—the self-sacrifices of their works, which are supposed to purify them for adoption into the True Family. That's not the sacrifice Jesus made on the cross and took to the heavenly altar, but the Moonies sure count on it. There's a statement in a Unification Church brochure which tells the story:

> We create our spirits by the quality of our life on earth; by the degree of goodness we 'build into' them through our actions. Therefore, learning to love God, our parents, brothers and sisters, spouses, children and all mankind is the most important preparation for our eternal life.[6]

139

Brainwashing

Some former members are sure the high degree of commitment comes from brainwashing. Of course there's no way you can prove something like that. It is a fact, though, that the sales pitch is very strong. And once you're in, the pressure to stay is more than most people can take. Ex-Moonies tell stories of how they were told to cut off all ties with family and former associates. Leaving was unthinkable; it was like deserting God. Leave, they were told, and you're going to hell. Then they were watched closely.

A. Terrence Murray of New York has made a notarized deposition that his free will was destroyed by the Unification Church, that he was conditioned not to use his mind, and that his mind was controlled by the leaders of the organization. I've got a copy of it. It's also a fact that Moon has said, "I am the thinker. I am your brain."

Heavenly Deceit

Ex-Moonies say deceit was justified by their leaders. They claim the thinking went something like this: Since Satan deceived Eve in the garden, it's time for a turnabout. The people of the Unification Church should practice "Heavenly Deception." Moon, in a talk to disciples only, has said, "You must be able to manipulate those people."[7] The Master's advice seems to be followed. Several former members have told stories of having been taught to go out on the streets and tell people anything that would get donations.

Above all there is great stress on impressing the public. Broad smiles, polite behavior, and friendliness are literally the rule. When the church purchased the Hotel New Yorker, it promptly began a widely-publicized campaign to "clean up the city." A public display was immediate.

An elderly Jewish couple, observing a group of Moon People all dressed in white jumpsuits, wielding brooms and sweeping up trash on the sidewalks, was very impressed: "They sure are dedicated. It's certainly better than becoming hippies."

How Master Lives

While members live hectic, marginal lives in crowded facilities, that's not the life for the Master. Moon lives with his wife and eight children in a luxurious mansion on an extensive estate. He, of course, must associate with high governmental figures and other dignitaries who wouldn't understand a simple lifestyle. And, of course, he has already paid the price for his church through great suffering. The members, on the other hand, are in the process of paying for themselves and others for whom they are responsible. So Master lives high and disciples live low. A far cry from Jesus, the Messiah Moon scorns.

Selling a New Religion

Where did you first hear about Moon? If you're like most people it was when you learned about one of his rallies. Massive publicity is given to these meetings held in major cities. Full-page ads come out in newspapers. Moonies put posters everywhere.

Moon doesn't mind a little deception here, either. He is promoted as an evangelist and these events are inferred to be unified Christian efforts. Moon people from many other places move in force to rally cities. They go everywhere urging people to attend, promoting Moon. Perhaps most impressive is the International Brigade, composed of people from other countries, who convey the concept of International Christian cooperation. Thousands of people are thus subjected to the emotional and misleading preaching of a man who has been widely renounced by Christian leaders everywhere.

Civic and governmental relationships are also given special attention by Moon. He invites government officials and community leaders to special dinners and receptions. At these events the guests are given the red carpet treatment, as the coffers of the Unification Church are opened to make the occasion memorable. When Moon is in a city for a rally, the office of the mayor is contacted, and a strong public relations pitch is made. Consequently, the mayors of many cities have handed him the "keys of the city."

Politics

Patriotism is also a big angle, particularly in view of Moon's vision of the United States as the nation prepared to receive the Second Messiah, and his consequent buildup of democracy as opposed to communism. During the Watergate controversy the Unification Church promoted a "Support the President" rally in front of the White House. Several such events occurred during the last days of the Nixon presidency. In June, 1976, Moon scheduled a massively publicized "Bicentennial God Bless America" rally in Yankee Stadium. In spite of increasing Christian opposition, many people are misled by such promotions, and are drawn into the Moon web.

Grass-Roots Evangelism

But the major job of building the movement is the job of the membership, who are commanded to bring in converts. Moon has been known to tell his followers that until they have three spiritual children, they cannot reach the kingdom of heaven. Such new converts are to be nurtured to the point that they would do anything for—would die for—the one who brought them in.

You can be sure, therefore, that the Moon people apply themselves diligently to the task of getting converts. On the streets they smile sweetly and use every possible device to get guests for dinner at the communal house. At these dinners, guests are treated royally and are shown a good time. There is singing, perhaps a short meditation, dinner, and more singing. The pressure is put on to get the guest to go to a weekend conference.

Once at the conference, the visitor is subjected to an extremely tight schedule in which there is no free time alone. Someone is always there at break time, talking about the content of the conference. Lectures on *Divine Principle* go on and on. By Sunday evening the tired and pressured guest can easily become confused by all this enthusiasm, apparent love, and attention. Most converts are initially drawn in at this time.

Since appearance is important in order to make favorable impressions both with potential donors and potential converts, the Moon people dress very conservatively; there are no beards, and hair is short. They visit other churches and make friends, well before discussing Moon or *Principle*. Their public appearance is not that of typical young people, but rather that of older, very conservative people. It is very serious business

142

because their salvation and that of others, particularly their descendants, depends upon being successful in getting money and "spiritual children."

Watch Out, Europe!

Moon's "God Bless America" rally in Washington (September, 1976) supposedly marked the end of his "ministry" to America. A recent article in the *London Daily Telegraph* says Moon plans to make Britain and Europe his next targets. A church spokesman was quoted as saying Moon would devote himself to church business for the next few months and would then probably move his missionary activities across the Atlantic.

The Printing Press

A wide variety of publications helps spread the Moon program. At the top of the list, of course, is an official text of *Divine Principle,* Moon's main theological treatise. There is also a philosophical work, *Unification Thought,* in which Moon's whole wierd system is given a scholarly gloss. Among the several other volumes on the publication list is a song book in which hymns and familiar sing-along songs are mixed with new songs written by Moon's followers.

Perhaps most interesting is the newspaper—*Rising Tide*—which is not your usual house organ. Typically, it gives little attention to the activities of the Moon movement, except to sneak in an occasional favorable article or an editorial by Moon. It is primarily an anti-Communist publication, devoting more than 90 percent of its space to articles on that topic, from a wide selection of sources.

Moon's pace in building his movement is related to his own role as the Lord of the Second Advent. He says he has been working on three seven-year "courses," the last of which began in 1973. He wants to make the "ideal world" come at least to the United States by 1980. It is toward that end he is driving his disciples. He leaves the door open, however, for the possibility of another twenty-one-year period beyond that, but believe me, he isn't sitting around waiting!

A REFUTATION OF THE UNIFICATION CHURCH

Where Moon Gets It

Every single religion, theology, or philosophy has some kind of authority to which it appeals. As a matter of fact, every one of us justifies what we say and do by some authority, even if it is only as simple as "I think." At the very point of authority, Moon departs from historic Christianity.

For reasons of his own, he tries to make it look like he is using the Bible as his authority for what he says. He quotes from it profusely, and you'd think he was building his complicated theology from Scripture. Sorry folks; it ain't so. His other source, as we have noted, is the ancient Chinese work called *The Book of Changes,* commonly known as the *I Ching.* It's just as important in forming his ideas about God as is the Bible.

But Moon's real authority is neither the Bible nor the *I Ching.* It is the "direct revelation" he claims to have received straight from God. You see, he is sure he has heard directly from God what the Scriptures mean and how the *I Ching* works together with that meaning. Also, he has received from God more information that nobody else knows.

Moon's God

When you learn the sources of his theological ideas, it isn't surprising that Moon's view of the nature of God is non-Christian. Oh, he tries hard to make it sound Christian, but there's hardly any resemblance.

Just for the record, the creeds of Christianity, built on the Holy Scripture as consistently interpreted by the Church, all agree that:

> I believe in one God the Father Almighty: Maker of heaven and earth, and of all things visible and invisible. And in one Lord Jesus Christ, the only-begotten Son of God, begotten of the Father before all worlds, Light of Light, very God of very God, begotten, not made, being of one substance with the Father; by whom all things were made . . . And in the Holy Spirit, the Lord and Giver of Life; who proceeds from the Father; who with the Father and the Son together is worshiped and glorified. . . .

> (Excerpted from the creed accepted by the Council of Constan-

tinople as a fuller statement of the faith of the Council of Nicaea, commonly called the Nicene Creed, and universally accepted in the Christian Church.)[8]

There it is, very simply. Three persons, all of the same nature, in one Godhead, worshiped and glorified together. Moon's idea of God being single and full of pairs is so far removed from that statement that the contrast is like night and day. Compare the above declaration, so reverently accepted by millions of Christians, with Moon's God—a single God with all kinds of pairs in Him. Moon's trinity is made up of that God, temporarily attached to a totally human Jesus, and a female spirit he calls the Holy Spirit. There's no way that trinity qualifies as Christian.

Jesus Christ

Moon tells us Jesus Christ is not God, and it is a mistake to believe He is. That's not a new idea. Other heretics have taught such views. The Church has always rejected them! In fact, one of the most famous pronouncements on the deity of Christ came because the Church had to put down a teaching not much different from Moon's.

It was early in the fourth century, 325 A.D., when a council of 318 bishops (and hundreds and hundreds of elders and deacons) gathered in a town called Nicea to do battle against a heresy dreamed up by a man named Arius. For *three months,* these bishops, elders, and deacons met day after day, searching the Scriptures and what had been said by preachers and teachers who lived before them. In the end, it took only a short statement to sum it up, and that creed has been held by Christians ever since. Here is a very important part of it:

> We believe in one God, the Father Almighty, Maker of all things visible and invisible. And in one Lord Jesus Christ, the Son of God, begotten of the Father, the only-begotten, i.e., of the substance of the Father, God of God, and Light of Light, very God of very God, begotten, not made, being of one substance with the Father; by whom all things were made in heaven and on earth. . . .[9]

As you can see, that creed says Jesus Christ *is* GOD, and has the same nature as the Father. The war was not over, for these followers of Arius kept on promoting their false doctrine. The Church did not back off. Still the Arians persisted, twisting Scripture to make their heresy seem true. A few years later, Athanasius, who had been a young deacon at that Council, wrote against them, and reaffirmed the truth.

> We, on the other hand, very confidently prove the true Catholic Faith out of the Holy Scriptures. We place it as a candle on a candlestick. We assert that the Son is naturally and essentially the Son of the Father, of the same substance with Him, His Only-begotten Wisdom. The true and only Word of God; that He was not made nor created, but begotten of one substance with the Father. Therefore, we say, that He is true God, being of one substance with God the Father (*Orations of S. Athanasuis, Oration One,* point 9).[10]

Obviously, the deity of Jesus Christ was very important to the Church in the fourth century. Nor has the matter been dropped or the doctrine changed by the Church in all the centuries since. His deity is important to us. Among the many creeds and confessions written at the time of the Reformation, perhaps none stated the continuing belief of the Church more clearly than did the Augsburg Confession of 1529:

> The churches, with common consent among us, do teach that the decree of the Nicene Synod concerning the unity of the divine nature and of the three persons is true and without doubt to be believed. That is, that there is one divine nature, which is called and is God. God is eternal, without body, not divided into parts, of infinite power, wisdom, goodness. . . . Yet there are three persons of the same nature and power, who also are co-eternal, the Father, the Son, and the Holy Spirit" (free modern language version of Part First, Art. I).[11]

The authors recognized they were tied in with what had always been believed in the Church and affirmed at Nicea. Nor were they alone. That same recognition echoed throughout the Reformation world. In the French Confession of Faith, put together primarily by John Calvin and his associates, we find that same truth, backed up by an appeal to what the Church had said before:

These Holy Scriptures teach us that in this one sole and simple divine nature, whom we have confessed, there are three persons: the Father, the Son, and the Holy Spirit. The Father is first cause, principle and origin of all things. The Son is His Word and eternal wisdom. The Holy Spirit is His virtue, power, and efficacy . . . The three persons are not confused, but distinct, and yet not separate, but of the same nature, equal in eternity and power. And in this we confess that which has been established by the ancient council, and we detest all sects and heresies which were rejected by the holy doctors, such as St. Hilary, St. Athanasius, St. Ambrose, and St. Cyril" (modern language version).[12]

What are the Holy Scriptures from which the Church obtained this teaching? There are so many we cannot possibly tell them all, but look at these:

In many and various ways God spoke of old to our fathers by the prophets; but in these last days he has spoken to us by a Son, whom he appointed heir of all things, through whom also he created the world. He reflects the glory of God and bears the very stamp of his nature, upholding the universe by his word of power. When he had made purification for sins, he sat down at the right hand of the Majesty on high (Heb. 1:1-3).

He was in the world, and the world was made through Him, and the world knew Him not (John 1:10).

All things were made through him, and without him was not anything made that was made (John 1:3).

So the Bible and the Christian Church of all the centuries tell us that Jesus Christ is God and the Maker of all things. Moon suddenly pops up in the twentieth century and tells us that Jesus Christ is not God. He doesn't stop there. He goes on to tell us that Jesus made nothing—except perhaps a mistake by getting himself crucified (though you'll recall Moon blames that on John the Baptist).

The Holy Spirit

Then this audacious upstart has the nerve to tell us that the Holy Spirit is *a* Mother Spirit, temporarily joining Christ with God to form a trinity. What an outrage! Again the Scriptures

147

and the Church refute him. Already, in the creeds quoted above, there is enough to demonstrate his error. It is the Holy Spirit who teaches the Church all it knows.

> God has revealed to us through the Spirit. For the Spirit searches everything, even the depths of God (1 Cor. 2:10).

You will recall that the Nicene Creed reads, in part, ". . . And in the Holy Spirit, the Lord and Giver of Life; who proceeds from the Father; who with the Father and Son together is worshiped and glorified . . ."

The Holy Spirit is not *a temporary female spirit,* suddenly appearing to "marry" the spirit of Jesus Christ. *The Holy Spirit is God.* All historic Christian creeds affirm that truth, and the Thirty-Nine Articles of the Church of England (1563) provide a clear example: "The Holy Spirit . . . is of one substance, majesty, and glory with the Father, the Son, very and eternal God."[13] In my opinion, only a fool would choose Moon when confronted with such weight of evidence!

What is Man?

Things don't get better when Moon describes the nature of humanity. Man, he says, is a direct incarnation of God. Christianity has never held such a position. Only One is the direct incarnation of God, and that is our Lord Jesus Christ. The rest of us are creatures God created. Moon tries to make it sound like we are gods in the flesh—that we are made out of the same "stuff" God is.

Moon isn't even close! Some of the greatest of the reformers, in the Confession of Concord, wrote, "And today no less, God acknowledges our minds and bodies to be His creatures and work; as it is written, 'Thy hands fashioned and made me. . . .' " (Job 10:8).[14]

To this we can add the fuller statement of the Westminster Confession,

> God has all life, glory, goodness, happiness, in and of Himself. He is alone in and to Himself all-sufficient. He does not stand in need of any creatures which He has made. He does not derive any glory from them. He just shows His own glory in them, by them, to them,

148

and upon them. He alone is the foundation of all being, of whom, through whom, and to whom are all things. He has absolute reign over them, to do by them, for them, or upon them whatever He pleases (free modern language version).[15]

Now that doesn't sound like we're gods in the flesh. Human beings are totally distinct from God. God is God and man is man. The one is the creation, not the projection or incarnation of the other.

History and the Messiah

Moon's view of history cannot be found anywhere in Christianity. Some dispensational systems have been proposed. None of them, however, has been anything like his system. Actually, none of them has been universally accepted by the Church. Most of all, though, nowhere in all of Christian history do we find the view that God has been looking for a man who will sacrifice himself to save the world, to erase the sin of other people. Moon's blasphemous claim that Jesus Christ failed in His attempt to provide salvation for humanity comes right out of nowhere! The agreement of the Church has always been as the Nicene Creed states concerning Jesus Christ:

> . . . who for us men and for our salvation, came down from heaven, and was incarnate by the Holy Spirit of the Virgin Mary, and was made man; and was crucified also for us under Pontius Pilate; he suffered and was buried; and the third day he rose again, according to the Scriptures; and ascended into heaven, and sits on the right hand of the Father; and he shall come again with glory to judge both the living and the dead; whose kingdom shall have no end. . . .[16]

Many strong Scriptures stand behind that strong confession. It did not come out of nowhere.

> But far be it from me to glory except in the cross of our Lord Jesus Christ, by which the world has been crucified to me, and I to the world (Gal. 6:14).

> For I decided to know nothing among you except Jesus Christ and him crucified (1 Cor. 2:2).

149

> For the word of the cross is folly to those who are perishing, but to us who are saved it is the power of God (1 Cor. 1:18).

> . . . having canceled the bond which stood against us with its legal demands; this he set aside, nailing it to the cross. He disarmed the principalities and powers and made a public example of them, triumphing over them in him (Col. 2:14-15).

Jesus Christ did indeed win the victory. And that victory was our salvation. Not only that, but He won it on that very cross Moon despises and calls a failure. If He had not won the victory, all Christians would have died without hope. Perhaps if that had been true, someone like Moon might have been justified in trying to construct a hope of salvation. But Jesus Christ *did* win the victory, and the nature of that victory is well-stated by that hero of the faith, Athanasius, who wrote:

> Demons confess Him, His works bear Him witness day by day. It must be evident, then, and let nobody brazen it out against the truth, that the Savior raised His own body. He is the true Son of God, being from Him, from His own Father, His own Word, Wisdom and Power. It was He who took a body for the salvation of all and taught the world concerning the Father. It was He who brought death to nothing, and who gave eternal life to all by the promise of the Resurrection. He raised up His own body as a first-fruits of this. Then He displayed it by the sign of the Cross as a monument of victory over death and its corruption" (modern language version of point 32.6, *Incarnation of the Word*).[17]

In direct contradiction to this consistently held truth, Moon says we need a new savior. Then he sets himself up as the man to do the job. He, a sinful *man*, whose moral behavior has been questionable, to say the least, wants to replace the Son of God! The Heidelberg Catechism (1563) very effectively cuts him down here:

> Question 14: Can any mere creature make satisfaction for us? Answer: None. First God will not punish the sins of humanity, which have made us guilty, in any other creature. Further, no mere creature could bear the burden of God's eternal wrath against sin and redeem others from it.

Question 15: What manner of mediator and redeemer, then, must we seek? Answer: One who is a true and sinless man and yet more powerful than all creatures. One who is at the same time true God. (modern language version)[18]

Moon should be glad he doesn't have to be the savior!

With his foundation in ruins, Moon's system of salvation resulting from "True Parents" forming a "Perfect Family" crumbles. He is not the Lord of the Second Advent. He is an imposter whose theology falls under the anathema of the Christian Church from at least as far back as the fourth century, when the Council of Nicea said concerning Jesus Christ:

. . . And those who say: there was a time when He was not; and: He was not before He was made; and: He was made out of nothing, or out of another substance or thing, or the Son of God is created, or changeable, or alterable;—they are condemned by the holy catholic and apostolic church.[19]

A BRIEF PROFILE OF THE UNIFICATION CHURCH

1. History
   —Founded by Sun Myung Moon in Korea in 1954. Established in United States in 1958.
   —Moon's past very unsavory.
   —A vision and a prophecy concerning a Korean Messiah helped develop Moon's image of himself.
   —Moon a wealthy businessman.
   —Claims about 2,000,000 followers world-wide.

2. Beliefs
   —Jesus Christ is not fully God.
   —God is single, not triune.
   —The Holy Spirit is a female spirit.
   —Jesus Christ failed in His mission.
   —Moon is the true savior of mankind around whom the world is to unite.

3. Method Of Operation
   —About 7,000 core members in United States called "Moon People" or "Moonies."
   —Moon does all the thinking for his followers, who are brainwashed.
   —Moon lives high; disciples live low.
   —New converts gained through aggressive personal evangelism and massive rallies.
   —Red carpet treatment for political leaders, and patriotism emphasized.

4. Refutation
   —Jesus Christ is true God. Attested by both the Church and the Scriptures.
   —God exists in Trinity, the Father, the Son, and the Holy Spirit. Attested by both the Church and the Scriptures.
   —The Holy Spirit is true God, part of the Holy Trinity. Attested by both the Church and the Scriptures.
   —Jesus Christ succeeded in His mission, with the cross being a glorious triumph. Attested by both the Church and the Scriptures.
   —Jesus Christ is the only Savior of humankind. Attested by both the Church and the Scriptures.

THE UNIFICATION CHURCH—FOOTNOTES

1. "The Unification Church, Who We Are." Undated brochure.
2. "New Hope for America." Undated newspaper format brochure published by Unification Church.
3. Rabbi Davis, "The Moon People and Our Children," *Jewish Community Center Bulletin*, Volume 20, No. 18, July 10, 1974, White Plains, N.Y., p. 1.
4. Choi-Syn-duk, "Korea's Tong-il Movement," *The New Religions of Korea*, Spencer J. Palmer, Editor, p. 168. Note: Tong-il Church is the Korean name of the Unification Church.
5. List furnished by Mrs. J. C. Crampton. Similar list compiled by Spiritual Counterfeits Project of Berkeley.
6. "The Unification Church, Who We Are." Undated brochure.
7. Sun Myung Moon, "Relationship between Men and Women," Second 100-Day Training Session, Master Speaks, translated by Mrs. Won Pok Choi, May 20, 1973, p. 6.
8. Schaff, *A Select Library*, Volume XIV, p. 163.
9. *Ibid*, p. 3.

10. Athanasius, *The Orations of S. Athanasius Against the Arians,* The Ancient and Modern Library of Theological Literature (London: Griffith Farran & Co.), p. 18.
11. Schaff, *The Creeds Of Christendom,* p. 7.
12. *Ibid,* pp. 362-363.
13. *Ibid,* p. 489.
14. *Ibid,* p. 99.
15. *Ibid,* p. 607.
16. Schaff, *A Select.Library,* Volume XIV, p. 3.
17. Schaff, *A Select Library,* volume IV, p. 53.
18. Schaff, *The Creeds Of Christendom,* pp. 311-312.
19. Schaff, *A Select Library,* Volume XIV, p. 3.

An Introduction to
the Children of God

Mary Channing was nineteen and a member of the youth group of Fifth Presbyterian Church. Mostly the youth meetings weren't all that exciting, but her friends were there. Sometimes they had fun after the meetings. Actually, that's why she went.

This night there were about a dozen strange kids there. They sure were different. During the meeting they popped in comments like "Praise the Lord!" and "Oh, Lord!" and "Amen!" Wierd.

After the meeting a couple of these strangers cornered her. "Do you know Jesus?" one of them asked.

"I guess so", Mary replied, "I've been a member of this church all my life."

"But do you really know Him?" this girl, Esther, persisted. "Have you ever asked Him to forgive you? Asked Him into your life? That's the important thing."

"Well," Mary faltered, "sometimes when I feel guilty . . ."

"Hey!" Esther called to one of the group with her. "Can Mary come over to our place for awhile?"

"Sure," he answered. "Come on, Mary, we'll sing and talk about Jesus!"

They surrounded her, and Mary went along. What an enthusiastic group!

They had her pray a prayer, asking Jesus in. They told her about how they were traveling around telling everybody about God's judgment and how to be saved. Someone picked up a guitar and started to sing. It seemed to Mary like she was the only one who wasn't with it. Pretty soon they put her name in appropriate places in the song. Half a dozen of them joined hands and danced around her to the music.

155

"Mary, you're really a Christian now!" Esther exclaimed. "You want to really do His will, don't you?"

Mary was confused. How sure they were! She guessed she did.

"Come and join us. Is there anything more important you could do with your life?"

Mary wasn't doing anything very important. The only job she'd been able to find was working as a waitress. That didn't seem very important.

"Leave everything," they told her. "Do the will of God! That's the important thing. Judgment is coming; America is doomed!"

They pushed her. But it was so sudden. What would her parents think? They took her home, but when she got off work the next day, there were Esther and Naomi. Two days later, Mary decided.

"This is crazy!" her father exploded. "You don't even know these people!"

There was a big hassle, but Mary left. As Esther pointed out, her father was really tied up in the world system. Her new friends had forsaken all. Why shouldn't she? She gave her stereo and portable TV to the leaders. All she had left were a few clothes, but what more did she need? After all, God would provide. Esther had told her all those stories about how He took care of His children.

Next day, less than a week after she had met Esther, Mary left town in a busload of Children of God, all singing at the top of their lungs. What freedom! Serving God and seeing the world.

THE HISTORY AND THEOLOGY OF
THE CHILDREN OF GOD

Getting Started

It was 1968. The Vietnam War was in full swing, and it was a disillusioning time for many young Americans. Thousands were on the road with a backpack or less. Drugs of many varieties were big among southern California youth.

In Huntington Beach, California, when all this turmoil

among youth was taking place, an insignificant event occurred. A Teen Challenge coffee house changed hands. With this turnover, the seeds were planted for one of the most radical heretical cults of this generation, the Children of God (COG).

The mastermind of this takeover was David Berg, a one-time Christian and Missionary Alliance minister. He had left his church and become a participant in "minor league" evangelistic endeavors. Now he and his family used the coffee house for a ministry focused on young people. Many of those who came around were involved in the drug scene or were in some way identified with the new counterculture.

Berg pushed hard-line Bible study. He condemned "the System" loudly and continuously. Communal living was the only way to go. Soon he had more than 50 faithful disciples. Nobody would have suspected it, but a new religious movement, more radical than America had ever seen, was being born.

On The Road

Berg considers himself "God's prophet for these last days."[1] He exercised his "gift" of prophecy by proclaiming doom. In a foolish display, he joined a whole host of psychics, seers, and other clairvoyants in predicting that California would soon drop into the Pacific. Twice he "knew" the exact time and led his followers to the mountains to save their lives. Both times he was wrong. California stayed where it was.

Finally, he said God told him to shut down the coffee house and get his people out before it really did happen. Dividing into two or three groups they took off in caravans. In various parts of North America they showed up proclaiming a message of doom and judgment. Everywhere they went, they urged people to join with them.

By early 1969, the separated groups were back together again, making their way to Texas. Berg gave them the idea they were like ancient Israel wandering in the wilderness. The idea captured their imaginations and the whole group took on personal biblical names. Berg took the name of Moses David. Their communes were given Jewish tribal names. That practice is still followed by COG.

Back in Huntington Beach, Berg had called his ministry "Teens for Christ." It wasn't suitable anymore, but the news media had provided a new name when writing about them: "Children of God." Berg liked it and took it up. It fit his concept of the identity of his following.

A New Home

You can't travel around forever. At least not without a home base. A rather unholy alliance provided a place to live. Berg had once worked with a radio and TV evangelist Fred Jordan, who ran the American Soul Clinic and TV's "Church in the Home."

Jordan had fired him then but now he was looking for a youth group. Berg had one. Jordan could make promotional hay from the group, showing his ministry's effectiveness in the current youth scene. That would be money in the bank for him. COG needed a place to stay. Both sides had something to offer. Jordan had the place; Berg had the young people.

An agreement was made to swap assets. Jordan would use the COG young people to give the impression he was winning converts. In return, COG was given the use of three Jordan properties—plus some money. They first settled in at Jordan's "Soul Clinic," a ranch near Fort Worth, Texas. They also moved into a five-story building in downtown Los Angeles. Later Jordan put them on a ranch near Coachella, California.

From the beginning that alliance was shaky. Jordan and COG weren't on the same track. Jordan was part of the System, which COG vigorously opposed. Besides, if Jordan's public learned who these young people really were and what they believed, it would ruin him. His rather right-wing supporters wouldn't like it. On the other side, Jordan's involvement in the System grated the more left-wing reactionary COG. Each wanted the other to bend his way. Neither bent, and the relationship collapsed in conflict.

On The Road Again

Evicted from Jordan's properties in the fall of '71, the COG colonies (that's what they call their communes) scattered. They scrambled for whatever quarters they could get. Soon they were in San Diego, Seattle, Detroit, Dallas, Austin, New York,

Vancouver, you name it. Sometimes businessmen donated quarters. A few churches interested in young people provided places. Where there wasn't anything free, COG rented inexpensive houses and apartments, sometimes crowding ten to twenty people in a single room. All these kinds of arrangements tended to be temporary, of course, and the COG colonies moved often.

That time back on the Jordan properties had been profitable for the COG, though. They had been there a year and a half, and they had gotten their thing together. Lots of basic teaching and training had been done. They had developed the patterns of communal life and ministry that would stick with them. It had also been a time of aggressive recruitment. When they left Jordan's places, there were nearly 1,000 COG members.

Mass Conversion

Whole groups were joining up. David Hoyt had a ministry in Atlanta. After having drunk deeply from the well of the counterculture with its drugs and oriental mysticism, Hoyt had been converted to Christianity in California. After operating Christian communes there, he had felt called to Atlanta. There he had developed the same sort of operation.

When the COG came to town and leaned on him, Hoyt bought the program lock, stock, and barrel. Joining the movement, he brought four of his communes and about 100 people with him. Hoyt has since left and is an outspoken opponent of COG. Unfortunately, his wife and three children were still in it at last report.

Up in Seattle, Linda Meisner of the Jesus People Army joined up. Only a few of her followers came along, but she brought outstanding ability, plus a front for COG to use.

This sort of raiding of what has been called the Jesus Movement has been a regular COG practice. They've gotten a lot of people from those ranks. By the end of '71, COG was the biggest and best-organized religious group to come out of the new radical youth culture!

What They Did

COG's impact and influence was far greater than you'd expect from their size. Their activities have always tended to be dramatic. At one point they began to make mass visits to "standard brand" church services. Marching up to the front as a group, they would sing loudly and make generally obnoxious comments. Sometimes they even tried to take over the meetings. Often they pronounced doom on the "apostate church."

Their bizarre demonstrations haven't been limited to churches. They have made themselves very conspicuous at many public events, such as the trial of the Chicago Seven. At the funeral of Sen. Everett Dirksen they showed up wearing red sackcloth, wooden yokes around their necks, and carrying staves.

> God had told us to wear the red sackcloth, symbolizing mourning, and the yokes, the coming bondage, and to carry staves as a symbol of His righteous judgments upon a wicked nation that had forsaken God—America!

Demonstrations like these got COG a lot of publicity, including major network TV coverage. The noise they made was as great as it was offensive.

Witnessing

Hard-line witnessing has always been bread and butter for COG. Out on the streets they corner a potential convert. The message is doom. You've only got one way of escape: repent, accept Jesus, and come join the COG. They preach a spiritual revolution against the System, calling for nothing less than 100 percent commitment—to COG.

World-wide Scope

Zeal for the growth of their cause has been a passion of the COG since its early days. And grow they have, first in America, but now around the world. At first a world vision was just a dream, a fantasy. But as their anti-Americanism grew, they began to want to get out. At the same time, the secular counter-culture was spreading around the world. That provided potential bases for COG colonies. Soon the dream was to become reality.

The first overseas mission was headed by one of Berg's daughters in 1971. Cultural differences meant there had to be adjustments, but a beachhead was established. Soon COG colonies were scattered across Western Europe. By the end of 1975, these colonies had settled in almost every country of Western Europe and even in parts of non-Communist Eastern Europe.

But Europe wasn't the end. The COG moved out in pioneer works (that's their name for it) to far-flung locations. Now they're in 70 different countries with colonies even in Hong Kong, Singapore, Fiji, and Thailand. There are supposed to be 4,000-5,000 disciples in nearly 400 colonies spread over every continent but Antarctica. Berg claims they publish in almost 30 languages. Their "records" are supposed to show that COG made over a quarter of a million converts to Christianity between '72 and '74.[2] It seems unlikely.

Most COG disciples are Americans. Part of the world-wide program has been to move these people abroad. As of 1976, most of the American COGs were in other countries. This move ties in with Berg's feeling about America. In 1972, when Richard Nixon (whom Berg called "Nitler") was re-elected, Berg completely gave up on his native land. America wasn't going to repent and God's terrible judgment would come very soon. It would be too dangerous there for the COG. Chaos would reign and there would be war in the streets. The COG had better get out. So they took "vacations" to other lands, and most just haven't come back.

Berg writes in a Mo Letter,

> That was the year the COG decided to leave America to her fate, having warned the wicked with their witness. . . and departed for parts unknown! Thank God for delivering us out of Babylon!

The New Revolution—A Reorganization

Berg's birthday in 1975 marked a new era in the COG scheme. It was the beginning of "The New Revolution." In Berg's own words,

> So dawned the idea of 'The New Revolution' on my birthday in February of this New Year 1975!—a revolutionary new restructuring of leadership and organization into smaller colonies with more leadership and manpower scattered into more new fields by put-

ting some pressure on you to divide those colonies into new fields and gain more disciples.[3]

This "New Revolution" seems to center in two areas: the nature of the colony and the structure of leadership. Over the years, colonies had tended to get big, sometimes having 150 people. Such large groups were hard to manage. Then, too, a large group at a low level meant that strong leadership could develop down there. In no way did Berg want that.

It was really in '74 that Berg first began his attack against "Blob Colonies"—the big ones. The new plan shows he won, at least in theory. Colonies are now to be no bigger than 12. When the thirteenth convert shows up, the colony is supposed to split into two. That change hasn't been easily accomplished. Berg admits, ". . . our great society may be in great confusion for the moment . . ."[4]

Leadership changes are also supposed to be part of the New Revolution. It has certainly been broadened. Some people think that means Berg isn't taking the dominant role he once had.[5] Others say it's just the typical tool used by strong leadership to neutralize potential rivals by drowning them in a sea of leaders.

Whatever the outcome may be, the old, simple organizational structure has given way to an involved pyramid. The complexity shows in a Berg description of what's happening:

> Some have already jumped several grades before we even had time to notify them of their first promotion or two, and many a Colony Shepherd of yesterday has already wound up the District and Regional Shepherds of today, including a whole batch of new Bishops, and bid fair to be the Arch-bishops and Ministers of tomorrow, including a few brand new Prime Ministers which are gonna necessitate the creation of even newer officers above them![6]

That makes seven levels of leadership. Quite a pyramid for a group so anti-establishment. But it does create positions for "restless troops" who want to lead.

Along with this change comes a new emphasis on democratic procedure. COG is working on an involved system for presenting and approving decisions at all levels. That, too, may just be a means of taming lower leadership. One thing mentioned by

Enroth, Ericson, and Peters in their analysis of the COG is sure to happen—they're headed for internal division.[7]

Opposition Develops

The bitterness and hatred of everything but COG which Berg has promoted among his followers has brought a backlash. They've accumulated a lot of enemies. Kidnaping, brainwashing, gross immorality and other charges have been leveled against them. Of course, not all the charges hurled at COG by irate parents and other enemies can be proven, but many can. They may not have gone into a home to deliberately abduct a child, but they have hidden teenage "converts" from their parents. Some people have simply disappeared into COG until they were securely indoctrinated and hooked. Brainwashing is just one more common COG method of indoctrination, especially used with people who resist some basic teaching.

Immorality is essential to the COG program. Berg's regular letters to his disciples are filled with raw smut. His own daughter-in-law has publicly accused him of immorality. Polygamy isn't encouraged, but it is condoned. Berg has often said, "The end justifies the means." That attitude rules in COG. If an objective can only be gained by an immoral or unjust act, they do it. Rebellion against the System has brought license to create their own adjustable system of morals and ethics.

That attitude has helped build much organized opposition to COG. Both the state of New York and the state of California have made official studies of this cult. A report issued by the New York Attorney General in 1974 substantiated many charges:

> The central theme of all COG doctrine . . . is to alienate a new 'convert' from parents, government, former religious affiliation, education and society in general. . . . the COG engages in a particularly reprehensible course of conduct by tampering with the personalities of converts. They proceed in a calculated, systematic manner, albeit without even the informal consent of the victims, to change established behavior patterns. . . . brainwashing techniques are deliberately employed under the rationalization that it is in the service of a good cause.[8]

Parents' organizations have sprung up on both sides of the COG issue. A group of worried parents have set up "Freecog" (Free the Children of God) to get their children out of the cult. A group of COG friends and other parents have organized "Thankcog." Seeing their children off drugs, some just don't understand the damage COG is doing to people.

The Mysterious Whereabouts of David Berg

Of all the mysteries about COG, there is nothing more puzzling than the whereabouts of their leader. Only disciples from the early days have seen him. Most of his followers don't even know what he looks like. There are no pictures. He disappeared somewhere in Europe in 1972 and only the top leaders know where he is. Rumors have him everywhere. He says one reason he stays hidden is so he can be completely devoted to God. That way he can get unhindered leadership from God. He also claims,

> . . . for both my health and safety's sake where there are such crazy people like those we've been describing running around with guns in their hands actually threatening to kill me if they can find me because of their insane jealousy over their children, who have a perfect right to be in our colonies.[9]

The mystique about Berg's whereabouts has advantages for an unchecked leader. His errors and changes seem a little removed from reality and so not as obvious.

Changes

Berg has made some dramatic changes. In 1970 he went to Israel and applied for citizenship, claiming he had some Jewish blood. Then he suddenly turned around to a position favoring the Arabs. He has also changed his attitude toward the pope and the Roman Catholic Church. Since 1972, they apparently aren't quite as much a part of the System as they were. Other changes have come to COG, and more will. How long will they last and what will they become? Who knows? One thing is sure: their end will not be what the COG think. In the end it will be shown that they were *not* the true and faithful servants of God, the only ones who knew His program for the last days.

WHAT THE CHILDREN OF GOD BELIEVE

God and Man

The COG don't have a systematic theology. If asked, they'd probably be proud of that. Like all the other cults that arise within Christendom, they claim that only their teaching is the true and pure doctrine of the Bible. Nobody else has it.

There are certain semblances of orthodoxy in their teaching. They say they believe in the Trinity. They certainly speak of a personal God. Man is the creation of God. The human race would fulfill its purpose if only it would obey God. Man needs salvation in Jesus Christ. The Christian is to live by the power of the Holy Spirit. These are typical statements in COG literature. Much of the language would at least sound familiar to people committed to the doctrines of the historic Christian Church.

Salvation

Redemption, they teach, is by faith in Jesus Christ. To be saved, one must accept Jesus into his heart. That acceptance can be made, they say, by the use of a prayer such as:

> Dear Lord Jesus, please forgive me for being bad and naughty and deserving a good spanking. Thank you so much for sending Jesus, Your Son, to take my spanking for me. I now receive Him as my Savior and as Your Son and ask You to come into my heart and make me be good and love you and others by Your Spirit. Help me to read Your Word and obey it and try to help others. In Jesus' name, Amen.[10]

It's that easy, they assure us, to become a Christian.

Once a person takes that initial step, the very next question will likely be, "Now don't you want to forsake all and follow Him?"

That question has a special meaning for COG. It means you leave your family, your job, school, church, and everything else. What for? Why, to join the Children of God, of course. Their way is the only true way to follow Christ today.

The End of the Age Is Upon Us

Probably the most important COG teaching is "End Time Prophecy." This concept is their key to understanding every part of the Christian life. If you don't understand this, you can't really follow Christ in these last times. It goes like this: The end of the age is upon us. Humanity has become just about as full of wickedness as it can get. You can see that extreme wickedness especially in the world system. Every part of it—the governments of the world, the churches, public education, and all other creations of man are in rebellion against God.

"God's rod is pointed for the strike and His judgments are about to fall, and the White powers of the Western World are about to collapse under the rising Red tide of colour! . . . The White Man's Doomsday impends!"[11] America and the West will fall to communism, so the argument goes. Then communism will give way to the anti-Christ. Satan himself will personally take over the government of the world. For a while things will get better.

> But then it will get much worse again because he (the anti-Christ) and his forces will be all-powerful. So all-powerful they're even going to think they can make war on God and His people . . . Then when it looks like we're (the COG) going to be really wiped out, the Lord's gonna come and wipe them out![12]

While the anti-Christ is in charge, Christians will suffer badly. Most professing Christians will accept "the mark of the beast." Only the faithful (144,000 of them) will stand firm. Who are they? The COG, of course, and maybe a few others. When the great Tribulation is over, Christ will come and establish His reign on this earth for a thousand years—and the faithful will reign with Him.

"But though mercy be shown to the wicked, yet will he not learn," declares David Berg. So, when the 1,000 years is over, Satan will again lead a rebellion. Then comes the last great battle in which God will utterly destroy the earth. Judgment and punishment will follow for the wicked. "Then God will renew the face of the Earth with a New Earth and a New Atmospheric Heavens, and His Own Heavenly City will descend from above inhabited only by His Own saved children to rule a New earth . . ."[13]

Who's there to rule over? Those who have finally, through God's judgments and punishments, learned righteousness. Here they come up with their brand of universal salvation. All creatures, including Satan, will be restored to live under the reign of God and His saints.

This end time teaching is not just academic to COG. It's their basis for interpreting world events. Political crises, earthquakes, comets, depressions, inflations, famines—all things, "fit perfectly" into the prophetic scheme. Who knows how to interpret them? Only David Berg.

All of COG life is geared to the end times. It's all going to happen in a few years. Berg says so, and he's the authority. In fact the end will come sometime after 1989. More specifically, it's going to happen in 1993.[14] Berg says only the hour and day are still hidden from him. All this means a lot in daily life. Since the end is so near, COG doesn't have to look very far ahead. Old age is out of the question. Pretty soon it's all going to be over.

The Church

The Church, to the COG, is basically the invisible company of all true Christians. They do admit there is an actual visible Church. The COG, of course, are the only true present expression of it. Other churches aren't really the Church. In fact, even before the New Testament was completed, there grew up a Church which had departed from the truth of God. That's where the historic Church came from.

It's out of that satanic perversion that all the branches and denominations of Christendom have sprung. The only true churches in all history have come up apart from the historic Church. After all, that establishment is the devil's handmaiden. It is so evil that any true Christian who loves God would leave it. Thus, with a contemptuous wave of his hand, Berg dismisses the historic Church.

Worship

In external form of worship the COG is similar to much of "farther out" Protestantism. No form is intended. They take pride in saying they don't have a form of worship. It's all "by the Spirit."

Like all religious groups, however, the Children of God do have a liturgy. That is, things are done about the same way all the time. There is singing, dancing, handclapping, vocal response from the congregation ("Amen," "Praise the Lord," etc.), Scripture reading, teaching, and prayers at the frequent meetings. It's just assumed that how they do it is what God wants worship to be, and the COG carry out their form with zeal.

Baptism is practiced because it is commanded by the Lord. They don't teach much about it, though. It seems to be just a passing matter in the life of a Christian. There's little or no emphasis on the Lord's Supper. It isn't put down; they only observe it once in a while.

METHODS OF OPERATION OF
THE CHILDREN OF GOD

Colony Life

Life for a typical COG disciple revolves completely around his colony. All things are held in common. The colony is his home, family, and security. It is the only anchor in his or her life. To the potential recruit there's a promise of genuine relationships and security here. That is an attractive hope to a young person who feels (or is) lonely or who just doesn't feel he can relate to society.

Colony life is made to sound ideal. Peculiar COG beliefs and practices make ideal communal life impossible, though. COG demands a complete break with the past. You have to cut off all feelings for the past. No former relationship is allowed to have any value. In most instances, your natural family and home have to be rejected as ungodly. When you join COG, nothing else is allowed to matter to you.

But it's even difficult to build lasting relationships within the colony. People are moved around frequently, often with little or no notice. The "New Revolution" program demands that relationships be constantly dissolved as colonies divide. Deep roots are never really established in COG. They're not supposed to be needed. After all, judgment is coming quickly, and the end is just around the corner. The work and the cause are what is important. It costs to be a disciple.

Physical conditions vary widely in the colonies. In lots of places food is poor or inadequate. Sleeping quarters are often crowded and uncomfortable. Unsanitary conditions are common. Health problems often persist because COG members mostly refuse medical attention. Sickness must be dealt with by faith, they say. As a matter of fact, if you're sick, it's probably because of sin or lack of faith. So members suffer greatly from things that could be easily taken care of. No, in most colonies the dream is not realized.

Colonies are of various kinds. There are Basic Front Line Colonies, which are in the majority. Then there are special purpose colonies: Translation Colonies, Publishing Colonies, Babe's Colonies, Widow's Colonies and others. A recent innovation is the Catacombs Colony. It's for younger teenagers and military personnel, for example, who aren't free at the moment to leave their present place and join a regular colony. It meets once a week for "fellowship" and COG literature distribution. It's a great recruiting device, especially for those very susceptible young teenagers.

Mo Letters

Literature distribution is a big deal to the COG. Their success and growth depend on it. You can't understand COG literature distribution without knowing the background of their major literature type.

By 1970, the movement was getting widely spread out. Moses David (David Berg) had to find a way to communicate with the growing and scattering colonies. He accidently hit on a method that has really worked for his cult. Berg began to write a bi-weekly letter to his followers, giving instructions, teaching, and general information. These letters, soon to be known as Mo Letters, covered everything from politics to religion to organizational structure to sex.

They are anything but literary masterpieces. Crudely written, they are profane, pornographic, and extremely radical.

169

Berg tiresomely pursues his reactionism against government, the home, education, and anything else that smacks of the System to him. But they provide the spark that keeps the cult alive. The naive simplicity of their content both sets the course and carries the spirit of the movement.

By now there are several hundred Mo Letters. This collection serves as the teaching base for the cult. COG doesn't actually say the letters are more important than the Bible. Still, it's made clear that you can't understand "God's program for today" without them. So they are as necessary as the Bible.

Mo Letters do the same thing for COG that Mary Baker Eddy's *Science and Health with Key to the Scriptures* does for Christian Science. Back issues of Mo Letters are catalogued by subject and used for formal instruction. They are now issued in the "Mo Letter Reading and Study Course"—with tests, no less!

Litnessing

Mo Letters are also important in getting money and converts. They go out in tremendous numbers. In 1974 the COG distributed nearly 55 million pieces of literature, most of which were Mo Letters. Berg called 1974 the "Literature Explosion."

"Litnessing" is the COG term for their witness with literature. It's the center of their outreach. Litnessing teams head for "good" places—public gatherings such as concerts, busy sidewalks, heavily traveled streets with stop lights, anywhere lots of people can be found. Most COGs spend three to six hours a day, or even more, litnessing. It's the meat and potatoes of the movement. A detailed instruction sheet on litnessing offers motivation:

> It spurs you on to feed yourself that each person that even sees a Mo Letter is getting witnessed to. It's only our job to deliver the message and once you've stuck it in front of their nose you've delivered the message. And if they don't accept it, that's their funeral even if they don't take it in their hand.[15]

The same instructions add, "It's sharing Mo and really digging together that makes us one heart and mind and keeps us moving." One of the more interesting instructions on litnessing is, "You should enjoy litnessing as much as lovemaking."

Recently there has been a re-emphasis on witnessing by talking to people. Nevertheless, litnessing is still a big thing in the COG program.

"The Heat":Typical Method of Conversion

A young person found alone is a prime target for a COG witness. Say, for example, it's at a college campus, during finals perhaps. A student is approached. He turns out to be a professing Christian. The COG response will likely be, "Well, if you're a Christian, what are you doing in this school? It's all part of the System."

A giant guilt trip will be laid out by quoting multiple verses from the Bible with no respect for context. Most COG disciples know a lot of Bible content and memorize Scripture all the time. They are trained in their arguments and few professing Christians are a match for them.

They'll quote, for example, the passage from Acts about the early Christians having all things in common and ask, "Why aren't you living that way?" The heat is on.

You're really pressed to go home with them to dinner. You're promised that you'll meet a bunch of kids who really love each other and really love you. You agree to go. Dinner is probably fair, nothing fancy, but passable. It does seem like a happy family. There's enthusiastic singing, dancing, and handclapping. Everyone is really into it.

Then the heat is *really* on. You are forthrightly told that it is the will of God for you to come and join. Accept Jesus (if you haven't) and drop out of the System. Right now!

"But I want to think it over," you reply.

"Now is the time," is the answer.

"I need to talk it over with my parents," you insist.

"Your parents are emissaries of Satan," is the likely response.

The trap begins to close. Scripture after Scripture is quoted. Everyone gathers around you. There's more singing and handclapping. They dance in a circle around you. Your name is inserted in the song at appropriate places. "If you love Jesus you'll come with us," they all insist.

The pressure mounts within you. They sound so dedicated to Christ, so authoritative, so sure, and you're so confused.

Besides, you know you haven't been living right anyway. You're almost caught. You want to go home.

In earlier years they would have done almost anything to keep you from going home. Intense criticism has altered that somewhat. If you leave, they'll press you to come back, of course. If you stay or come back, the heat will really be on. Pressure is the name of their game. You may be put in a room with taped messages coming at you constantly. The brainwash is on. There is no let-up, even for a minute. Pressure, little sleep, long meetings, the singing and dancing—your will is being attacked. You just may bend, particularly if the guilt is great enough.

But there's still another card to play. Fear! "This may be your last chance." "Are you going to turn against God?" You're really afraid something catastrophic might happen to you. They give illustration after illustration of tragedy to those who have refused. The trap snaps. You're in.

Now it's indoctrination time. Long meetings, Bible study, memorization. Tapes—morning, noon, and night. All decisions are made for you. You don't think well anymore. You just react. Everything fits, at least it seems to—why didn't you see it before? The mindbenders have you. Regardless of why, how, sincere or not, they've got you and you're now one of them. You will believe and do whatever you are told to believe and do.

That's just one possible illustration. There are many potential situations and variations. It might have started at a rock concert, at the beach, on the street, or at the fair. It may focus on a professing Christian or a professing non-Christian, or in between the two. It may be someone into drugs or oriental religion or someone who is a "straight arrow." It makes no difference; the thrust is the same. The System is bad, doom will come on it and those who are part of it. Guilt. Fear. It's the constant dripping of the rain again. And you're caught in it.

Six months later you think about going home. You want out. No one stops you. But suddenly you realize you're scared to get out. Seriously, lightning might strike, or some other calamity. And those people out there. The ones in the System. They're bad, that much you know. You love these people, at least most of them, and they do love you. More singing, dancing, and prayer. More Bible, more letters, more litnessing. Maybe the end will come and it will all be over. They'll see we were right after all. Besides, you know what tragedy has befallen everyone else who has left. You've heard the stories again and again.

It is difficult to get out. Many do, but so slowly. For many the after-effects remain for years. The scars may never go away. Few people understand what's really happened. It's good that they don't. It's too bad you do.

Money

COG has to have money. You can't escape that part of the System. And the COGs don't hold regular jobs. Such things were left behind with the establishment. How are they going to get money?

First, there's the "Revolutionary Contract." When a person comes in he signs an agreement to give all his possessions and income, past, present, and future, to the cult. This usually doesn't amount to much, but some converts have brought a lot with them.

Then there's "Spoiling the System." The idea is to use the System for whatever can be taken. The COG asks for donations of food and supplies from merchants. A "procurer" tells the merchant this is a group "helping kids get off drugs," or they're from a Bible college. And, of course, the merchant gets a tax deduction. A lot has been obtained that way: food, clothing, even the free use of buildings. Sometimes money comes from those same sources. Everything possible is gotten free.

As with most groups, contributions from parents and friends are very important. COG gets hundreds of thousands of dollars this way. Most people who give don't have any idea what they're really giving to. Many think they're supporting a Christian cause to help young people. Parents in particular are exploited. Children write home for money, tape recorders, cameras, anything they think they might get. The person writing may never see the items sent from home. He may be asked to write a thank-you note home for gifts he has never seen and never will. It was "needed somewhere else," you see.

Probably the biggest source of money is litnessing. Now, the COG do pass out some material free, but almost always they ask for a donation. "Help our kids." No loafing either. There are quotas for each person, and some who didn't collect enough to carry themselves haven't eaten.

A fairly good litnesser will take in an average of $40 per day. One girl who said she wasn't very good at it averaged over $25 a day in a normal two-week period. One very exceptional girl took in $614 in thirty-six hours of work! Another time this same girl passed out 1,900 pieces of literature and took in $176 in one seven-hour period. It adds up.

Berg boasted they got over $5 million from literature distribution in 1974. Only $1.5 million went for printing costs.[16] That's an average donation of ten cents per piece of literature, and adds up to a lot of income. Many of the COGs take in far more than they would from a regular job.

Where does the money go? Mostly for living expenses, printing, and other necessities. Ten percent of gross collections goes, however, to "World Services," the central fund of COG.

Bluntly, but truthfully, the COG are beggars. Not common beggars, but beggars nonetheless. Not common, because they don't pick up just a little pocket change. It's a multi-million dollar, tax-free operation. Every litnesser must account for each piece of literature and each penny. It is a well-organized and well-executed begging business.

A REFUTATION OF THE CHILDREN OF GOD

It's astonishing that the Christian community still debates whether the Children of God is a dangerous heresy. The Children of God have already settled that for us. Heresy is by definition "an opinion or doctrine contrary to the truth or to generally accepted beliefs." COG has offered just such doctrines. They openly boast they have no connection with the historic Church. They ridicule churches and the doctrines taught in those churches. The fact is that the Children of God are self-confessed heretics who heap abuse upon the Church of God and the people of God.

Sure, there are some Christians amongst the Children of God. But that doesn't make COG a Christian movement. It is not Christian. It is sub-Christian. It is not godly. It is not good and the Christians who are in it are totally deceived about it.

To support such a claim it is not necessary to expose the whole multitude of errors of the COG system. An exposure of just three of their more serious errors is more than sufficient.

Total Rejection of the Historic Christian Church

Fringe fundamentalism (the more radically narrow and aggressive fundamentalism) is the mother from which COG was born. Berg's parents were both evangelists associated with that fringe. His lengthy association and labor with the likes of false-religionist fundamentalist O. L. Jaguers (himself a heretic) and Fred Jordan and his American Soul Clinic shows his ties to that fringe are clear and deep.

But Berg has rejected even that fringe which mothered him. The COG proudly deny any positive relationship to any part of contemporary Christendom and, in fact, denounce it as the false, satanic church. That's why we so emphatically denounce COG as a sub-Christian cult. It takes more than claiming to be Christian to make something Christian. Wings on a car don't make it an airplane; neither does biblical vocabulary and some talk about God and Jesus make a religious group Christian.

COG Doctrine of the Church

This brings the focus in on one of the more sinister heresies of the Children of God, namely their doctrine of the Church. The COG acknowledge the Church as being little more than the sum total of all the true Christians of all time. That kind of a Church is purely a mystical thing. There is truth in that, but taken alone it is not the truth. They give no importance to the historically continuous visible Church. Of course they agree there has been such a thing called the Church, but what it said and what it did is completely irrelevant and unnecessary to them today. Each church is as if it were the only one in all history. It gets its doctrine and practice from God through the Bible with no reference to either the churches of history or other churches today.

This childish view is a denial of the unity of the Church of Jesus Christ. It acknowledges the possibility of church*es* of Jesus Christ, but not of *the Church* of Jesus Christ. Each church is independently responsible only to God, and any relationship between churches, if there is any, is purely accidental and mystical. It is because of such a Spirit-denying, God-disgracing view of the true unity of the Church that the COG view themselves and their prophet to be completely sufficient to interpret the Bible, truth, and doctrine with no regard for anyone but themselves. Arrogantly and foolishly they measure themselves by themselves (and, of course, they always measure up).

The Church of Jesus Christ has consistently rejected cults such as the Children of God because of their deviation from the truth of God as it has been understood in the Church. In the City of Chalcedon in the year 451 A.D., there was a gathering of church leaders quite similar to the one at Nicaea which we described in an earlier chapter. The purpose of this council (as it was called) was to settle a huge Church-wide argument about how it was that Jesus Christ could be both God and man at the same time. After weeks of debate, a creed was read to the assembly. When the reading of the creed was finished, the bishops, elders, and deacons stood and cheered as one man, crying out, "This is the doctrine of the apostles. This is the faith of the fathers."

That creed began with the words, "Therefore, following the holy Fathers, we all with one accord teach men to acknowledge one and the same Son, our Lord Jesus Christ . . ."[17] Those first words give us a clue as to why they met for such a council. They fully realized that some arguments cannot be settled just by each person interpreting the Bible on his own. In fact, that was exactly the problem that was causing the argument.

Each side (there were more than two sides in this argument) was absolutely convinced its teaching was the clear teaching of the Bible. They were just as individually convinced that they were right as David Berg is individually convinced he is right. But they knew they would have to get together and check their understanding of the Scriptures with one another. They also realized they must check their teaching in the light of what the Church had said before them. That's why they said, ". . . following the holy Fathers . . ."

It is right at this point that the COG have gone off so easily into blasphemous error. They check their understanding with only themselves. Pompously claiming to teach only what the Bible teaches, their teaching has strayed far from the true teaching of the Bible. It's sort of like grading your own final examination. There's no one but yourself to check you.

David Berg and the COG reject any need for ties with either the past or present that might in any way check their teaching. They condemn the historic Church, where it is in disagreement with them, as satanic. They are a law only unto themselves. The truth is that David Berg is a servant of Satan and a blasphemer of the Church of the living God. His followers, knowingly or unknowingly, dutifully follow him in this deception.

A Warning

The very existence of a movement such as the Children of God should be a fair warning from God to Protestantism, which itself increasingly ignores the historic Church in terms of any "checks and balances" on its doctrines. A cult such as the COG can only grow on the outer edge of a Protestant environment that has in practice emancipated itself from any genuine need of and unity with the visible historic Church.

The blunt truth of the matter is that the Children of God is a bastard orphan heresy. It is a bastard because it admits its mother to be a whore; an orphan because it pronounces its whore-mother dead; and a heresy because it has departed from the true teachings of the Scriptures as those teachings have been passed down through the historic Church.

Rebellion Against Authority

Closely related to their heresy regarding the Church is another monstrous error of the Children of God: radical rebellion against authority . . . any established authority at all. In their unhumble opinion, authority is represented by the establishment and is properly and necessarily attacked.

Step number one in that attack is to drop out, totally out, of the establishment. Every conceivable phase of it. Then, expose it for what it is at every possible point. Tell it like it is. Expose it for all its ugly corruption. This emphasis of attack and rebellion against the establishment comes over and over and over in the literature and conversation of the Children of God. It's like a broken record.

Rebellion against established authority is the heart and soul, breath and blood, of the COG movement. David Berg has managed to transform a gigantic personal temper tantrum against authority into a world-wide movement.

Rejection of Parents and the Home

Berg blasts away at parents as the true rebels. Your natural family is evil, wicked, and bad. The youth rebellion today is not to be faulted at all. It is thoroughly proper and totally justified, according to him. Here is just a sample of his condemnation of parents:

> You parents are the most God defying, commandment breaking, insanely rebellious rebels of all time who are on the brink of destroying and polluting all of us . . . To Hell with your devilish system. May God damn your unbelieving hearts.[18]

Hating authority (except, of course, any he can get), Berg strikes at the most important authority in a young person's life—his parents. It is his desire to bring people under his total domination. To do that he must rip away all other authority from their lives. That is a far cry from the simple, "Honor thy father and thy mother." David Berg and the COG cause their disciples to sin against God by disgracing their parents. The fifth commandment doesn't say "Honor thy father and mother if, according to David Berg, they are worthy of it." It just says to honor them. The Children of God don't.

Condemnation of the traditional established Church almost exhausts the vocabulary of the COG. Judgment and doom is the constant theme of their diatribe against the Church, which they call the "Satanic System." At least as early as 1961 and 1962, long before the Children of God began, Berg was constantly haranguing against the churches. If they do not do things his way or agree that his way is proper, it is obvious they are backed by the devil.

Since the established Church stands against a great number of Berg's nonsensical doctrines and against his spirit and moral temperament, his solution is simple. Pout! Rebel against it. Get a following, and do it your own way. But denying the authority of the Church cannot destroy either the Church or its authority. Berg and his movement stand guilty before God and the Church. All the big talk in the world will not alter the judgment against them.

Rejection of the Authority of Civil Government

And of course civil government comes in for its due scathing denunciation from the COG. America, in particular, is attacked, though in more recent years they have broadened that condemnation to include the governments of virtually every country to which they've gone. Governments are viewed by the COG as organized rebellion against God. Cartoons and caricatures of government officials are everywhere in their literature. Here, from a Mo Letter, is a sample Berg attack:

> Kids have been kidnaped from their homes by the laws of compulsory school attendance; drugged to damnation by godless, and useless public education; hypnotized by TV, movies, magazines, and modern music; imprisoned by modern curfews, child labor laws, parental jurisdiction laws, minimum marriage age laws, minor's laws, and draft regulations and military bondage! These have made our modern children virtual prisoners and slaves of the average home, school and military for at least a third of their lives . . . This is freedom and liberty and equality? . . . It is slavery and death.

God knows there are plenty of young rebels just waiting to hear someone say those things. The Children of God make sure a rebellious youth age is not disappointed in that hope.

We all admit it would be foolish and untrue to insist that everything done in the church, the home, and the government in the present establishment system is faultless. That is not the case. Constructive changes are in order.

But the Children of God don't appear interested in either constructive criticism or constructive changes, only destructive doom. They are prepared to accept nothing short of complete acceptance of their own way. Since that isn't going to happen, they flee the System and stand outside of it, pretending to be its god, about to descend upon it in fiery judgment.

It is really quite immaterial that the COG people may not understand that establishment is necessary to human society,

179

or even that they have a mini-establishment of their own (a fact which some might perhaps admit). The fact is that a parasite on society, David Berg, has managed to become a king over his own establishment. And his followers, who are convinced they have cleverly escaped an authoritarian establishment, find themselves in another that is more authoritarian than that from which most of them have come. Claiming to be free, they are in greater bondage than ever. There are perhaps few others on this earth whose lives are so utterly determined and whose wills are so utterly dominated by their "church" government.

A Substitute for the Holy Spirit

The mindbending aspect of the COG must also be considered if the extreme danger of the group is to be fully understood. Brainwashing, to most Americans, is a memory of a practice used by the Red Chinese against our POWs during the Korean War. With COG, it is not a thing of the past; it is an integral part of the methods used on its converts.

Hour after hour, day after day, the relentless process of indoctrination goes on. There is no time to rest, to think, or to will. The disciple slowly but surely sinks into complete dependence on the movement for his whole life. Significant behavior modification is achieved in this way. COG disciples cease to think on their own. They only react. They are programmed to respond with predictability.

The COG indoctrination program is devastating to the personalities of those subjected to it. Granted, not all are equally affected, but almost no one remains unaffected. Some are virtually destroyed. The end result of the program is that the organization's personality gains dominance and replaces the individual personality. The degree of control the organization gains over its adherents defies the understanding of the average observer.

A member of the COG may be a prisoner of that "mini-system" all his life. In such a case, he cannot live as a fully functioning human being. However, if he leaves the organization and attempts to go back to his past life, he is faced with an almost impossible task. He has been programmed against all that it represents. He can leave the movement, but the movement doesn't leave him.

Some who have left the Children of God testify it has taken them twice the time they were in the movement to shake its domination after they left. Some haven't fully shaken it; some never will. Normal life on the "outside" becomes difficult because of the deeply ingrained indoctrination against what they must do to successfully live and relate there.

The indoctrination program of the COG is a sad substitute for the ministry of God's Spirit. They speak of the Holy Spirit constantly, but in reality He has no role amongst them. Behavior modification through brainwashing is their *un*holy spirit. There is absolutely no place for the Spirit of God to actively work in the lives of people, calling them as whole human beings to voluntarily respond to God. The tyrannical spirit of COG replaces the Holy Spirit of God. This is not Christianity; it is a perversion of it and is a false religion. It is a sub-Christian religion harming many deceived people.

Conclusion

It is clearly time it be understood that the Children of God is a heretical cult, carrying out an illicit rebellion against both God and human society. Regardless of the motives of the people in it, the inspiration of David Berg and the cult comes from Satan himself.

It is not only dangerous to those within it; it has a detrimental effect on the Church of Jesus Christ. The unbelieving world outside the Church has difficulty understanding that a group using the Church vocabulary and pretending to be Christian is not of it. They identify the Children of God with the true Church of God and reject the latter because of the bizarre excesses of the former. The Children of God are not of the Church. That fact must be made known to the world.

There are even negative results from the Children of God which show up inside the Church. Surely this is a day when there is a need for attention within the family of God to reform and renewal. The excesses of such a cult cause fear of necessary change on the part of many within the Church. They become overly cautious and the Church bogs down. The Children of God stand not only to endanger their own lives and to deceive the world with their claim to be Christian, but they injure the cause of true renewal in the Church of Jesus Christ.

A BRIEF PROFILE OF THE CHILDREN OF GOD

1. History
   —Founded by David Berg in 1968 in California. Berg now known as Moses David.
   —Preaches message of doom against the American System, the established Church, and the home.
   —Expanded overseas in 1971. In 70 different countries in 1976.
   —Established colonies of 12 each in 1975, with 7 levels of leadership.
   —Immorality and polygamy practiced by some members.

2. Beliefs
   —No systematic theology.
   —Only COG has true and pure doctrine of the Bible.
   —Salvation is by faith in Jesus Christ and by forsaking all to follow COG.
   —All will ultimately be saved, including Satan himself.
   —COG only true expression of visible Church with the historic and contemporary Church being false and satanic.

3. Method Of Operation
   —Life revolves around the colony, which demands complete break with the past.
   —Relationships in each colony only temporary. Much moving around.
   —Money raised through literature passed out by COG members.
   —New converts gained through high-pressure witnessing.
   —New converts brainwashed with intense indoctrination.

4. Refutation
—COG departs from generally accepted Christian beliefs; therefore, a heresy.
—COG has condemned the historic and contemporary Church; therefore, it is a sub-Christian cult.
—COG has rejected an historically continuous visible Church; therefore, denies the unity of the Church.
—COG has turned against the fathers of the Church; therefore, no check on their teachings.

FOOTNOTES TO THE CHILDREN OF GOD

1. Mo Letter, "Saul and Michael," October, 1971.
2. Mo Letter, "Explosion," 334-B, May, 1975.
3. *Ibid.*
4. *Ibid.*
5. Rex Davis and James T. Richardson, *A More Honest and Objective Look at the Children of God,* a paper presented at the Society for the Scientific Study of Religion, annual meeting, Milwaukee, Wisconsin, October, 1975.
6. Mo Letter, "Explosion," 334-B, May, 1975.
7. Enroth, Ericson, and Peters, *The Jesus People* (Grand Rapids, Michigan: Eerdman's, 1972),
8. Study by the New York Office of the Attorney General by the Honorable Lewis J. Lefkowitz, September 10, 1974.
9. Quoted in *Oui* Magazine, February, 1975.
10. From the tract, "You Gotta Be A Baby," put out by the Children Of God.
11. Mo Letter, "Who Are the Racists?" No. 105, September, 1971.
12. Mo Letter, "The American Way," No. 214A, January, 1973.
13. Mo Letter, "Heavenly Homes," No. 316, October, 1974.
14. Mo Letter, "The 70-Years Prophecy of the End," No. 156.
15. From the pamphlet, *Litnessing Tips,* p. 2, put out by the Children of God.
16. Mo Letter, "Explosion," No. 334-B, May, 1975.
17. Schaff, *A Select Library,* Volume XIV, p. 264.
18. An early Mo Letter.

An Introduction to The Way, International

Irene Myrton was a member of Campus Christian Fellowship at Maxwell City College. She had grown up across town in a family active in Suburban Bible Church. There had been a constant stress in the church on the value of knowing the Scriptures, but somehow she had always felt guilty about the skimpiness of her own biblical knowledge.

Since moving into her dormitory, she had participated in some campus Bible studies, but her own devotional life had always been superficial. To her secret shame she had never really studied the lessons, always talking glibly off the top of her head when discussion time rolled around. She lived by warmed-up leftovers from dog-eared sermon notes. Most of her spare time was actually taken up with backpacking and ski trips which, she had to admit, really did interest her more.

One spring evening at the Fellowship meeting someone introduced her to Max, a very intense-looking fellow whom she hadn't seen there before. As they talked after the meeting, he mentioned a physical fitness camp.

"It's a great camp," he explained enthusiastically. "We concentrate on physical fitness and fitness for life. Our bodies get developed while we also learn the Word."

"Both at the same camp?" Irene was interested.

"We sure do!" Max replied, "If you want to learn how to rightly divide the Word of God, this camp is the place!"

As the conversation progressed, Irene became more and more intrigued. This camp sounded like a place where she could finally get a systematic knowledge of the Scriptures and at the same time be out in the wilderness. She decided to go. After all, she had some money, and her parents would help.

Mr. and Mrs. Myrton were amazed at the change in Irene when she returned from camp that summer. She certainly knew a lot more about the Bible than before, but she also had interpretations of Scripture which were strange and new to them. They tried to talk with her about these new ideas, but she had answers for every argument. Not only that, she was openly contemptuous of orthodox interpretation.

"We've been taught all wrong about so many things," she complained. "Our pastor is so ignorant of the plain teaching of Scriptures."

"For instance," she continued, "we've always been taught there were two crucified on the cross when Jesus was, but the Bible teaches there were four."

"How's that?" wondered her father.

"Well, just look at the gospels," Irene explained patiently. "First in Luke. It says there were two other malefactors led with Him to be put to death. They crucified Him and the malefactors, one on his right hand and one on his left. In Mark, after it tells about Him being crucified, it tells about two thieves being crucified."

"So?" her father asked, puzzled.

"Don't you see?" Irene demanded. "There were four—two malefactors and two thieves!"

"Now wait!" her father protested, "That's not what that means. Can't you see that?"

"Oh, stop it, Dad!" Irene interrupted. "You're just repeating the same mistakes you've been taught."

"I'd hardly say they were mistakes," her father replied mildly, "but what on earth difference does it make anyway if there were two or four?"

"A lot. The same people who've taught us wrong about that have taught us a lot of other falsehoods too. They just won't let the Scripture speak for itself. Don't you agree the Bible says what it means and means what it says?"

"Well, yes," her father faltered, "but . . ."

"There can't be any 'buts'—we have to rightly divide the Word of truth." Irene was emphatic. "Using 'but' is how they get by with teaching us falsehoods like the one about Jesus Christ being God!"

"Irene!" gasped Mr. Myrton.

"Dr. Wierwille shows conclusively that our salvation rests on Jesus Christ being a man and not God," Irene replied firmly.

186

"Dr. Wierwille?"

"The president of The Way. Dad, you need to take the Power for Abundant Living Class. There's one starting next week right here in town. How about it?"

Mr. Myrton felt defeated. "I don't know, Irene. We'll talk about it later."

THE HISTORY AND THEOLOGY OF THE WAY, INTERNATIONAL

A Promise Made is a Debt Unpaid

Just what would you do if someone approached you and said, "How would you like to be set free from all fear, doubt, and bondage; delivered from poverty, sickness, and poor health; overflowing with life, vitality, and zest; rescued from condemnation and self-contempt; cured of drug and sex abuse? You can restore your broken marriage, enjoy a happy and united family, where there is no generation gap."[1] And then they guaranteed you they could produce what they were promising.

Would you be at least a little bit interested? Most people would. Those lines were taken from a brochure put out by one of the modern cults called The Way, International.

Those are mighty bold claims, especially in the context of a somewhat sick society and a youth culture that is really hurting. If someone could do all this group says it can do, it would be just the ticket for many people.

Well, just who makes these claims? What is this thing called The Way? And can they perform what they so confidently promise? What do they believe? You need to know the answers to these questions. It's not all that unlikely that you will hear from them one of these days. They're growing at an alarmingly fast rate, and they just may be at your door tomorrow. That's one of the ways they grow.

From Church to Behavior Modification Cult

The Way is one more of the modern behavior modification cults. Just one name is associated with the beginnings and development of this cult. That is Victor Paul Wierwille, called "The Doctor" by his many ardent disciples.

Having grown up in a rigid fundamentalist environment, Wierwille, now in his late fifties, became a minister in the·old Evangelical and Reformed Church (now the United Church of Christ). He brought theological training with him from Mission House College and Seminary as well as from Princeton Theological Seminary, where he received a Masters degree in Practical Theology.

The ministry was a terribly frustrating experience for Wierwille because he couldn't produce the behavior in people he thought should be forthcoming from his efforts. It was a "vanilla" ministry, to say the least. He quite frankly admits, "As I looked about me at the communities where I had worked, the abundant life was frequently not evident. In contrast to these Christian people, I could see that the secular world of non-Christians was manifesting a more abundant life than were the members of the church."[2]

Not being one to accept a less than spectacular ministry, and determined to produce certain behavioral results, Wierwille set out to get his act together. He concentrated on one statement from Jesus which we have recorded in John 10:10, "I am come that they might have life, and that they might have it more abundantly." Wierwille had a concept of what that abundant life should be. He was confident that if he could come up with a scheme to produce that concept of abundant life, he would have the key to dynamic ministry.

A New Scheme

Ignoring the very basic foundational doctrines of the Church, he put together a patchwork system of heretical biblical interpretation. But the system could effect certain behavior modifications that were satisfactory for his purposes.

Putting this novel teaching together into a Bible study course called "Power for Abundant Living," Wierwille began to teach it. There were surely enough people looking for an abundant life, particularly of the kind Wierwille promised. And he could produce some results.

There are, of course, many avenues to behavior modification. Wierwille had found one of them and worked it to the full. Cloaked with a familiar-sounding evangelical vocabulary, the product had a market.

While still in the ministry of his church, Wierwille got a radio ministry and Biblical Research Center going to push his new program. The Power for Abundant Living ministry caught on quite well. It finally demanded so much of his time that he gave up his Van Wert, Ohio, Evangelical and Reformed Church to give full time to his independent work.

He did, however, have some encouragement in giving up the church. It seems that while on a trip to India to visit mission stations of his denomination, he made some remarks criticizing the church and the government of India. Those remarks precipitated a riot at one of the mission stations with a considerable amount of property damage involved. When he returned home, a hearing was conducted into the matter. The outcome was that Wierwille was advised to withdraw as a minister of the denomination because of his feelings and attitudes toward the church. The account of this incident doesn't appear in the publications of The Way.

It is difficult to pinpoint an exact date when The Way actually began. October 5, 1975, was designated by Wierwille as the thirty-third anniversary of The Way, International. That would put the beginning way back in 1942, with Wierwille in his early twenties. In light of the facts, it takes a pretty fair stretch of the imagination to buy such an early beginning date for this cult.

The Jesus Movement Boom a Boon

Regardless of what may or may not be the full truth in the matter, 1968 is the year that The Way, now having moved its headquarters to New Knoxville, Ohio, began to experience significant growth. As with several other struggling offbeat groups of that time, The Way found the Jesus Movement a boon. Capitalizing on the nondiscriminating religious interests of many in the movement, The Way picked up a host of young people from those ill-defined ranks. Particularly significant gains were made in terms of capable young leadership.

Youth predominates The Way scene, though there are some older adults involved, particularly at the highest levels of leadership. That being the case, the effort of the cult has been aimed at the younger generation. This is particularly in evidence at the annual "Rock of Ages Festival," the well-organized and youth-oriented get-together for the followers of The Way from everywhere. In 1971, the festival drew some 1,000 people, but by 1975, the Ohio affair had some 8,500 in attendance.[3] Most observers estimated the "youth factor" at about 80 percent. The program was surely aimed at young people.

THEOLOGY OF THE WAY

Doctrine of God

Victor Paul Wierwille, the originator of The Way's teachings, generally begins his discussions of God in words you've heard so many times you hardly realize what he is saying. You casually note he is speaking of a personal God, the Creator of the world, the Maker of man, and the Author and Giver of life. He is the God of Abraham, Isaac, and Jacob. He's the God of Israel and the God and Father of our Lord Jesus Christ.

But, like a bolt out of the blue, all of a sudden you hear some words that hit you like thunder. "Jesus Christ is not God," he is saying, and all so matter-of-factly. Now you may not know a whole lot about Christianity or about Christian theology, but you surely do know enough to know those words have a distinctly unfamiliar ring to them.

Jesus Christ is Not God.

You listen as he goes on. "Jesus Christ was not with God in the beginning. . . . The Son of God is not co-eternal (with God)." You aren't exactly sure just what "co-eternal" means. Besides, it sounds sort of theological. You let that one slip by. Then he adds, "If Jesus Christ is God and not the Son of God, we have not yet been redeemed." Well, you'd never thought of it that way. Maybe he's got a point. It surely is different from anything you've heard before.

So goes the typical approach of Wierwille to teaching what he believes about Jesus Christ. He is emphatically against the doctrine of the Trinity, or any teaching that equates Jesus Christ with God. He says with the utmost confidence that the origin of the "Three-in-One God" is to be found in paganism, not the Bible.

Then he gets involved in a discussion of Church history in an attempt to show that such men as Irenaeus, Tertullian, Cyprian (those three really were famous men, even though you've probably not heard of them), and Augustine were the perpetrators of the crime. He claims that no one in all the first three centuries of the Church believed that Jesus Christ is God, or believed in the doctrine of the Trinity. (That is an odd contention since Irenaeus was living in 160 A.D., Tertullian in 200 A.D., and Cyprian in 250 A.D.!)

The Pagan Origin of the Doctrine of the Trinity

The truth, we are told by Dr. Wierwille, is that the whole idea of the Trinity was brought into the Church early in the fourth century by the Roman emperor Constantine. Wierwille goes on to explain exactly how it happened.

It seems, he says, that Constantine had this doctrine of the Trinity he wanted to get into the Church to make Christianity fit better with general paganism. That would be politically expedient for him. To achieve this he called the leaders of the Church together at a place called Nicaea "which is now Nice, France," in 325 A.D. There were about 220 bishops present, most of whom were from the Occident (the West). The Creed of Nicaea established this pagan doctrine in the Church and was "truly the work of a minority." Those bishops present, Wierwille admits, did sign the creed, but only "because they were overawed" by the whole affair. So goes Wierwille's history of that affair.[4]

Sloppy Scholarship

Wierwille simply hasn't done his homework on the subject. His scholarship in general is irresponsible, slipshod, and false. One rather typical illustration of that fact is this "historical" treatment he gives of the Council of Nicaea. The history of the greatest and most significant council in the history of Christianity deserves a more accurate treatment, even from its enemies. His carelessness here demonstrates his extreme shallowness and the questionable credibility of his teaching in general.

191

Bad, Bad History

The facts are so far removed from Wierwille's less than infantile historical treatment that it is almost unspeakable. Perhaps it is even deliberate on his part.

First of all, just for the record, Nicaea isn't the present Nice, France. It was just a few miles from ancient Constantinople. Today that is the site of Istanbul, Turkey! O well, France, Turkey, what's the difference? It's only history.

Secondly, there were not "about 220 bishops" present. That is both false and a misleading misrepresentation of the true situation. There were actually some 318 bishops present. But that's only part of the matter. Wierwille neglects to mention that more than 1,500 bishops, elders, and deacons were there, and they were *not* predominately from the West (apparently Wierwille wants the doctrine of the Trinity to be a Western invention). They had come from all over the whole Christian world. All of Christendom was represented.

Thirdly, there was indeed some "overawe" there, but it wasn't from the bishops. It was Constantine, the emperor, who was overawed. He'd never seen such a group of men in all his life. There were those there who had gone through some of the most terrifying persecutions imaginable at the hands of the Roman Empire.

Some had empty sockets where their eyes had been before they had been gouged out by torturers because they refused to renounce their faith in Jesus Christ. Others had had members of their bodies cut off. Still others had been augered—giant drill bits had been drilled into their arms and legs or other parts of their bodies, because they wouldn't deny Christ.

Constantine had never seen such commitment, or devotion, or dedication to anyone. He was so moved that he walked about the assembly and kissed the scars of these heroic confessors. (That's what they called those who had suffered because they preferred to be tortured rather than renounce Christ.)

And we are to assume from Wierwille that the men who met at Nicaea were spineless men who were snookered into signing a creed in which they did not believe, because of overawe and political expediency!!?? What garbage!

He claims the creed was the work of just a few. The truth is that more than 1,500 leaders met for three months and considered every possible Scripture on the matter. Further, they searched back through the whole history of what the one holy catholic and apostolic Church had taught since the days of the apostles. Then they debated every conceivable option. Work of a few? Nonsense! It was the agreement of the whole assembly. And if that weren't enough, it is still today the most agreed upon doctrine in all of the Christian Church! Wierwille is a disgrace to God, a disgrace to the heros of our faith, and a disgrace to the Church of God.

Then Who is Jesus Christ?

He insists Jesus can't possibly be both God and the Son of God at the same time. Somehow he feels this is proven by his statement, "One point of dissimilarity disproves identity." (We'll deal with that later).

Jesus, he claims, is only the Son of God, not God. He is the Son of God because God fathered Him by artificially inseminating the Virgin Mary with the divine sperm.

The Scriptures say, "The Word became flesh and dwelt among us" (John 1:14), and the Church has always held that means the second person of the Trinity became flesh. But Wierwille takes great exception to that teaching. What became flesh, he teaches, was not a person, God the Son, the second person of the Trinity, but rather a piece of foreknowledge from the mind of God.

John 1:1 says, "In the beginning was the Word and the Word was with God and the Word was God." Wierwille admits there is a definite relationship between Jesus Christ and the Word in John 1:1. But he insists there is a difference made in John 1:1 between the Word which he says is God and the revealed Word which he says is Jesus Christ and the Bible. Jesus Christ is not the Word. God is. Jesus Christ is the "revealed Word."

Now, says this teacher of novelty, that revealed Word didn't pre-exist with God, nor was He God. There was, however, a sense in which He was with God in that He was there in the foreknowledge of God. That simply means He was only a thought in the mind of God. That is, God knew that someday He would artificially inseminate Mary and have a Son who would be called the Word. And that, says Wierwille, is the only sense in which Jesus Christ is eternal.

Prove it By the Bible

The Christian, maintains Wierwille, has "the responsibility to test to see whether ... . various doctrines originated in the right or wrong dividing of God's Word"; in this case by Word he means the Bible. It takes some mental gymnastics to prove his view is what the Bible teaches. But a mental gymnast he surely is. It's all so simple. All you need is a "literal translation" of what the Bible says. Wierwille obliges by giving us his own "literal translation" of John 1:1, which he arrives at through speculative word and grammar games with the Greek language:

> John 1:1 literally says: "The revealed 'Word was with God' in His foreknowledge, the revealed Word was later to be manifested in writing as the Bible and in the flesh as Jesus Christ."[5]

With that as the background he smoothes it out to read,

> In the beginning was the Word (God), and the (revealed) Word (*pros*) God (with Him in His foreknowledge, yet independent of Him), and the Word was God.[6]

Now wasn't that simple? It's proven. The Bible says so!—in Victor Paul Wierwille's own private "literal translation" only.

What About the Holy Spirit?

But Wierwille doesn't stop by denying that Jesus Christ is God. He also comes out with a teaching about the Holy Spirit that is completely foreign to the Christian Church's doctrine. He does speak of the Holy Spirit, but he means something far different from what is taught in the orthodoxy of the Church.

He acknowledges the Holy Spirit as God, but not as a distinct person in the Godhead. God is a spirit and God is holy. Since both those things are true, he reasons, we can say that God is the Holy Spirit. But since Wierwille has thrown out the Trinity, the Holy Spirit as a distinct person gets thrown out as well. The Holy Spirit is just another convenient name for God.

But that's not the end of his teaching in this matter of the Holy Spirit. He says orthodoxy is wrong in believing Christians are filled with the Holy Spirit. It's just one more mistranslation of the Bible text. If you had access to his literal translation, he's sure you would realize Christians are not filled with the Holy Spirit. He sees that as being neither desirable nor possible. What they are filled with is something called "*holy spirit*." That small *h* and that small *s* make all the difference in the world.

Now this is a little hard to grasp, but you must get it to understand his teaching. Pay close attention to the use of capital letters in the use of the words "Holy" and "Spirit." This is exactly the way Wierwille teaches it.

When Holy Spirit in his writings is *capitalized* it is a designation for God. When it is *not capitalized* it refers to a gift a Christian receives from God. But remember, that gift is not the person of the Holy Spirit. Wierwille insists there is no such person. It refers to a gift given which is called holy spirit (not capitalized). Specifically, that gift of holy spirit is a matter of certain spiritual abilities such as speaking in tongues, prophecy, and healing. There are exactly nine of those spiritual abilities. There is one gift, holy spirit, but nine "manifestations" of that one gift.

A Christian is not filled with the Holy Spirit, according to Wierwille; he is filled with holy spirit. Every Christian has that gift with all these abilities. It's just that most haven't learned to use them yet. Remember that—we will come back to it later.

Enough For God—Or Whatever; What About Man?

The Way's "theologian" says man had a really great start. He was created by God. He was given a body, a soul, and a spirit. Now somehow because of this make-up (Wierwille never clearly explains how) it turns out that Adam was confronted with two ways in which he could gain knowledge. (Get this, too; it is vitally important in this teaching.)

One way of attaining knowledge was through the five senses (seeing, tasting, touching, smelling, and hearing). But that was the wrong way, says Wierwille. The other way, and the right way, was to get spiritual knowledge directly from God. That spiritual knowledge would come through man's spirit. That was the choice for Adam and Eve. They could either choose to receive natural knowledge into their minds through their five senses or they could receive spiritual knowledge into their minds from God through their spirits.

There's something else Wierwille teaches that relates here. Since God created the earth, it was, of course, His. But God *legally* deeded the earth over to Adam. It was to be man's to dominate and control. Naturally, he was supposed to run it right. To do that it was necessary that he walk in fellowship with God. That was so man's mind could receive spiritual knowledge from God through his human spirit. He was not to use knowledge gained through the five senses of the body to run the earth.

You're no doubt ahead of me and have figured out that Wierwille teaches that Satan fouled up the plan. Darned if that devil didn't get Adam to get his knowledge through those five senses instead of through the human spirit. There was a disastrous twofold result to that action.

First, Adam had his spirit taken away from him. He became a brute beast with only a body and a soul. Secondly, what Adam actually did under this deception from Satan was to legally deed over the earth (which God had deeded to him) to Satan. Man forfeited the earth to Satan. Legally. Now the earth and humanity were legally under Satan's domain.

That put man in bad shape. Without a spirit he could no longer walk in fellowship with God. He had no choice but to walk by those five senses. To top matters off, he and his world were under the rule of Satan as legal master.

Redemption

A legal loss demands a legal redemption, teach The Way and Wierwille. They say it works like this: God had to find a legal means to redeem back the earth and humanity from Satan. Since it was a man who had done the forfeiting, it demanded a man to legally gain it back. Jesus Christ was just that man. Jesus' sacrifice on the cross of Calvary was just the ticket. With that sacrifice Jesus bought back what had been forfeited to Satan.

People can get the benefits of that legal transaction by being what they call "born again." That happens when a human being confesses with his mouth Jesus Christ as Lord and believes in his heart that God has raised him from the dead.

Some of you might be thinking, "Well, that's right, isn't it?" But the way The Way sees it, it isn't. You must understand this transaction is *strictly a legal matter and nothing more.* It merely sets the salvation stage.

The Salvation Kit

In this scheme there are two basic benefits of being born again.

One is legal standing with God that gives you legal sonship. That is based on His being considered absolutely righteous, as righteous as Jesus Christ. That's done legally. It has nothing experiential about it. From there on it's up to you and The Way's way to do it. Very importantly, you must understand that Wierwille's new birth has absolutely no effect on your mind at all, no transforming effect whatsoever in and of itself.

So, you need the second ingredient for your salvation kit. God gives you a new spirit for the one that was taken when Adam made the wrong choice. With it, you can now get to the real business of claiming back from Satan all that territory which now once again is rightfully and legally yours.

But there is a right and wrong way to do this. Don't make the same mistake twice of using those five senses. They make for a bad scene. No, you must use your spirit to get the right kind of knowledge. The way to do this is by a process of getting your mind renewed. You see, the mind doesn't get renewed in the new birth. That is something *you've* got to do with the spirit you got in that new birth.

The Renewing of the Mind

To claim those legal rights you've got to know *what* they are, and *how* to get them. Wierwille says you make this legal claim by gaining a correct understanding of the Word of God, the Bible. Through your spirit you receive the true understanding of the "pure Word of God." You find out what the Bible says to do and then you must do what it says.

But there's a snag. It seems that only Wierwille and The Way have the straight scoop on what the Bible really means . . . .

or even says. So, for a price, you may take a course in which you learn that "pure Word of God." You see, the Church lost it way back there in the first or second century somewhere, and people have really been out of luck since then. Now, at the end of the age, Victor Paul Wierwille has gotten the act back together again so the Christian can claim his true rights from the devil.

Oh yes, after that introductory course (which can only get one started), there is, for another price, an intermediate course. But who wants to stop as an intermediate! After all, the world is in a bad state, and something more than intermediate must be done. People with commitment and a true knowledge of the "pure Word of God" are its only hope. So, for a price, there is an advanced course, and then for a price there is an. . . .

If you pay enough and "study" enough you'll get your mind renewed and be able to claim all that's coming to you.

Worship

Closely related to this renewing of the mind process is The Way's understanding of worship. Worship for The Way is something you do only in your new spirit. You may be with other people in a meeting. In fact, that just may be helpful. But worship is something you do in your own spirit, individually.

Remember those manifestations of *h*oly *s*pirit (there are these small letters again)—that gift of abilities? Well, here's one place they get used, at least in part. Wierwille explains it this way,

> And to worship by the spirit we must operate a manifestation of the holy spirit [again, these are small letters; that's not God]. The manifestation of the spirit which produces true worship is speaking in tongues.

Everyone Speaks in Tongues

A purely mechanical method has been worked out by Wierwille so that *everyone* in The Way can—and does—speak in tongues. This is absolutely crucial to the success of the program. (Note: There are tongues that are true and biblical, and there are tongues that are false. The tongues of The Way are false.) Followers of The Way learn to speak in tongues not only out loud, but also in their heads. Tongues is where they find the ultimate of their worship and their means of getting their minds out of gear. Speaking in tongues is the only true and pure worship, they say.

Here's The Way concept: Have a problem? Don't think about it. Don't even pray about it, (thus using your mind). There's too much danger in accidently using your five senses if you do that. You need to commune with God in your spirit. Speak in tongues. Many followers in this cult speak in tongues for hours a day. In this way, they maintain, one's spiritual facilities are strengthened and he can meet his problems with a renewed mind. So this tongues business is really big for The Way.

Wierwille does not speak of the possibility of false or faked tongues. He has the people of his cult totally convinced that all these tongues are the real product. They see tongues as the proof that this whole trip is of God. At least that's what the average person in The Way believes. Thus, the rationale is something like this: all tongues are supernatural. If something is supernatural, it's got to be from God and has His approval. If it's from God, it's got to be right.

(It is not my purpose here to discuss the differences between true tongues and demonic, faked, or imagined tongues. It is sufficient to say here that the tongues-speaking which The Way practices is every bit as much a perversion of the truth of God as is their blasphemous teaching concerning Jesus Christ and the Holy Spirit.)

METHOD OF OPERATION OF THE WAY, INTERNATIONAL

The Way Tree

Having a penchant for organization, Wierwille has put together an overall organizational structure for his movement that is extremely effective. That structure is illustrated by The Way Tree.

The tree *roots* are the International Headquarters in New Knoxville. The *trunk* is the complex of national organizations, which are separately incorporated. The Way is presently operating in close to thirty-five different countries of the world. The *limb* is the state organizations—fifty at last count. The *branch* is the city organization. Then comes the all-important *twig*. That's the basic unit, the local fellowship or Way group. Last come the *leaves*, the individual followers of The Way. There are somewhere in the neighborhood of 1,500 of these twig fellowships operating with a total participation (The Way claims no formal membership) of about 20,000 individual people.

The Way and the Church

Quite properly, the Way claims they are not a church. Nothing could be more true. There is no way they meet even the first requirement to be a part of the Christian Church.

But, typical of the Way's word games, they also insist "The Way is not . . . a religious sect of any sort." Such claims may make good copy, and they may impress people who have no understanding of what the word "sect" means; but the Way qualifies as a sect in every sense of the word, though the term "cult" is a better description of this religious movement.

How They Get Their Followers

This cult is particularly aggressive in its evangelistic endeavors. Personal witnessing is a major part of its push to introduce new people to its ranks. Door-to-door canvassing is regular. Recreational areas, the college campus, and the military are also prime targets for Way recruiting efforts.

Workers for their heavy recruitment program are supplied in a significant measure by their WOWs. These are the Word Over the World Ambassadors, young people who are enlisted for a one-year term to be sent wherever the cult may want them. They do not know until almost the last minute just where they will be going. When they arrive on assignment, they must find part-time work to support themselves and spend the rest of their hours in an aggressive recruitment program. In 1975, more than 1,000 young people were in the WOW program, both in the United States and abroad.

Where the Rubber Hits the Road

The bread and butter drawing card for The Way is their so-called Bible study emphasis carried on in the twigs. The personal recruitment program is designed to get people into the fellowship of the twigs, so that the rest of The Way program can be sold from there.

The potential recruit will get a lot of sweet talk and "love-you-brother" stuff on arrival. Every effort is made to make him feel he's really wanted. He is. But not because of his own personal value. He's just one more on whom the program can be dumped.

Once the potential recruit is caught in the fellowship, the hook is ready to set. The sell job starts for the "Power for Abundant Living" video-tape course by Wierwille. "And it costs so little that it's well worth it." Everything costs in the Way. This one costs $85 a shot. The course is 12 sessions long, about three hours a crack. There is no note taking, and questions may only be asked at the end—if you remember what you wanted to ask. Accurate figures are hard to come by, but 12,000 would be a "ball park" estimate for their 1975 total enrollment in this one course. At $85 a head, that's more than a million dollars.

Of course, after the "miracle class," there is an Intermediate Power for Abundant Living Class. Then there is the "Renew your Mind" class. And the "Christian Family and Sex" class. That's only the beginning of things. And they all come for a price.

For those who want to press on to really, *really* abundant life, there is The Way College in Emporia, Kansas. This ex-United Presbyterian College, taken over by The Way, opened in 1975 with some 400 students registered. The cost is $300 a month, which the student supplies by soliciting "sponsorships" (these are tax-deductible contributions) from family, friends, or wherever he can find them. The program is strict and highly regimented. As one ex-participant put it, "Someone is watching you all the time."

With little modesty, The Way describes this program as the finest schooling available in the world today. And it is suggested that it is, no doubt, the first of its kind since St. Paul's School of Tyrannus in Ephesus (Acts 19:9).

The Man Who Heard From God—Outloud

Motivating people to begin and advance in the program is based on simply outlandish claims of its value. After all, Wierwille himself makes it clear he has heard audibly from God. Now that is some big deal in anybody's book.

"God told me," he says, "if I would teach the Word, He would teach it to me as it hasn't been taught since the first century."[7] How can anyone be blamed for wanting in on teaching like that? That puts Victor Paul Wierville ahead of some pretty fair company: the likes of Polycarp, Augustine, Chrysostom, the Venerable Bede, Luther, Calvin, Owen, and Hooker. If he's better than these, he's mighty good. The preposterous claim is nauseating.

Teaching the Word as it has not been taught since the first century is not what Wierwille does. There are three reasons why. First, what Wierwille teaches was not taught in the first century. Second, his teaching is quite reminiscent of the teaching of the ancient heretics, Paul of Samosota and Arius, as well as others since—all of whom, without exception, have been condemned by the Church as heretics. Thirdly, Wierwille does not teach the Word of God at all. He does use the Bible as the starting point for what he calls his "biblical teaching and research ministry." From there on, it is a matter of Wierwille's own weird "literal translations" and interpretations of the Bible that are taught.

A System of Principles

Wierwille has attempted to extract principles of conduct and doctrine from the Bible. These become the foundation for the teaching of The Way. Some of his principles are accurate. Many are far removed from the teachings of the historic Church, or are in direct contradiction to them.

He constantly plays the tune, "the Bible says what it means, and means what it says." The statement is a truism. But someone must decide what it means before anyone can decide what it says. In The Way, Wierwille decides both. The whole Way scheme is based on the propagation of these principles, and Wierwille's intent to spread them everywhere.

The World is a Bad Place to Live

Typical of many emerging religious groups today, much attention is given to the world situation. That sits deep in the motivation game of The Way. The corruption and violence of mankind, and the personal hurt of the individual is vividly portrayed in living color. And no one seems able to do anything about it. "Well", they say, "we are a group who can." Here is a teaching that can give you abundant life here and now, in the midst of all this mess. You can be successful while the whole world is going to hell.

The promises of The Way program are great. And they *are* able to modify behavior. There is no question about that, at least, for anyone who will submit to their teaching.

A Gimmick or Two

And who can doubt this dynamic teaching will work when Wierwille comes up with such convincing proofs of its truth? He loves to play tantalizing word games, using gimmicks such as his insistence that Jesus was not crucified between two thieves, but between two thieves and two malefactors. That means there were five crucified at the time. At least Wierwille says so. And would you believe those crucifixions weren't on crosses at all, but on stakes? Now isn't that life-changing?

But such intellectually dishonest games are crucial to the method and operation of this movement. It must be shown that Wierwille's insights and research surpass those of all others since the first century. This is the kind of tool used to establish that claim. There these things were, in the Bible all these centuries, and Victor Paul Wierwille finally discovered them.

Spiritual Gifts

Of course, such teaching alone is not enough to keep people in the movement forever. There must be more proof that God is somewhere in the program. They have a way to demonstrate that, too. A fake charismatic-type emphasis is urged.

Followers are taught as we have noted, how to speak in tongues, plus how to interpret tongues, how to prophesy, and how to perform all the various possible gifts or "manifestations." Of course, they deny that they teach methods of doing these things. According to them, they only *lead* people into these "manifestations." Again, this false charismatic emphasis is vital to The Way program because this is their proof they have the power of God behind them.

A Way Meeting

The result of this emphasis is that a Way meeting can be a real dog and pony show. Aside from singing and fellowship, there is constant speaking in tongues, interpretation of tongues, prophecies, and whatever else is cooked up.

Daily meetings, if possible, are sought in the twigs. The more meetings, the better for the program. That creates much more opportunity for reinforcement of the principles program.

Breaking of bread is practiced as an imitation of the Christian practice of the Lord's Supper. Baptism is not practiced unless requested.

The Politics of The Way

One eyebrow-raising recent development is the quiet entrance of The Way into active politics. For some years, The Way has practiced a patriotism borrowed from the political right wing and has adapted it to a "Save America through The Way" type of emphasis.

Wierwille has insisted, "To help put God's Word into positions of authority and leadership in our country, we as American citizens must become involved in positions of leadership of lawmaking."[8]

But until Maine State Sen. Hayes Gahagan cast his lot with the cult, little was done actively. Gahagan has now established the Christian Political Alliance (CPA) in Ohio as a nonprofit corporation. According to Wierwille, "the CPA is designed to help people become knowledgeable and actively engaged."[9]

As one might expect, Gahagan insists the CPA is not associated with The Way. A moment's digging into the personnel of the Alliance and its Board of Directors, however, will prove the facts to be contrary. Gahagan does admit that the purpose of the Alliance is "to promote and support candidates for public office." The political action has paid off already in some local elections in Maine.

Way Enterprises

One accusation that can never be hurled at The Way is that they are unenterprising. They really do get into it. They've got their own Way Bookstore in Ohio, and their own quality musical enterprise called Way Productions. Then there's *The Way* magazine, with a circulation of some 10,000.[10] They do their own radio and TV production, and they even have their own press, The American Christian Press.

Summers are loaded with other enterprising programs. Family camps in various parts of the country are sponsored by The Way. And they even have their TFI, Total Fitness Institute. That's a camp program stressing spiritual, mental, and physical fitness. Of course, the Power for Abundant Living course is an option at all of these camps, for a price. Anything is used to get people exposed.

Who is a Candidate for the Way?

Who are the candidates for The Way? Everyone. You are. At least as they see it. Particularly vulnerable are people from the more conservative religious backgrounds, especially if they are dissident or dissatisfied with what they have found in their religion. The Way seems to offer them new hope without throwing out all they grew up with. But no background is completely immune. The Way is after any and all whom they can get. And for those who buy it, it just may cost them their spiritual lives.

A REFUTATION OF THE WAY, INTERNATIONAL

The Way may be a religious movement, but it is not a Christian movement. Wierwille and The Way want people to think the God they speak of is the Christian God. No such resemblance exists. The Christian's God is Father, Son, and Holy Spirit. Wierwille's is not. The Jesus Christ of Christians is God. He is the second Person of the Trinity. Wierwille's is not.

At the greatest of all the councils of the Christian Church, the Council of Nicaea, that noble assembly of bishops, elders, and deacons agreed on just exactly what the Bible and the apostles taught about Jesus Christ. Let's review part of it:

> We believe in one God the Father All-sovereign, maker of all things visible and invisible; And in one Lord Jesus Christ, the Son of God, begotten of the Father, only-begotten, that is of the substance of the Father, God of God, Light of Light, true God of true God, begotten not made, of one substance with the Father. . . .[11]

No matter what Wierwille says, that is the truth as to the identity of the Lord Jesus Christ. That is what the Bible teaches, and that is what the Church affirms. Victor Paul Wierwille has some other Jesus, if indeed there could be such a one. The truth is that Wierwille and his followers believe only in a non-existent phantom and are still in their sins.

The Most Agreed-Upon Doctrine in Christendom

Wierwille's childish prattle about the doctrine of the Trinity being slipped into Christianity from paganism at the Council of Nicaea is completely unsupportable. Wierwille conveniently neglects to mention that at least five more Church-wide (ecumenical) councils similar to the one held at Nicaea acknowledged the exact same biblical doctrine.

Add to that the fact that every major confession of the Protestant Reformation reaffirms the Nicene Creed. The statement that Jesus Christ is "God of God, Light of Light, true God of true God" is no doubt the most agreed-upon truth in all of Christianity. The Eastern Orthodox Church, the Roman Catholic Church, and the churches of Protestantism all agree on that creed.

The Johnny-Come-Lately, Victor Paul Wierwille

And now, wonder of wonders, here comes Victor Paul Wierwille after nineteen centuries of Christianity. With a few pathetically argued "literal translations" and some shoddy Church history he makes the startling disclosure that everyone has been wrong about the touchstone of Christianity for all these centuries.

He doesn't even have the courtesy to admit his heresy did not originate with him. The fact is there have been others from time to time throughout the history of the Christian age who have taught the same drivel. And time after time, without exception, the Church has rejected that error flatly. The Trin-

206

ity is not doctrine that was sneaked into the Church during the fourth century while no one was looking. It has been believed by the Church throughout her whole history. The affirmation that Jesus Christ is God was taught by the apostles and recorded for us in Scripture. There is not even the slightest doubt as to the truth of that fact. Wierwille is so wrong it almost defies description.

Perhaps one reason Wierwille doesn't acknowledge others from the past who taught similar doctrine is because of the gross and sick excesses that so often accompanied that teaching. The Arians are a clear-cut example. They were the ones who really pushed the Wierwille-type teaching in the fourth century. They were responsible for the outright murder and torture of many Christians; many believe more Christians were killed by them than in the hideous persecutions under the Roman empire in earlier years. Wierwille's doctrine does not bring a record of righteousness to commend it!

It is hardly necessary to refute Wierwille's argument against the Trinity. That was done centuries ago. His shallow arguments and trite biblical reconstructions don't approach even those of earlier times who held a similar view. Wierwille offers no original arguments. He has only come out with inept repetitions of arguments long ago thoroughly and decisively discredited and condemned as heresy.

The Toughest of the Tough: Athanasius

It is interesting that in none of his writings does Wierwille mention the name of Athanasius, the great fourth century bishop of Alexandria. Athanasius is acknowledged by theologians and historians of Church doctrine as one of the greatest theologians in the entire history of the Church. Some think he was the greatest. Certainly, in his time, he was the most able defender of the true doctrine against those who claimed that Jesus Christ was not God.

For over forty years during that century he battled the "Wierwilleites" of his day (the Arians, followers of one Arius). The Arians threw everything they could muster against him, even plotting often to take his life. They managed to get him exiled from Alexandria five times. But when the smoke of the battle had cleared, the Arians' arguments were destroyed and their blasphemous cause was in shambles.

Athanasius was assuredly the most able voice at the Council of Nicaea in 325 A.D. Wierwille's arguments were all anticipated and answered by the ancient godly bishop there and in the years that followed. He has already been answered, and that long ago!

Jesus Christ Can't Be Other Than Both God and The Son of God

But look for a moment at one of Wierwille's main contentions against Jesus Christ being God. It will give you some insight into his utterly illogical thought. He would have us believe that according to the Church's own view, the doctrine is contradictory. He asks, "How can Jesus Christ be God and the Son of God at the same time?" Now such a question might be pardonable if he had made even the least effort to describe why we believe Jesus to be at the same time God and the Son of God. But he makes no such effort.

The Church believes the Father and the Son and the Holy Spirit are not three Gods, but are three distinct persons in the Godhead, sharing the same nature or substance. One God in three persons. The Father is not the Son. Neither is the Son the Father. Yet both certainly do share the very same nature. They are two persons, but one God.

On that basis, the real question is, how could Jesus Christ be anything besides God and the Son of God at one and the same time? For Wierwille to disagree with the doctrine of the Trinity is one thing. But for him to make the trite accusation that it is internally contradictory shows the utter shallowness of his own mind.

No Holy Spirit—Then No New Birth

Wierwille's efforts don't improve when he seeks to straighten out twenty centuries of the Christian Church's teaching about the Holy Spirit. He plays little word games with Scripture passages to attempt to show that the Holy Spirit is not a distinct person in the Godhead. They are anything but convincing. The Holy Spirit is just another name for God in his system. The Church in the earlier centuries had a name for those who believed like Wierwille on this subject, and they condemned them. The name? Pneumatomachians. What does it mean? Enemies of the Holy Spirit!

He does away with the very basics of Christianity, the deity of Jesus Christ and uniqueness of the Holy Spirit as a distinct person. But then he wants to steal other doctrines from Christianity.

Take, for example, Wierwille's teaching about the new birth. The new birth is one of those precious doctrines he would rob for his religion. But that robber will find his bag empty when he gets home.

You will recall he refers to the new birth as a legal transaction. That is perhaps a part of what Christianity believes about the new birth. Many Christians do believe that *one facet* of the new birth is that it is a legal transaction. But *all* Christians agree it is far more than that.

Christians believe that in the new birth a whole life in Christ, not just a legal transaction, is received. This new birth is accomplished by the Holy Spirit. He is the one who makes it happen. Jesus said, "Except a man be born of water and of the Spirit, he cannot enter the Kingdom of God" (John 3:5). It is the Holy Spirit who brings the new life in Christ to the Christian.

The new birth brings a changed life. It involves more than a legal transaction. St. Paul said, "If any man be in Christ, he is a new creature; old things are passed away; behold, all things are become new" (2 Cor. 5:17). That is what happens in the new birth. Listen, for example, to the Articles of Religion of the Reformed Episcopal Church in America (1875).

> Regeneration is the creative act of the Holy Ghost, whereby he imparts to the soul a new spiritual life. And whosoever believeth in Christ is born again, for saith the Scripture, "ye are the children of God by faith in Christ Jesus"[12]

Wierwille and The Way may talk about the new birth until their collective tongues melt, but without the person of the Holy Spirit, a distinct person in the Godhead, *there is no new birth*. Those who have the "new birth" of The Way do not have the life of Jesus Christ. They are not Christians! That is not to say there are not Christians in The Way. But it *is* to say that those who have only the "new birth" as taught by The Way, are not.

No Holy Spirit: No "Enablements" or "Abilities"

The same is true in regard to the gifts of the Holy Spirit. Wierwille's linguistic somersault with this capital *H* and small *h* stuff is ridiculous. It's just another of his word games.

The Holy Spirit is truly both a gift to the Church and the giver of gifts to Christians in that Church. Those gifts can only function when He, the third person of the Trinity is present. It's as simple as $2 + 2 = 4$; if there's no such giver, there are no such gifts. The so-called "enablements" or "abilities," those "manifestations" of holy spirit which Wierwille and The Way speak of, don't come from God. They may exist. But their source is anything but God!

The Way's Bible Gymnasium

Word and grammar games with the original languages of the Bible are a pet pastime for Wierwille. He speaks as if he were an authority on Greek, Hebrew, and Aramaic. No doubt he makes an impression on some who have no knowledge of any of those languages. To those who do, his games are little more than comedy relief. He arbitrarily makes up rules for grammar and assigns meanings to words with caprice.

Here's just one example of his word games. You don't need to know Greek to see through this one. Look at his "literal translation" of John 20:22.

> And when he had said this, he breathed on (he breathed in), and saith unto them, "Receive ye the Holy Ghost."

The scene, of course, is the upper room. The time is the night of the resurrection of Jesus Christ. He is the speaker. Now, just because he feels like it Wierwille decides that "breathed on" means "he breathed in."

There's a method to his madness. He is seeking to prove that on the night of the resurrection, Jesus was showing his disciples how they were to receive the gift of *holy spirit* (there they are again, those small-case letters), *a la Wierwille,* on the day of Pentecost. You see, part of Wierwille's mechanical method of speaking in tongues is that one must "breathe in deeply." Jesus, according to Wierwille, was just giving the disciples a demonstration of the way to do it. That night, according to his altering of the text, Jesus "breathed in" to show them how.

But that's not the punch line. You get that in his description of what took place on the day of Pentecost as recorded in Acts 2.

> And suddenly a sound came from heaven like the rush of a mighty wind, and it filled all the house where they were sitting (Acts 2:2).

That, of course, refers to the disciples on the day of Pentecost. Wierwille now takes this verse to his "biblical gymnasium," does a few back flips and cartwheels with it, and here is how it comes out in his "literal translation."

> And suddenly there came a sound from heaven as of a rushing mighty wind, and it filled (What filled? This heavy breathing by the apostles) all the house (the Temple) where they were sitting.[13]

Now get this. Wierwille says it is plain that this sound from heaven, this noise like a rushing mighty wind was the heavy breathing of the apostles doing their thing to receive the gift—just like Jesus told them to. He's just *got* to be kidding. But he's not!

The Bible, Interpretation, and Tradition

Most of Wierwille's "biblical proofs" are done in a fashion akin to the one above. There are some places, however, where he chooses to translate a Greek word with a meaning that might be quite possible, but which does alter the meaning of the Bible as most of our versions have it.

Anyone who has ever done any translating from one language to another knows there are often words which have several meanings. A choice must be made. What the translators desire is, of course, to choose the meaning that the writer or speaker had in mind. When it comes to the Bible, that's sometimes difficult to know since the Bible was written so long ago.

This brings us to an issue that is important to understand. Translation of the Bible is not as cut and dried as it may seem.

There is much interpretation possible in the choice of meanings for various words and grammatical forms.

It is mighty dangerous for any individual, Wierwille or anyone else, to make such decisions all on his own. The Church has had the Bible in her hands for over 1,900 years and incredible amounts of study have been given to translation. Sure, there is a tiny, tiny fraction of the Bible where there are some legitimate disagreements on what the best translation should be. But there is agreement on the vast portion of it. A moment's comparison of various versions, Roman Catholic or Protestant, will show that to be more than clear.

It is just because there is so much agreement within the Church in terms of her translations of the Bible that we must be as cautious of novel translations (so-called "literal translations" or whatever) as we are of novel doctrines. The truth of the matter is that the various accepted translations and versions of the Bible which we have *are literal translations*.

Closer to the Heart of The Way

The deviations of The Way and Wierwille from the truth about the deity of Jesus Christ and the person of the Holy Spirit are of great significance. Their sloppy handling of the Bible is not unimportant, either. But they are only the door openers to something even more sinister about this sub-Christian cult.

Wierwille and The Way are into mind control. They, too, are mindbenders. A thoroughly brainwashed devotee of The Way ceases to be able to function in his own control. His mind and behavior are changed without his knowing about it or actively willing it to be so. He becomes a pawn of someone else's program.

The Way accomplishes this by skillful psychological manipulation of the minds of its followers. The whole process is all wrapped up in this thing they call the "renewing of the mind." To be sure, the Bible does speak of a Christian's mind being renewed, but that has nothing to do with this teaching of The Way. Theirs is an out-and-out brainwashing trip. They teach a renewing of the mind all right, but their disciples are not willingly aware of what is actually taking place.

Phase One of the Brainwash—Deprogramming From Historic Christianity

Phase one is to deprogram the subject from any concepts or background that will resist the new program. It is necessary, therefore, to rip away any understandings, beliefs, and response patterns the subject brings with him. Since historic Christianity is at least the nominal background of most of the converts to The Way, that means the tearing out of the foundations of historic Christianity.

The "Jesus Christ is not God" shock treatment is where it begins for many people. The most basic belief of the historic Christian faith, as we have noted, is that Jesus Christ is God. Successfully tear that away, and you've pulled the bottom block out of the foundation of Christianity. The superstructure must then collapse with it. Therefore, the mindbenders can begin to build a new one without having to constantly hassle with the old.

This is precisely what happens to followers of The Way. They have left Christianity. Many aren't consciously aware of what they've done. Occasionally an old building block is used in the new structure, but always with a new design or purpose. Of course, "it was used wrongly in the old structure."

Phase Two—The New Program

I'm making no charge as to the underlying motives of either Victor Paul Wierwille or The Way. It is neither profitable nor necessary to do so. But motives, whether they be bad or good, don't change the fact that this is a mind control cult. Manipulation is their business. It is a program of non-volitional behavior modification. That means people's behavior is changed without their directly willing that change. Of course, the cult doesn't announce this is what it's doing, but nonetheless it is the end result.

As said before, their "renewing of the mind" process is the means by which they accomplish this manipulation. Watch how it works. The Way teaches:

By conditioning our minds through a renewal of the mind process, we can correct imperfect chains or patterns in the brain.[14]

Now you couldn't ask for it to be much clearer, could you? But when they describe their own method it gets clearer.

> To enlarge and control our thinking we must not only study the Word, we must allow it to sink into our hearts out of which come the real issues of life.[15]

That statement may seem innocent until you think for a moment about that "study of the Word" business. How does a person "study the Word" in The Way? Simple. He takes their teaching. They are the ones who provide all the data for that which conditions the mind.

Further, it is not the Word (that is, the Bible) they are teaching. It is their false interpretation of the Bible. The Bible will not grip a person's mind. But the teachings which The Way claims come from the Bible not only can, but do. This cult gets the mind out of gear with the false use of tongues; then, with the guard down, they slip in their own insidious teachings to reprogram the mind.

Change just two words of that first quote above and you've got the picture. It would then read like this:

> By conditioning *your* minds through a renewal of the mind process [remember, that's their teaching program] we can correct imperfect chains or patterns in *your* brain.

That, in a nutshell, is the program of The Way.

But it takes time. That's why they push one "Bible Study" program after another on their people. They say,

> You cannot totally change your mind all at once . . . As you absorb more and more spiritual knowledge, your mind will become more and more pure.[16]

Change that first "you" to "we" and you've got their program again. And that "more and more pure" stuff simply means, "You'll think just the way we're programming you." That's the *"literal* translation"!

Behavior Modification

Slowly the behavior of the devotee of The Way changes. He begins to act almost as if he were becoming another personality. He isn't. It's just that another personality is dominating him.

Parents see it and grieve. Old friends see it and say, "He's just not his old self any more." But the disciple of The Way sees nothing of it. He just speaks in those false tongues in his mind (or outloud) and bumbles along doing "automatically" just what he has been programed to do. How does all that take place? It's that incessant drip, drip, drip, drip.

The old White Owl cigar commercial had a line that really fits here for those who stick with The Way: "Sooner or later we're gonna getcha." They do.

Some will say, "Well, isn't what you're saying true of Christianity?" No way! The Christian has a living relationship with a Person. It's the difference between speaking with a computer or a person. Christianity is not built on a programming of the brain. It involves a relationship with the Triune God. And the Christian responds to God with the full power of his own mind and his own will. The Westminster Confession of Faith has a most appropriate comment that is helpful here.

> The liberty which Christ has purchased for believers under the gospel consists in their freedom from the guilt of sin . . . and their yielding obedience unto him, not out of slavish fear, but a childlike love and a *willing mind.*[17]

What the program of The Way does is to actually brainwash into its subjects a deadly legalism which prevents any true and abiding relationships from developing. Their people must become slaves of a law, related only to a program which they are led to believe is from God through the Bible. They utterly miss the true joy of loving and serving Jesus Christ, who is God in the flesh, with their whole heart, mind, soul, and strength. They become just robots programmed to respond according to a pre-set program.

Conclusion? Anathema!

Victor Paul Wierwille and his Way have devised an evil, corrupt, and humanly degrading scheme of duping and controlling the minds of many people. Most of those who are so affected are no doubt innocent, and a number of those so tricked are probably Christians.

As a dutiful servant of Satan himself, Wierwille has departed totally from the God and Father of our Lord Jesus Christ. His doom is sure. In his book, blasphemously entitled, *Jesus Christ Is Not God,* Wierwille quotes what he claims to be the Creed of Nicaea. That is only partly true. The words he quotes are actually the words of the creed of the Second Ecumenical Council held in Constantinople in 381 A.D. Of course, Wierwille is opposed to this creed. And well he might be, because it is a true and proper representation of the Creed of Nicaea. But perhaps the real reason he chose to quote that version of the Nicene Creed rather than the one from Nicaea itself is because of the closing words of the latter, which reads,

> And those who say, "There was a time when he [Jesus Christ, the Son of God] was not". . . . or those that allege that the Son of God is "of another substance or essence" [from the Father] or "created" or "changeable," or "alterable," these the Catholic and Apostolic Church anathematizes." (In those days that meant the whole universal Church of Jesus Christ.)[18]

That word "anathematizes" means to condemn with a great condemnation. Victor Paul Wierwille thus already stands condemned by the Church of Jesus Christ, for he indeed teaches there was a time when the Son was not, and that He is of another nature from the Father, and that He is a created person. And the Church of Jesus Christ affirms that condemnation until this very day.

Victor Paul Wierwille: the Church of the Lord Jesus Christ, who is God of God, Light of Light, true God of true God, anathematizes you. You are condemned with the great judgments of our fathers for your blasphemy against our Lord Jesus Christ, and for the tyranny you hold over those whom He loves.

A BRIEF PROFILE OF THE WAY, INTERNATIONAL

1. History
    —Founded by Victor Paul Wierwille in New Knoxville, Ohio in 1968.
    —Ignored the foundational doctrines of the Church and

put together a novel system of biblical interpretation for the purpose of behavior modification.
—The emphasis is on "Power for Abundant Living."
—Secured many converts from the Jesus Movement boom.
—An annual "Rock of Ages Festival" drew 1,000 in 1971 and some 8,500 in 1975.

2. Beliefs
   —Jesus Christ is not God.
   —The Trinity is denied.
   —The Holy Spirit is God, but not a distinct person in the Godhead.
   —Salvation is only a legal transaction secured by the death and resurrection of Christ.
   —Salvation is experienced by gaining the right knowledge, offered by the various Bible study courses of The Way. Behavior is modified by this "renewing of the mind" (brainwashing).

3. Method Of Operation
   —The Way tree illustrates the organizational structure with the "twig" being the basic unit. Claims not to be a church.
   —Aggressively evangelistic.
   —Money raised through courses offered.
   —Converts put through heavy indoctrination program with Wierwille doing all the interpreting of the Bible.
   —Dabbles in politics and has numerous enterprises to further its growth.

4. Refutation
   —Both the Church and the Scriptures affirm Jesus Christ to be true God.
   —Both the Church and the Scriptures affirm there is one God in three persons, the Father, the Son, and the Holy Spirit.
   —Both the Church and the Scriptures affirm the Holy Spirit is God and a distinct person in the Godhead.
   —Redemption and the new birth are far more than legal transactions, but rather the impartation by the Holy Spirit of a new spiritual life.

—The Way's interpretations of the Bible are all novel and designed to deprogram the converts from historic Christian doctrine.

THE WAY, INTERNATIONAL—FOOTNOTES

1. Taken from The Way college brochure, "Be A Winner" that has been distributed on campuses throughout the country.
2. Wierwille, Victor Paul, *Power for Abundant Living,* p. 3.
3. *Christianity Today,* "The Word and The Way According to Victor Wierwille," p. 42, September 26, 1975.
4. Wierwille, Victor Paul, *Jesus Christ is Not God,* p. 34.
5. *Op. Cit.* p. 85.
6. *Ibid.*
7. This is quite a common quote from Wierwille. I first came across it in a taped interview with a former disciple of The Way.
8. This was taken from a personal letter from Wierwille to followers of The Way in which he was explaining the purpose of the Christian Political Alliance. The letter is dated March 31, 1976.
9. *Ibid.*
10. *Christianity Today, Op. cit.,* p. 40
11. Schaff, *A Select Library,* Volume XIV, p. 3.
12. Schaff, *Creeds Of Christendom,* p. 817.
13. Wierwille, Victor Paul, *Receiving The Holy Spirit,* pp. 82, 83.
14. Walter J. Cummins, "The Mind of the Believer," *The Way* magazine, July /August 1974, pp. 10,11.
15. Ibid, p. 12.
16. Ibid.
17. Schaff, *Creeds Of Christendom,* p. 643.
18. Schaff, *A Select Library,* Volume XIV, p. 3.

An Introduction to the *"Local Church"*

You were told it was to be a Christian meeting. You had agreed to come for two reasons. One, you considered yourself a Christian. Two, the invitation had been extended so persistently. Now that the meeting is over, you wish you hadn't come at all. You've never felt so on-the-spot in your whole life.

The meeting itself was unusual, to say the least. It was a full-scale psychodrama. At least that's how you were describing it in your mind while it was in progress. But then you'd felt guilty about thinking that way about any group of sincere Christians.

You had arrived ten minutes ahead of the announced starting time. But the room was already at least two-thirds full, and the meeting seemed to be in full progress all by itself. It was mostly singing at first. And what singing! You'd never heard any like it in your whole life. Such enthusiasm. The audience of at least two or three hundred swayed back and forth almost as one man in rhythm with the music. Song after song was sung. You knew several of them. They were familiar gospel songs, but the words had been changed freely in places. There were modern pop tunes, too. But all new words had been put to them. You had joined in. You simply couldn't help it. Everyone was really into the singing.

Between songs, various people spoke out spontaneously with a testimony about God in their personal lives. The whole room responded with oddly intoned, but hearty, responses such as "Hallelujah," "Praise the Lord," or "O Lord Jesus." You were impressed and embarrassed for them at the same time.

Then, that rather elderly, but extremely energetic Chinese gentleman appeared. The singing and the vocalized responses crescendoed. Never had you seen or heard anything like it in

219

your whole life. "They're crazy," you thought. "Just a bunch of 'holy rollers'." But somehow, you knew those descriptions didn't quite fit.

The Chinese gentleman had spoken for more than an hour. His English was heavy with an oriental accent. You could hardly understand him, but the others seemed to clearly understand what he was saying. The message was constantly punctuated with the listeners' vocalized responses. Again, there was that odd intonation. You couldn't put your finger on it.

You begin laughing a bit inside because you had thought the meeting was over when the message was finished. How wrong you had been! After the message, people everywhere stood and enthusiastically repeated bits and pieces of the message with some comment on it. At times the vocalized responses were deafening. The whole group even broke into chanting at times. More songs were sung.

At long, long last the meeting was over. But not for you. About twenty-five people surrounded you and sat down. Then it started.

They began a rhythmic chant, "O Lord Jesus, O Lord Jesus, O Lord Jesus, O Lord Jesus." They seemed hypnotized. And you were beginning to feel the same way. They pitched and rolled together with the beat. That odd intonation? It was Chinese. You recognize it now. You'd not figured it out before because the majority by far were Caucasian. But that intonation was sure enough Chinese.

"O Lord Jesus, O Lord Jesus, O Lord Jesus." On it went. It was beginning to become clear to you what they wanted. You were supposed to join in. The friend who had invited you was smiling at you and encouraging you with his hand to join in. The heat was on. It was all of them against you. You could feel the flush of embarrassment coming up your neck and face. How did you ever get yourself into this? "What kind of a heathen am I anyway?" you ask yourself. You better do something. They're not about to give up. It could be a long night.

Finally you venture an "O Lord Jesus," but only with your lips. Smiles and encouragement come from the whole group. They like what you're doing. "That didn't hurt so much," you muse. You vocalize it softly, "O Lord Jesus."

You're really into it now. You're even enjoying it. You're pulsating back and forth with them. What acceptance! You're a part. You've even got that odd intonation. Your mind is relieved. The pressure is off. Your will has been broken. And it's likely that you have just become the most recent convert to the Local Church.

That's right. The Local Church. That's what it's called. It's not *a* local church. It's THE Local Church. It's the only true church in your whole city of two and a half million people. And you found it tonight. They're the only truly non-sectarians in the whole city. Just ask them, if you've got any doubt about that.

And the older Chinese gentleman? Who's he? That is Witness Lee, the autonomous dictator of this world-wide religious cult.

HISTORY AND THEOLOGY OF THE LOCAL CHURCH*

The roots of this movement go back several decades to China. Missionary programs from the Western world were in deep waters early in this century. Many Chinese Christians were disenchanted with what they saw. It was true that many of the missionaries did cooperate, but they still represented various Western denominational mission boards, and that didn't sit well with the people. Whether that was good or not is another question. But confidence in the missionary program was shaken.

One result of the loss of awe of the Western missionary was the emergence of the Little Flock movement, a religious sect claiming to be free of all sectarian principles. Its prime mover

---

*In order that a clear understanding of what this cult believes and the errors involved may be firmly grasped, I will alter the procedure somewhat from that which I have followed in considering the other six cults. Rather than devoting a section to a theological analysis and then following with a section for a refutation, I will combine the analysis and refutation together in "A Refutation of the Local Church."

The reason for this procedural change is that the Local Church doctrine has an unusually great number of contradictions and inconsistencies. They must be pinned down point by point.

was the late Watchman Nee, now widely known in America through his many books which have been translated into English.

Quite small and struggling initially, the Little Flock movement began to gain momentum after the Second World War. China was in great internal turmoil. The Communists were advancing. Western causes were extremely unpopular. Many of the Chinese Christians were looking for a "home grown" church. The Nee movement was promising to many. Nee could arouse interest, but he couldn't seem to get the act together. That's where Witness Lee enters the picture.

Nee and Lee had been associated closely for a number of years. But Lee had not been really prominent in the leadership of the whole movement. In the late forties, the two joined together in a much stronger relationship. Nee was the dynamic teacher; Lee was the gifted organizer.

The complete Communist take-over was becoming fully apparent. Nee recognized the implications of that for the new movement. In 1948 he sent Lee off the mainland of China in order to preserve the movement after the Communist take-over was complete.

Lee made his way to Formosa and took up the Little Flock effort there. The growth was significant. Between 1949 and 1955 it appears that the size of the Little Flock grew from 500 to 23,000 on the island. There was also significant success in the Philippines. In 1968 the Local Church claimed 10,000 adherents in the city of Taipei alone and 6,000 in the Philippines.[1]

On To America

Los Angeles, San Francisco, and New York were the main points on Lee's first visit to the United States in 1958. Little was done on that trip other than getting the lay of the land. Lee did, however, come into contact with two groups that would be significant to the importation of the movement to the United States.

One was an already-established, all-Chinese, Chinese-speaking Local Church in San Francisco whose roots were established in Taiwan. He discovered the other group in Los Angeles, where a group of Christians were meeting at a place called Westmorland Chapel. The San Francisco group was, of course, already committed to Lee's teaching. The Westmorland group had some common ties with Lee through one T. Austin Sparks of England. One offered Lee a starting point in the Bay Area. The other could be used as a springboard in sprawling southern California.

Lee returned to the United States in 1960 and was invited to speak for a number of Christian groups who had become interested in the teaching of the late Watchman Nee. The Navigators, for example, had him at their headquarters in Glen Erie, Colorado. But few people in this country really understood what Lee was after.

The contacts gained through speaking were not particularly profitable for Lee's purposes. But they did give him exposure to many Americans. And one circumstance proved exceedingly profitable. Subsequent to Lee's first visit to the United States, a brother-in-law of Watchman Nee joined with the Westmorland group in Los Angeles, bringing several Chinese families with him. But they never fully merged into the identity of Westmorland Chapel. An issue came up over Witness Lee himself. The Chinese faction sided with Lee, while others from Westmorland opposed this faction. As a result, the group split and in 1962 the divisive element from Westmorland Chapel, under Lee's not-too-well-disguised leadership, "claimed the ground" in Los Angeles. The movement was now fully underway in the United States.

Claiming the Ground

It is necessary here to explain the expression, "claim the ground." There is no way to understand the workings of the Local Church without a grasp of that concept. (Other Local Church doctrines will be considered under the theological analysis, but this one must be discussed here in order to understand their history.)

The idea is wrapped up in the concept that there can be only one church in a given city. One city, one church. The teaching is based on an appeal to an ideal of the unity of the Church. Los Angeles, California, and Dacula, Georgia, have one thing in common. They can have only one church. Anything besides that one church is considered a division.

Now there are certain requirements a church must meet if it is to be the true church in a city. Foremost among those requirements is that it must have no sectarian doctrines whatsoever. (Of course, the Local Church is the deciding factor as to whether a doctrine is sectarian or not.)

Denominations are automatically excluded from being true churches because, according to the Local Church, they are founded on sectarian principles. A church, they say, can be founded only upon their concept of Christ. Anything else disqualifies it.

As you would expect, then, the Local Church proudly pretends it has no sectarian doctrines. In reality, however, it is one of the most heavily doctrinally-oriented cults in the world. It is absolutely convinced it "feeds only on Christ." That means it has the automatic spiritual territorial rights to a piece of geography called a city. All other Christians must join them. Anyone who does not is wrong, sectarian, and dishonoring to God. All other churches are part of the great harlot, Babylon.

Proselytizing Procedures

The Local Church had firmly established itself in America by 1962. Growth over the next five years was slow but steady. Securing converts among people seeking "a New Testament-type church," the Local Church took people away from a number of already-established groups. The pattern was almost always the same.

Contact was made with a group that had some ideas similar to those of the Local Church. There would be a great deal of talk about unity. Slowly the group would lean towards some kind of co-working with the Local Church.

As soon as the Local Church was in a position to take a sizable portion of the other group, some issue would be made. It didn't make any difference what issue. Just an issue. A stand with one side or the other was then demanded by the Local Church. It, of course, could no longer work together with a false church that had now shown its real colors. The ugly head of sectarianism had risen. No way would the Local Church accept that. Division resulted, and the Local Church took its spoils of victory away.

This is precisely what happened in 1962 and 1963 in the Los Angeles area. The Local Church, a group from the San Fernando Valley, and another group from Whittier began to cooperate. It looked like a fine arrangement until the charismatic question became an issue. The Local Church sided against the charismatics. The other group, seeing the authoritarian manner of the Local Church's operation, backed off. When the smoke cleared, only the Local Church came out whole. The other groups lost numbers to the Local Church.

The growth and scope of the Local Church is best seen by a quick look at its conference and training program held annually in Los Angeles during earlier years. (More will be said about this important phase of its method later.)

Its first conference, held in 1962, drew only 70 people. By 1964, it had 132 people, with several U.S. cities and a few foreign countries represented.[2] In 1969, 462 people came from a much wider range of American cities, and quite a few from foreign countries were on hand. Brazil, Canada, and Denmark were represented.[3] The number grew to 1,300 in 1970, with people from Thailand, Singapore, and Malasia attending.[4]

The growth of this movement coincides quite closely with the other cults described in this book. The late sixties and early seventies were a heyday for such dissident groups. Many of them dug in firmly during that time and established themselves. The Local Church is certainly no exception to this. Its splash is not as great now, but its growth rate is greater.

The Overall Size of the Local Church Movement

The full size of the Local Church movement is difficult to ascertain. Taiwan is still a stronghold, as are the Philippines. It would appear there are some 5,000 or more members in the United States. Their overall number might be in the vicinity of 30,000 around the world.

Witness Lee is no longer a young man; his days are obviously numbered. I personally doubt that his close control can be assumed by anyone else in the ranks. The movement will almost surely splinter into two or three major factions when he dies. But splinter or not, the Local Church will be on the scene for some time to come. I predict that in America its influence will outlive the other six groups considered in this book, though its scope will not be as great as some in terms of sheer numbers.

THE METHOD OF OPERATION OF
THE LOCAL CHURCH

The brainwashing, or mindbending, of the Local Church is, I believe, the most powerful and lasting of any cult on the contemporary religious scene.

Centering on the endless barrage against the established Church, the Local Church's deprogramming process is quite similar to that of the Children of God and The Way. Established Christianity, it says, is Babylon, the great whore of the Book of Revelation. There is nothing in her but death. (The Local Church acknowledges there are Christians in the churches, but they need to get out.)

Its means to mind control is as frightening as it is effective. It begins with what I believe to be an involuntary forfeiture of all normal use of the human mind. The Local Church uses two tools to gain this.

The Local Church "Mantra"

The first of these mindbending tools is the Local Church *mantra*. They would violently reject any such suggestion that it is a "chant." No doubt they would even condemn that practice as heathen. Nonetheless they have their *mantra*. And it's not all that different from that of the Hare Krishna cult.

Listen to Witness Lee's view of the effectiveness of the mantra: "We have seen that to reach the unbelievers, no preaching is necessary. If we help them to say 'O Lord' three times they will be saved. . . . All they have to do is to open their mouths and say, 'O Lord, O Lord.' Even if they have no intention of believing, still they will be caught!"[5]

The Local Church's *mantra* is the phrase "O Lord Jesus." I know that phrase sounds terribly Christian, but from my repeated observation, the phrase becomes a psychological device. It is repeated over and over again, day in and day out. Meaning and content of the phrase are immaterial.

We have seen that the leaders say if they can get you to say it just once, they're well on their way to getting you. Witness Lee has said:

> In other words, whenever we say "Lord Jesus" in a real way, it means that you are in the Spirit. . . we all have to learn to say "Lord Jesus" in the meeting, in our home, and a thousand times a day. . . we must all say this. If we are going to lose our temper, we must say, "O Lord Jesus"! Then our temper will be gone . . . I tell you, you can become holy just by saying "Lord Jesus." Whenever you say "Lord Jesus," you are in the *Holy* Spirit.[6]

That doesn't sound Christian, does it? There is truth in his statement, however. Even as the TM *mantra,* or "Hare Krishna, Hare Krishna, Krishna, Krishna, Hare, Hare, Hare Rama, Hare Rama, Rama, Rama, Hare, Hare" will change your life, so will the repetitious mouthing of the phrase "O Lord Jesus." *It can produce a state of altered consciousness.*

The Local Church rationale behind the use of the phrase is that it is calling upon the Lord. (Oddly enough, that is the same rationale of Hare Krishna!) Such "proof texts" as, "Whosoever shall call upon the name of the Lord shall be saved," and "No one can say Jesus is Lord except by the Spirit," are used as evidence that such employment of the phrase is thoroughly Christian, proper, and necessary.

It becomes evident quickly, however, that this is actually no normal calling on the Lord. It is usually voiced repetitiously to get one "into his spirit," as an expression of approval, or a display of delight or excitement.

Witness Lee explains one is to "breathe in God and exhale the four syllables 'O Lord Jesus.' " The phrase is also used as a powerful chant by a crowd. Imagine 2,000 to 3,000 people rocking from side to side and chanting it in perfect unison for several minutes and you may have some idea of the impact it can have in crowd psychology.

The phrase and its variations are used as a substitute for the rational use of the mind. The mind seems to go out of gear as the mouth shifts into high. "Get out of your mind, brother," is a constant admonition. And it is not enough to *think,* "O Lord Jesus." It must be vocalized. The effect is far greater. It is not unusual for someone in the Local Church to repeat that phrase fifty to one hundred times a day.

A New Testament of the Bible—Pray-Reading

But the Local Church does not stop with a *mantra.* The mindlessness extends into the use of Scriptures, too, through an interesting invention called "pray-reading." This technique was introduced by Witness Lee during the late fifties in Taiwan.

For example, here is a way Witness Lee might suggest you pray-read Gal. 2:20:

> I am crucified with Christ. (With your eyes upon the Word and praying from deeply within, you say), Praise the Lord, I am crucified with Christ. Amen! O Lord, I am crucified. Praise the Lord! Crucified with Christ. Amen! I am crucified with Christ. Hallelujah! Amen! Nevertheless. Amen. Nevertheless. Amen. I live. O Lord, I live! Hallelujah! Amen! Yet not I, but Christ. . . .

You are not to think when you pray-read. You are to respond with whatever enters your "spirit." It makes little or no difference if what you say is right or wrong. This is a matter of the spirit, and you must not seek to think out whether or not it is true. Just keep your mouth going.

Lee explains this is how one actually partakes of Christ. He quotes 2 Tim. 3:16, "All Scripture is God breathed. . . ." Quickly, he turns the phrase to say, "All Scripture is God's breath." Since God is Spirit, God's breath is Spirit. Therefore, we actually partake of God's nature or essence when we pray-read. Says he, "From now on, we must consider the Bible to be the very essence of God instead of the revelation of God."[7] Again, "It is clear from the Scripture that the Word [the Bible] of Christ is nothing less than Christ Himself."[8] Thus, to pray-read is to eat and drink spiritually the essence of Christ. The Bible and Christ become synonymous!

The Scriptures, then, are read with little apparent concern for what they really mean.

> Pray-read every word, and you will be filled with the Word which is the Lord Himself. When He is filling you, everything will be taken

228

care of. It is not to practice the teaching or obey the Word, but to enjoy Him through the Word.[9]

Further, Witness Lee is constantly teaching the Scriptures against the backdrop of his own private theological system. Lee insists he has received the interpretations by revelation from God. Therefore, anyone operating in his "spirit" and not his "mind" will surely recognize Lee's interpretations are correct. In this way, one man's doctrine easily becomes the foundation of the whole movement.

The Suppression of the Individual

Closely related to the "O Lord Jesus" chant and pray-reading is the suppression of individuality. There is no place whatsoever in the Local Church for anything uniquely individual. Natural talents, attractiveness, and abilities must be negated. No one must stand out.

There is a clear, unwritten, unspoken, heavily adhered to (and always denied) code of conduct and dress. Pressure for conformity to the group is demanded in many subtle ways. Disciples are like so many peas in a pod.

Witness Lee told at one meeting, for example, of trying to buy himself a pair of shoes while traveling from Seattle to Los Angeles. Dramatically he described how he looked and looked for something appropriate. But they were all too stylish. They had the world on them. He just could not bring himself to stand and preach the gospel in such unsuitable shoes. You may be sure that stylish shoes are not a part of the wardrobe of the truly dedicated Local Church disciple!

The conformity in vocabulary and intonation in pronouncing certain words and phrases is likewise amazing. Once you know the sound you can recognize it anywhere in the world. I have never met a group where people speak so much alike, look so much alike, and sound so much alike. The individual is absorbed into a corporate whole.

Group Acceptance

Such individual suppression is compensated by group acceptance. The only identity these individuals have is within that group. That makes group acceptance all-important. The maintenance of that acceptance is one of the powerful forces to keep people in the movement. Proper performance is the key to maintaining the group's acceptance. But the welcome can be withdrawn at a moment's notice if performance fails.

One's first impression is that there is a great deal of spontaneity with them. They seem to speak up so freely. It's only a guise. Let someone say something that is not acceptable and the group's displeasure is instantaneous. A particularly intoned groan will go up from all over the room. If the word spoken was extremely unacceptable, it is not uncommon for the crowd to rise to the occasion and simply shout the dissident voice down with the ever-effective "O Lord Jesus."

Propagation

The propagation process of the Local Church is relatively simple. No one is really considered fully converted until he is into the Local Church. Their meeting is the key to gain that end. If a person buys the meeting, he'll likely take the whole thing. Confidence about their meetings is great. They are not hesitant to bring people in, and they cannot fathom anyone not liking what goes on. Surely, anyone attending will realize this is truly the right way to worship God!

Indoctrination Process

The blood in the veins of the Local Church movement is their conference and training program. It is here the uniform direction (or "flow" as they call it) is set. The conference is a week-long affair in the summer, and is of popular nature.

The training program immediately follows it. It is a four-week program of concentrated teaching from Witness Lee. He speaks day and night. These messages and teachings provide the base for the teaching everywhere in the movement for the whole year. They are printed up in the Local Church magazine, *The Stream,* and circulated throughout the groups.

The doctrinal unity of the movement is tight. One quick glance at a list of their available publications gives the reason. They are virtually all done by Witness Lee. They offer some of the Watchman Nee books, but in the case of occasional conflicts between the two, Lee is the official interpreter. With only one person doing all the basic teaching and writing for the whole movement, it is quite simple to keep things tied together, particularly if no one is really free to think.

The Local Church on Parade

It was August 20, 1968. Two hundred marchers converged on the downtown area of Taipei. Divided into seventeen groups, each led by a drum corp, they paraded through the heart of the city. Huge banners with slogans such as "The World Is Empty," and "You Need Jesus" preceded each group. Shouts of "Hallelujah" and "Praise the Lord" reverberated through the city streets. The marchers sang in full voice. The Local Church was on parade.[10]

They call them "Gospel Marches." The robed marchers choose a crowded place in a city and march on it with zeal. Lost in the facelessness of their own group, the marchers lose all fear of individual embarrassment. Even the normally timid may shout out slogans at the top of their lungs. The singing is almost deafening, at least to those in the group itself. There is a feeling of power and exhilaration and rightness. For the moment, at least, the Local Church is stage center.

Can you imagine the amazement of Saturday shoppers in downtown Los Angeles when a hoard of 1,200 or 1,300 robed marchers streamed down Broadway in just such a fashion! They've done it and most likely will do it again.

The greatest impact of the Gospel March, however, is not on the viewer. It's on the participant. They've done something bold that no one else has done. They've made an impression. But it took them all. Each one had to cast aside his dignity and reserve. The cohesiveness it provides to the group is inestimable.

The Power of Fear

What keeps these people in the Local Church? The cause? Yes. Excitement? Yes. But beyond that, people who have encountered the group say it seems to be fear that keeps them in. Fear of what might happen if they leave. Individual identity and the adherent's past have been rejected. It is next to impossible to ever go back. The indoctrination has been too thorough. Those weeks, months, and years of daily emphasis on how bad it is where the others live takes it toll. Many find it is

231

almost psychologically impossible to return to and maintain normalcy.

The fear and guilt that accompany leaving are too much for most people to take. It's not just the humiliation of having to admit you were wrong after you had so openly and boldly committed yourself. In fact, that's trivial compared to the black dread that you may be washed out with God forever. Within the movement, stories are multiplied as to tragedies which have occurred in the lives of those who have left. The most dramatic of these tales are told by people who have left only to come crawling back on their hands and knees telling of the awful judgment of God they experienced on the outside. There are no stories told within the group of those who have successfully left and made it.

Once in the Local Church, the member is likely to stay on for life. This is no movement of kids going through a stage. Sure, there are some young people in it. But all ages are represented.

Fear, it seems to me, is the ultimate weapon in the Local Church. It is a fear few Christians have ever known or even knew existed.

Once in, you must not think about your circumstances. Do not ask if it's right or wrong. Never admit you're trapped. Just go along with it all. It will all be over someday. "O Lord Jesus, O Lord Jesus."

A REFUTATION OF THE LOCAL CHURCH

"Oh, but you're in your mind, brother; you must learn to turn to your spirit." So goes the typical retort of a Local Church devotee to any questioning of their doctrines. He'll likely go on naively, "We aren't concerned with doctrines; we partake only of Christ, just Christ."

Thus it is that the people of the Local Church have effectively deceived themselves into believing they have somehow left doctrine behind. Indeed, they believe they have advanced to a higher level. In fact, all they've done is to redefine terms, in this case, the term "doctrine." Doctrine, they believe, is teaching which is understood with the *mind*. On the other hand, teaching which is taken in through the *spirit* is Christ, not doctrine. The tragedy is that they have so lost touch with reality that they believe they actually understand without their minds. The mind is to be by-passed. The spirit, that aspect of the human being which supposedly can alone experience true spiritual understanding, is to be exercised to "partake of Christ."

A Change in Procedure

In order that a clear understanding of what this cult believes may be grasped and their aberrations plainly demonstrated, I will alter slightly the procedure of analysis. Rather than devoting a section to the theological analysis and then following it with the refutation, I will combine the two in one section. Such a procedural change seems necessary because Local Church doctrine has an unusually great number of contradictions and inconsistencies. It wiggles all over the place. It has to be pinned down point by point, right on the spot. A doctrine presented one way in one place may appear with quite a different or even contradictory twist in some other place. As in the case of the other cults, I will deal here with only their most serious departures from historic Christianity.

The Heart of the Problem

At the very heart and core of Local Church teaching is a monotonously repeated claim: God's great eternal purpose for man is that he become completely and forever mingled with God. Man is to cease being mere man and become totally merged with God. God, in turn, ceases to be only God and has now become totally and completely mingled with man. Everything else hinges on this teaching; it is the crux of their heresy.

How It All Supposedly Happened

Local Church theology starts out innocently enough, but gets quickly off the track. In the beginning, they say, there was God. This God created a creature called man. Man was created with a body in order to experience physical life. He was created with a soul at his very center to express the human personality, the self. He was created with a spirit for contacting, receiving, and containing God.

233

This man was not yet the finished product of God's purpose, however. He still had no intimate relationship with God. Man had only created life in him. God's final goal for man was that he should have uncreated life—the very life of God. Lee writes:

> God's purpose for us human beings is that we may obtain His uncreated life and be transformed into His image to be like Him, as He is.[11]

God's purpose, according to Lee, was that this man would one day completely mingle with God, and God with man. *The two would ultimately become absolutely as one.* This aim of God's would not just automatically come to pass, however. Man was going to have to cooperate in the process. Lee's words about this mingling are specific:

> Man was created neutral to God and Satan. It was God's intention for this neutral, innocent man to take God into himself that God and man, man and God would be mingled together as one.[12]

As we shall see, this mingling process was to occur fundamentally in man's spirit. That is, man was to take God in through his human spirit. If man would operate the way God planned, the purpose of God would be fulfilled.

A Fouled-Up Program

But man fouled up the whole program. He ate of the Tree of the Knowledge of Good and Evil and fell away from God. Instead of assimilating, mingling God into himself, he assimilated Satan into himself. Man, according to Lee, became mingled with Satan. Man actually received Satan into his body.

> . . . the fall of man was not just a matter of man committing something against God, but of man receiving Satan into his body. Satan, from the time of the fall, dwells in man.[13]

Of course, such circumstances could only lead to further disastrous complications. Lee tells us, you see, that the soul is imprisoned within the body. Thus, the result of Satan's invasion of the *body* is a contamination of the soul as well. The soul indeed becomes Satan.

234

. . . the fallen soul, the self, is Satan. . . . . Beyond a doubt, it means that Satan is mingled with self! . . . It means that self and Satan are mingled as one.[14]

Before we go any further, let's get clear on what Lee means by this word "mingle." He uses it over and over again, and its meaning is crucial to an understanding of his theology. Whether the mingling is with God or Satan, it turns out that the basic idea is the same.

Mingling is much more than mixing together; it is an intrinsic union.[15]

We see then that he does not use "mingling" to show that two substances or persons merely associate. Rather, they totally blend together as one.

Now, with the term "mingle" defined that way, you can see that Lee does not mean that man simply had some dealings with Satan. Nor does he mean that man willfully followed a satanic suggestion. No, man and Satan mingled. They became one. An intrinsic union. *Blended.*

It is now possible to understand the problem of the human condition as set forth by Lee. God created man whom He intended to mingle with His very nature and essence. Because of the fall, however, that man actually became mingled with the very nature and essence of Satan. The result is that the whole of humanity has now become polluted to the extent that *it is Satan.*

All humanity, permeated by Satan, is just the same as a serpent in the eyes of God. Whatever is in the serpent is in us. Have we ever come to the Lord and confessed, "O Lord, I am as sinful as Satan. Lord, in your eyes I am a serpent also!"[16]

But wait! It was really only the body and the soul which became united with Satan. What happened to the human spirit? Well, according to Lee, it died. Now, he doesn't mean it became non-existent. He just means it ceased to function at all.

So there we are. Humanity is a total wreck. Satan is dwelling in the body, the soul has become Satan, and the spirit is dead. What a predicament!

Lee and the Local Church Propose a Way Out

Lee and the Local Church do not, of course, leave humanity without hope. God had a plan. God came in the flesh. That's Jesus Christ. When God came in the person of Christ, it was to solve the problem by mingling Himself with humanity.

> Therefore, the incarnation of Christ simply means the mingling of God with humanity. Mingling is much more than mixing together; it is an intrinsic union. . . . The first person who was mingled with God was Jesus. Do you realize why He is so precious to us? Because in Him is the universal mingling of God with humanity.[17]

Lee thus redefines the purpose of the death, resurrection, and ascension of Jesus. It is to make God's now-mingled-with-man nature available to human beings so the original purpose of God for humanity can proceed on to fulfillment (granted the proper conditions).

The true essence of being a Christian, according to Lee and the Local Church, is expressed in mingling. Christ, who is now spirit, comes into the human spirit, mingles with it, giving life to that dead spirit. That, says Lee, is regeneration.

> Regeneration is the mingling of God, Himself, with our spirit.[18]

So, according to this teaching, if you are a Christian, your once-dead spirit has been brought to life by being mingled with Christ's spirit. You have become blended with deity. You are, in a very real sense, divine! You and God are alike. Lee describes the new condition this way:

> It is indeed inconceivable to our natural mind that the almighty God would one day mingle Himself with a man. But this was accomplished in Jesus Christ, and this is the very desire of God for you and me—that He be mingled with us.
>
> Do you know what it means to be a real Christian? To be a real Christian simply means to be mingled with God, to be a God-man.[19]

Once you were nothing more than a purely devilish human being. But now, in Christ you are no longer only human, just a

236

human being. You are a God-man. You are partly God, mixed in essence! Says Lee:

> What He is, we are; and what we are, He is.[20]

> Before the incarnation, God was God and man was man, but by the incarnation God was brought into man, and man was brought into God.[21]

It is clear, isn't it? Yet, because this concept is so crucial, I must quote Lee one more time.

> He is the God-man and we are the God-men. . . . In number we are different, *but in nature we are exactly the same.*[22] (italics mine)

In a Nutshell

Make sure you've got this clear. Lee and the Local Church are saying that in Christ, God and man mingle so that a new identity is formed: God-man. That is, God is no longer just God. He is now both God and man mingled as one substance or nature. The Christian also gains a new identity. He is no longer merely a human being. He is also God-man. He possesses the very same nature as the altered God.

Four-Serious Consequences of Such an Idea of Mingling

It is important to make a strong statement at this point: The Church of Jesus Christ stands against such allegations! She has consistently confessed that deity and humanity *never* mingle. Just exactly why she has done so and how her confession has been expressed, I will shortly set forth. First, it is important to show some disastrous consequences which accompany this idea that God and man both now have a common nature, the God-man nature.

1) The God Who is No More

First, we must understand that if the uncreated nature of God is mingled with the created nature of humanity to form a new nature from the mixture, God no longer exists as truly God. He has lost His unique identity. He is robbed of His God-ness. The plain truth is that in such a case, God ceases to exist. He is replaced by a new substance composed of a mixture of the one-time God and corporate ex-humanity. How preposterous!

2) The Man Who Is No More

Secondly, the uniqueness and dignity of humanity is also thoroughly destroyed by such an idea. Why, if such an idea were true, it would mean that in eternity, the man God created would be nothing more than a memory of a bad trip back in time. Such a man would have no real value, even before his fall. The man who mingles with God becomes something entirely different from that original man. Being man was only something temporary. In Witness Lee's system, man isn't redeemed, he is replaced!

3) Contempt for Mere Humanity

Thirdly, there is an unavoidable attitude of disdain and pity toward those poor souls who are still merely human. The Local Church has apparently forgotten that it was, after all, mere humans whom God so loved that He gave His only begotten Son that they might be redeemed.

4) The Unbearable Burden

Fourthly, the burden of being of one nature with God is simply too much for a human being to bear. The demands are too great. God never intended it. The Local Church can talk about being God-men till the cows come home, but they're still as human as the rest of us. Those who believe such tragic doctrine must retreat to an unreal world of shadowy mysticism where they forfeit their normal functions as human beings and become a part of an anesthetized corporate Local Church—oblivious to the true needs and purposes of the human race.

They cease being able to relate normally either amongst themselves or those outside their "church" in the everyday relationships of life, such as husband-wife, parent-child, and employer-employee. Indeed, Lee encourages abnormality in such relationships:

> Have you seen God, Christ, the Church, and the Churches? The sisters must forget about their husbands, and the brothers must forget about their wives. We must forget about our preoccupations and see God, Christ, the Church, and the churches. Hallelujah![23]

Yes, responsibility and reality fade from ordinary human relationships for the members of the Local Church. As the gods of Olympus had difficulty in relating with humans, so these God-men necessarily are crippled in their human associations.

A Bits and Pieces Program of Spiritual Growth

Perhaps that is why Lee and the Local Church don't want you to get the idea that the mingling of God and man occurs all at once when a person truly becomes a Christian. It's a bits and pieces affair. That is, this assimilation of Christ, this mingling with Him, is a progressive matter.

> Day by day he [the Christian] eats and drinks Christ. Christ is gradually digested by him and mingled with him so that he and Christ become one.[24]

Regular "eating and drinking" of Christ is therefore necessary. But where and how? It turns out that a properly functioning local church is the *only* place where this progressive assimilation can occur. And guess who are the ones with the properly functioning local churches? That's right—the Local Church. Of course, they would agree that any church could become a properly functioning local church if it would only do and believe exactly what the Local Church does and believes. But then, naturally, they would join in with the Local Church and Witness Lee.

The Exercised Spirit

Lee teaches that this assimilation process takes place only as the mind goes out of gear and the human spirit supposedly goes in gear. There is an oft-repeated emphasis: The spirit must be exercised. What this means is that a person must refuse to try to understand anything with his mind. Whether it be the Scriptures, a song, the teaching of Lee (or whoever is teaching), or whatever, the mind must put forth no effort to grasp what is being said. If the mind is exercised, knowledge or doctrine will be taken in. That is said to be "death." But if the spirit is exercised, only Christ will be taken in. Man is to receive and understand God in his spirit, not in his mind. The mind is considered incapable of receiving and understanding God because it is part of the soul.

According to Lee and the Local Church, pray-reading and repeating "O Lord Jesus!" are two of the very best methods of exercising one's spirit.

> We really enjoy pray-reading the Word together in the meetings. It is much better than preaching or teaching, because it includes breathing. When we pray-read the Word, we just breathe the Lord Jesus into us. . . . We come together not to receive some teaching, but to be breathed upon by the Lord Jesus—to take in the Lord Jesus by breathing.[25]

The conscious effort to not use the mind doesn't shut the mind off. It simply causes it to work without heed to its critical process. Operating under such conditions, a person accepts what he is told without question. That is the advantage to Lee. In this case the person is persuaded that it is Christ alone that he is receiving, because that is what he is told is happening. Since he is not supposed to use his mind, he usually does not question.

A Fly in the Ointment

This progressive mingling with Jesus Christ, the one-time God, now become God-man, is made to sound good. But progress in the mingling is very hard to come by. There's a tough road ahead of anyone who plans to really advance in that mingling.

You see, according to this cult, when a person becomes a Christian, only his spirit is affected. That means there's a fly in the ointment: the body and the soul. They are not affected at all, and they don't buy the new program of the spirit one single bit. Now, if that were really true, the Christian would be in a bad way. The way Lee teaches it, there is indeed a first-class bad situation within the Christian. A great warfare is produced within, a three-way war at that. The devil is in the body, plain old human life is in the soul, and Jesus Christ is now in some measure mingled with the spirit. Lee writes:

> We are quite complicated. The man, Adam, is in us; the devil, Satan, is in us; and the Lord of life, God Himself, is in us. . . . We have become a little garden of Eden.[26]

The result is an all-out struggle on the part of the body and the soul, who generally cooperate, in opposing the spirit. The devil gets to the soul through the body. He tells lies that trick a man into doing his bidding, "and thus causes him to become a devilish man and lead the life of a mixture of man and devil."[27] Thus, this theological system has the body and soul resisting the spirit and trying to prevent it from operating properly.

The Foundation Doctrines of the Local Church

The whole foundation for this teaching of Lee and the Local Church about the mingling of man and God rests totally on their teaching that God and man are completely mingled in Jesus Christ. If that foundation collapses, any doctrine built upon it collapses with it. I will show clearly that this fundamental teaching of Lee and the Local Church is far from the truth as believed by the historic orthodox Church.

The God Who Changed His Nature

It is imperative to understand Lee's doctrine on this issue. So let's review and clarify. Agreeing but for a moment with the orthodox Church, Lee teaches that Jesus Christ had two natures. One was human and the other divine. But at this point, Lee's agreement with the historic Church comes to a screeching halt. He insists that those two natures, the divine and the human, were mingled in such a union in Christ that both natures ceased to have their own unique identity. There was no longer a divine nature that was only divine. And the human nature of Christ was no longer just human. Lee's exact words are . . .

> so the human nature was added to the divine nature and the once separated natures have become one.[28]

In plain and simple English, what that means is there is no longer a God who is just God. The very basic nature and essence of God's being has been altered eternally. He hasn't become a man, but He has mingled human nature with His divine nature. He is neither God nor man, but God-man.

Tea Water

An illustration from Lee will make his teaching on this matter clear.

> Take a cup of plain water and mix it with tea. Now the water is something more than just water. Originally, it was water, but now it is water mingled with tea. Before God was incarnated [i.e., come in the flesh], He was God and God alone. But after His incarnation, He is God mingled with man. In Him there is not only the divine nature, but also the human nature, the human essence, the human element. He is the Father, He is the Son, He is the Spirit, and He is man.[29]

The God of the Local Church is a being who once was God but has now altered His divine nature. He has added human nature to the divine content. The God of the Local Church is not the true God of historic Christianity.

The Belief of the Historic Church

God Himself has said, "For I, the Lord, do not change . . ." (Mal. 3:6). The creeds of the Church have constantly confessed that God is unchangeable. The *Westminster Shorter Catechism* speaks of a God who is . . .

> infinite, eternal, and *unchangeable* [italics mine], in His being, power, holiness, justice, goodness, and truth (Question 4).[30]

The Belgic Confession begins by stating:

> We all confess with the mouth that there is one only simple and spiritual Being, which we call God; and that He is eternal, incomprehensible, invisible, *unchangeable* [italics mine], infinite, almighty, perfectly wise, just, good, and the overflowing fountain of all good (Article I).[31]

Witness Lee, on the other hand, calmly says God has changed at the very heart of His being. His divine nature has now changed; it is utterly mingled with human nature. Whatever kind of creature that may be, it is not the God of the Christian Church.

The Fifth Century Revisited

There have been others besides Lee and his Local Church who have claimed that the divine and human natures mingled in Jesus Christ. In the heat of the battle of one such challenge, the leaders of the whole mid-fifth century Church met at the city of Chalcedon in 451 A.D. for an ecumenical council. Here in the Chalcedonian Creed is their answer to those teaching a mingling of nature:

> . . . This one and the same Jesus Christ, the only begotten Son [of God] must be confessed in two natures, unmingled, unchanged, indivisible, inseparably [united], and that without the distinction of natures being taken away by such union, but rather the peculiar property of each nature being preserved and being in one person.[32]

It was at the reading of this creed that the bishops gathered at Chalcedon cried out with one voice, "This is the faith of the fathers . . . this is the faith of the Apostles; by this we all stand: thus we all believe."[33]

Ever since that time, the Eastern Orthodox Church, the Roman Catholic Church, and virtually every branch of Protestant Christendom have embraced that creed as representing the essence of what the Bible truly teaches about the joining of the human and divine natures in Jesus Christ. Witness Lee stands almost alone against all the centuries of Christendom as he arrogantly claims to be right while the whole historic Church is wrong. The truth of the matter is that it is Lee who is dead wrong.

Surely, Jesus Christ did (and does) have two natures, one divine and the other human. *But those two natures did not, do not, and never will mingle.* In the great mystery of the Incarnation, those two natures came together, not in one new nature, but in the one person, the person of our Lord Jesus Christ. He remains wholly and truly God and wholly and truly man, but without any mingling. The divine nature is still purely divine, and the human nature is still purely human. God is God, and man is still man.

The noble leaders of the Church gathered at Chalcedon had a further word for those who teach that Christ's two natures mingled. Witness Lee should pay great heed. Speaking of those who might teach contrary to the faith which they had affirmed, they decreed:

> But such as dare to put together another faith, or to bring forward or teach or to deliver a different creed . . . let them be anathematized [accursed].[34]

Lee and his followers have dared, and the verdict against them has already been rendered.

The Foundation in Ruins—And The Superstructure Too.

There is no way the teachings of the Scriptures as interpreted by the historic orthodox Church will allow Lee's doctrine of the mingling of the divine and human in Christ to stand. Measured against historic orthodoxy, his foundation collapses in ruins.

But that is not all that falls. The whole idea of a "super-race" of Christians now possessing deity by a mingling with Christ collapses with it. The Christian is not partly divine. We remain human throughout all eternity.

Double-Talk, Sloppy Illustrations, and the Local Church Trinity

We have not, however, come to the end of the Local Church's ideas regarding the nature of God. This time look at the Local Church's view of the Trinity.

First, understand that for the almost twenty centuries of its existence, the Church has believed the Scriptures teach God is Father, Son, and Holy Spirit. It has firmly held that the Father, Son, and Holy Spirit are *three distinct persons with one nature*. Not three Gods, but one God in three persons.

The doctrine of the Trinity is of far more than academic interest. It is perhaps the most crucial doctrine of Christianity. Amongst other vital concerns, it is through the persons of the Trinity that God can be known and experienced by us. The Father is a person; the Son is a person; and the Holy Spirit is a person. They are *one* God in *one* nature. Yet each can be experienced as a person. If we deny the full personness of one or all, the persons of the Godhead will drop out of our practical experience. That is precisely what Lee and the Local Church have done.

Confessedly, the doctrine of the Trinity is a great mystery. However, Lee and the Local Church feel they have unraveled much of that mystery. Over and over they profess to believe in three persons in the Godhead, but their words to that effect are meaningless because they redefine the word "person."

Accusing historic Christianity of believing in three Gods, the Local Church ends up with what amounts to a *one-person Godhead* who expressed Himself in three stages or functions. This one person they name Jesus Christ. He is all-inclusive, they say. Lee writes:

> The Lord Jesus is the Father, the Son, and the Spirit, and He is the very God. He is also the Lord. He is the Father, the Son, the Spirit, the almighty God and the Lord.[35]

As they would have it, Jesus Christ is the very Father Himself, and He is also the Son and the Spirit. They insist they believe that the Father, Son, and Spirit are real persons. That claim, however, turns out to be double-talk because they redefine the word "person." Lee's own illustration of the so-called persons of the Trinity goes like this:

> Some men have little purpose; therefore, their appearance is continually the same. But a man full of purpose may have several appearances. If you could visit him at his home in the early hours of the day, you would see that he is a father or a husband. After breakfast, he may go to a university to be a professor. Then at the hospital in the afternoon, you may see him in a white uniform as a doctor. At home he is a father, in the university he is a professor, and in the hospital he is a doctor. Why is he these three kinds of persons? Because he is a man of great purpose.

> Do not think that because there are three Persons in the Godhead, there are three separate Gods. No, they are absolutely one. Matthew 28:19 says that we are to baptize people in *the name* of the Father, and of the Son, and of the Spirit. There are three persons, but only *one name*. It is not in the *names* of the Father, the Son, and the Spirit, but in the *name*. The father in the home, the professor in the university, and the doctor in the hospital are also three persons with one name."[36]

This father, professor, and doctor is not three persons; he is one person only. Father, professor, and doctor are merely three functions of one person, but in no way are they distinct persons. So it is with the Local Church "Trinity." They can call the Father, Son, and Spirit persons, but it is meaningless when they redefine the term.

The Also-Rans—Father, Son, and Spirit

It would be serious enough if this were the end of the Local Church false teaching about the Trinity. But it gets worse. Not only are the Father, Son, and Holy Spirit only functions rather than distinct and unique persons in the Local Church teaching, but their functions aren't even unique. In Lee's Godhead, Jesus Christ not only functions as Father, Son, and Holy Spirit, but also as "other items." Lee makes this very clear,

> As God, He is the Father, the Son, the Spirit, the Lord, the Christ, *and other items* . . . He is the light, the life, the air, the water, the food, the clothing, and the lodging. He is all of this and more to us.[37] (italics mine)

That makes the Father, Son, and Spirit nothing more than also-rans (important also-rans, but nonetheless also-rans) along with those "other items." Being functions of God, rather than persons, they cannot be experienced as persons even though the Local Church claims such experience. The Local Church multiplies words about their experience of the Lord Jesus Christ, who they say is the Father, Son, and Holy Spirit and other items. But their understanding of Him is pantheistic rather than orthodox.

The Local Church Judged by the Historic Church

Before we leave the subject, we must take a special look at the teaching that Jesus Christ is the same as the Father. In the fifth century this same doctrine was taught.

Cyril of Alexandria, fifth-century Christian and theologian, wrote in reply to that teaching, "But we do not call the Word of God (Christ) the Father . . . and fall under the charge of blasphemy."[38] These words were officially approved at the third and fourth ecumenical councils of the Church in 431 A.D. and 451 A.D., respectively. As long ago as those years, there were heretics claiming that Christ was Himself the Father—in much the same way the Local Church does today. They gave up the identity of the Father, Son, and Holy Spirit as unique persons. The Church condemned them as blasphemers. That has continued to be the position held by the Church, as the Augsburg Confession, among many others, demonstrates:

> We unanimously hold and teach, in accordance with the decree of the Council of Nicaea, that there is one Divine Essence, which is called and which is truly God, and that there are three Persons in this one Divine Essence, equal in power and alike eternal: God the Father, God the Son, God the Holy Spirit. All three are one Divine Essence, eternal, without division, without end, of infinite power, wisdom, and goodness, One Creator and Preserver of all things visible and invisible. The word "Person" is to be understood as the Fathers employed the term in this connection, not as a part or a property of another but as that which exists of itself.

> Therefore all the heresies which are contrary to this article are rejected. Among these are the heresy of the Manichaeans, who assert that there are two gods, one good and one evil; also that of the Valentinians, Arians, Eunomians, Mohammedans, and others like them: also that of the Samosatenes, old and new, who hold that there is only one Person and sophistically assert that the other two, the Word and the Holy Spirit, are not necessarily distinct Persons but that the Word signifies a physical word or voice and that the Holy Spirit is a movement induced in creatures (Article I).[39]

The sides are all too clear. One must side with Lee and the other false teachers of these heresies or with the historic Church. They may profess their orthodoxy in the loudest of voices, but they are far from orthodox.

The Idolatry of the Local Church

Not only is there a strong emphasis in the doctrinal system of the Local Church on the mingling of the individual with God, but the mingling is given a corporate sense in an alleged mingling of the God-man with the Local Church. In fact, they say it is fundamentally with the church that God mingles His nature. The individual participates in that mingling as he participates in the Local Church.

God planned to have a corporate body, a corporate vessel, with which He could mingle Himself and all that He is. This is called the church.[40]

Lee explains that "the essence or substance of the church must be Christ Himself assimilated into our being." A single individual is not seen to equal Christ. But the Local Church, the sum total of all individuals in a given locality who are in this assimilation process, is an expression of Christ. It is actually Christ Himself.

Only Christ Himself could be this house [the local church]. Therefore the church must be Christ. When we say that the local church is the house of God, we must realize that this house must be Christ. This house must not be a group of people, but Christ alone.[41]

You must understand they do not simply mean that the Local Church is a place *where God dwells.* The Local Church must also be *what God is.* There is an identity of essence. Cut it any way you want to, in a very real sense that makes the church deity itself. So thoroughly does Lee hold this view that he unbelievably adds a fourth "person" to his Godhead. *The church joins the Godhead.*

They are now four in one. The Father, the Son, the Spirit, and the Body.[42]

Now "get into your mind" and follow the thought here. God and man now have the same nature, they say. The fullness of this mingling is in the Local Church. They also insist that the church is Christ. The Godhead is to be worshiped and the church is a part of the Godhead. Okay, the logical conclusion is unavoidable. In the worship of their God, they must worship their own corporate self—the Local Church. They'd scream in protest about such a conclusion, but it is a fact. And that is how they treat the Local Church.

A Root of Arrogance

It is perhaps right here at this point that we find the taproot of the arrogance of the Local Church. Claiming to be mingled with deity, they see only those who do and believe as they do and believe as genuinely sharing in that divinity. Others may be Christians, but they are judged to be bogged down in their souls, not having begun to assimilate God. The Local Church is not something so common as "God's Green Berets." They are the Christian "super-race."

A Case of False Divinity

Never has the Church of God seen herself as possessing deity. The very thought is blasphemous. The Church is not divine. It is not God. It is not a part of the Godhead.

How, then, does the Local Church come to its conclusion? This heresy is founded on the same basic error that pervades all their teaching: the mingling of deity and humanity. Grant that, and they are correct in exalting the Church to deity. But the foundation is false. We have already shown that error for what it is.

Surely, the historic Church believes the Church is the body of Christ. But that is according to His *unmingled humanity,* not His divine nature. The Church, according to the Scriptures, is "one new *man*," not one new God, or God-man. The Church is human in its corporate nature. It is redeemed humanity, but still humanity.

A Church which sees itself as participating in the nature of deity will scorn humanity and see itself as superior to all.

The Prodigal Church or The Church of the Recovery

The Local Church claims that for the greater part of fifteen centuries the truth of God was totally obscured by the historic Church. Lee insinuates that even before the end of the first century A.D., the real truth of God for the Church was already submerging. It is clear he is sure the truth virtually disappeared by the end of the second century. Then, until the Reformation in the sixteenth century, there was little light. The true Church was lost.

> But not long after the New Testament was completed, the Church began to lose all the important things found in the Bible. Eventually, by the fifteenth century, everything was lost. Very little of God was known.[43]

249

Such a plight calls for what they call "the recovery" of the true Church. "The recovery" is Lee's term to describe the gaining back of the true Church as it was known, say in 50 A.D., and which he is sure has been lost for these many centuries. You must understand they do not believe the historic Church of those fifteen centuries was the true Church just having some bad days. It wasn't the true Church at all. It was Babylon, the great harlot.

This so-called recovery, Lee tells us, began with Luther and the Protestant Reformation. But the Reformation didn't recover the Church. It was only the *beginning* of stage one of a five-stage process. Lee's stages are named: 1) Fundamentalism; 2) Pentacostalism; 3) Evangelism; 4) The Deeper Life emphasis; 5) the Church. He acknowledges that there was some truth in each of the first four stages, and says he is not against them. But, he says, "We must go on." We are now in stage five, the age in which the true Church is to finally be recovered. That's where the Local Church comes in. *They view themselves as the church of the recovery.* They are the ones who are following God today. When the rest of us wake up, we'll leave where we are and join them.

> When we were in the denominations, we were blind. I do not believe that any dear Christians who have really received sight from the Lord could still remain in the denominations. . . . Allow me to say this: If anyone is still in the fold, he is blind. Of course, a blind person requires the fold to keep him. But when he receives sight, he will swiftly leave the fold for the pasture, for the sunshine, for the fresh air.[44]

Now, as stage five progresses, God is finally being properly worshiped after an eighteen-century lag. There will now be a Church who, in all her glory, can finally usher in the kingdom of God in its fullness. That, according to the Local Church, is the next step in the program of God.

And while that day is coming, the people of the Local Church believe the Christian life can be experienced in a way that the saints of yesteryear did not ever know. These "stage fivers" have much more light than those who have gone before. All other Christians miss this "perfect plan of God" which they have so newly discovered.

250

The Self-Refuting Cult

The emphasis of this book has been to show where and how far these various cults have deviated or separated from historic orthodox Christianity and its understanding of the Scriptures. It has been the premise here that any group or teaching that stands outside of that Church, or contrary to it, is in error.

On this basis, the Local Church refutes itself. On the one hand, it claims faithfulness to the Scriptures. But, on the other hand, it proudly admits its interpretation of those Scriptures is different from and superior to that of historic orthodoxy. The Local Church plainly says the latter was wrong.

This has not been a matter of matching my interpretation of the Bible against theirs. It has been the interpretation of the Local Church matched against the mainstream of almost twenty centuries of Christendom. The Local Church, by its own admission, is not in that mainstream. Babylon, it calls her. Judged by the historic Christian Church, Lee and the Local Church have been weighed in the balance and found wanting.

By its attacks on the historic Christian Church, the Local Church sets itself apart. The decision as to who is right must be made on the basis of whose interpretation of Scripture to believe: the witness of orthodox Christianity for nineteen centuries or the distinctive teachings of a twentieth-century group that has adapted some age-old heresies to their needs.

The Exclusive Non-Exclusivists

The claims of Witness Lee and the Local Church are so bold that most people simply will not believe they could possibly be serious about them. Nevertheless, Lee plainly says he rejects historic Christianity.

We are simply putting off religion, putting off Christianity. In the early days, the church had to put away Judaism. Today we have to put off Christianity.[45]

Now that should be clear enough, shouldn't it? Still, many people hear those words and insist, "But that's not what he means." It is exactly what he means. Lee and the Local Church loathe the historic Church with almost unbridled passion. "Babylon" is their favorite description for it.

> What is this great Babylon? It is the mixture of Christianity. The great Babylon is a harlot mother with many harlot daughters. The Roman Catholic Church is the mother, and the denominations are the daughters.[46]

Proudly they shout and sing that they have forever left it. As they see it, only a tiny, tiny fraction of professing Christians have fully experienced true Christianity since the early Church. They, of the Local Church, are of that favored few.

Quite sincerely, they do not see themselves as the only Christians in the world, but they are equally sincerely convinced there is no way to really fully know Christ other than in a local church that operates on exactly the same basis they do. "We must be in the local churches [their kind of local churches] in order to be built up to be disciplined, to learn the lessons, and to grow in life. Hallelujah! Praise the Lord! He has shown us the local churches!"[47]

They see churches of historic Christendom as not even vaguely approaching that mark. They pity Christians trapped in Babylon (in the historic Church). It is inconceivable to them that anyone outside their scheme could possibly truly experience the full blessing of Jesus Christ.

Lee and the Local Church plead innocence when accused of sectarianism, but in plain language they are super-exclusivists, ultra-sectarians. Theirs is the only true way. You don't have to be a part of them, but you're wrong if you don't do things their way. All who don't are a lesser class of Christian, and they'll let you know it. They are the ultra-elite, the really favored. Those in historic Christianity may be Christians, but they've missed God's best by ever so far.

What then, of the people of the Local Church? How should the Christian Church view them? Sure, there are Christians in the Local Church. But for the most part they are those who were spiritually arrogant or super-dissident in the true churches they left. It's better for the true Church that they've gone unless, or until, they repent of their spiritual arrogance.

Many will leave the Local Church over the years. Few will ever find rest, peace, or a place where they fit once they do. The emotional and spiritual devastation is too great. Most have become emotionally dependent on the Local Church system.

Those who remain in the Local Church will fare even worse. They have deliberately removed themselves from the people of God. They must bear the consequences of that action in full. Their minds no longer function normally because of the effect of this mind-manipulation cult, and they will go on being emotionally dependent on the Local Church. It's a sad situation. Most who could have been productive Christians are neutralized for the rest of their lives. It's a great price to pay for religious zeal.

A BRIEF PROFILE OF THE LOCAL CHURCH

1. History
   —Roots go back several decades to Watchman Nee's and Witness Lee's association in the Little Flock movement in China.
   —In the late 1940s Nee was the dynamic teacher and Lee the gifted organizer of the movement.
   —After the Communist take-over was complete in 1948, Lee escaped to Formosa and established the movement there. Between 1949 and 1955 it appears the Little Flock grew from 500 to 23,000 on Formosa.
   —Lee came to the United States in 1958 and ultimately established the movement here in 1962.
   —Present membership today in the United States is about 5,000 and world-wide about 30,000.

2. Beliefs
   —God's purpose is for God's uncreated life and human life to be joined together in an intrinsic union through an alteration process called mingling.
   —The human and divine natures of Christ were mingled together; therefore we are to become a God-man too.
   —This mingling takes place by by-passing your mind and by turning to your spirit.
   —The Lord Jesus Christ is both the Father, Son, and Holy Spirit—thus there is only one real person in the Godhead.
   —Historic Christendom is Babylon, while the Local Church led by Witness Lee is the true church of the recovery.

253

3. Method Of Operation
   —Movement gains a foothold in a city by "claiming the ground." Initial talk is about unity, but unity around themselves.
   —Conferences and training programs held annually in Los Angeles very important to their growth.
   —The Local Church has own "mantra" or chant and has a new treatment of the Bible called "pray-reading."
   —Totally suppresses individuality and makes group identity and acceptance all-important. People held by the power of fear.
   —Group marches and public displays are also used.

4. Refutation
   —Four disastrous consequences of the idea of mingling; (1) God is no more; (2) man is no more; (3) one's humanity is held in contempt; (4) an unbearable burden. This so-called mingling leads to idolatry.
   —Historic Church doctrine has always said the Bible teaches that the two natures in Jesus Christ never mingle, but that He has two natures united in one person, the one Son of God.
   —The historic Church has always taught that God's nature is unchangeable and unalterable and therefore cannot be mingled with human nature.
   —The historic Church has always consistently rejected the lie that the Lord Jesus Christ is both the Father and the Holy Spirit, but has affirmed that He is the Son of God. Historic Christian doctrine has always believed in one God, consisting of three real persons.
   —The Local Church stands outside the historic Christian Church and is therefore no church at all but a cult that stands self-refuted and self-condemned.

THE LOCAL CHURCH—FOOTNOTES

1. The Stream, Vol. 6, No. 4, Nov. 1, 1968, pp. 27, 29.
2. The Stream, Vol. 2, No. 3, Dec. 1, 1974, p. 26.
3. The Stream, Vol. 7, No. 4, Nov. 1, 1969, p. 31.
4. The Stream, Vol. 8, No. 4, Nov. 1, 1970, p. 26.
5. The Stream, Vol. 8, No. 1, Feb. 1, 1970, p. 6.
6. Lee, *How To Meet*, p. 84.

7. The Stream, Vol. 5, No. 3, **Aug. 1**, 1967, p. 4.
8. The Stream, Vol. 5, No. 3, **Aug. 1**, 1967, p. 13.
9. The Stream, Vol. 5, No. 4, Nov. 1, 1967.
10. The Stream, Vol. 6, No. 4, Nov. 1, 1968.
11. Lee, *The Knowledge of Life*, (Los Angeles: Stream Publishers, 1973), pp. 24, 25.
12. Lee, *The Economy of God* (Los Angeles: Stream Publishers, 1968), p. 106.
13. *Op. cit.*, p. 109.
14. Lee, *The Parts of Man* (Los Angeles: Stream Publishers, undated), pp. 40-41.
15. Lee, *The Four Major Steps of Christ* (Los Angeles: Stream Publishers, 1969), p. 6.
16. *Ibid*, pp. 19-20.
17. *Ibid*, pp. 6-7.
18. Lee, *The Economy of God*, p. 114.
19. Lee, *The Four Major Steps of Christ*, p. 7.
20. Lee, *Christianity Versus Religion* (Los Angeles: Stream Publishers, 1971), p. 87.
21. Lee, *The Vision of God's Building* (Los Angeles: Stream Publishers, 1972), p. 158.
22. Lee, *The All-Inclusive Spirit of Christ* (Los Angeles: Stream Publishers. 1969), p. 103.
23. The Stream, Vol. 7, No. 4, Nov. 1, 1969, p. 11.
24. Lee, *The All-Inclusive Spirit of Christ*, p. 189.
25. Lee, *How to Meet*, p. 42.
26. Lee, *The Economy of God*, pp. 168-169.
27. Lee, *The Knowledge of Life* (Los Angeles: Stream Publishers, 1972), p. 89.
28. Lee, *The Economy of God*, p. 11.
29. Lee, *The All-Inclusive Spirit of Christ*, p. 12.
30. Schaff, *Creeds of Christendom*, pp. 676-677.
31. *Ibid*, pp. 383-384.
32. Schaff, *A Select Library*, Volume XIV, pp. 264-265.
33. *Ibid*, p. 265.
34. *Ibid*, p. 265.
35. Lee, *The Clear Scriptural Revelation Concerning the Triune God* (Anaheim, Ca.: Living Stream Ministry, undated), p. 3.
36. Lee, *The Practical Expression of the Church* (Los Angeles: Stream Publishers, 1970), p. 8.
37. *Ibid*, p. 15.
38. Schaff, *A Select Library*, Volume XIV, p. 203.
39. Schaff, *Creeds of Christendom*, pp. 7-8.
40. Lee, *The Practical Expression of the Church*, p. 7.
41. *Ibid*, p. 14.
42. *Ibid*, p. 43.
43. The Stream, Vol. 7, No. 4, Nov. 1, 1969, p. 14.
44. Lee, *Christ Versus Religion*, pp. 109-110.
45. Lee, *The Practical Expression of the Church*, p. 133.
46. The Stream, Vol. 7, No. 4, Nov. 1, 1969, p. 19.
47. *Ibid*, p. 24.

An Introduction to the Peoples Temple Christian Church (Disciples of Christ)

Between the mid-1950s and the end of 1978 there grew and flourished, within the very ranks of American Christendom, one of the most evil cults of our day. Yet from its inception, neither the Peoples Temple nor James Warren Jones, its founder and leader, was ever Christian in either doctrine or practice.

CULT OF DEATH

In November, 1978, the whole world was shocked when Jim Jones's lifelong project culminated in the deaths of more than 900 people, including himself. As we examined the reports set forth by the news media, it became apparent that Peoples Temple was quite typical of the modern cults we have considered and exposed in *The Mindbenders*. Still, this movement most likely would not have come to the attention of very many people in Christendom if its depraved and perverse leader had not chosen this spectacular ending.

While experts in psychology, psychiatry, and sociology were suggesting sundry explanations for the sudden tragedy, I, being persuaded at heart that the cause was a theological aberration, set out, along with a few associates, to piece together a total picture of what Jim Jones and his cult were all about.

We collected literature, interviewed former members of Peoples Temple, talked with former associates of Jim Jones, sought out and obtained extensive data from people who had come into contact with the group, and analyzed the history of the movement. What we discovered was shocking. This group displayed every one of the characteristics set forth earlier in the book as descriptive of mindbending cults.

Further, its deviation from Christian orthodoxy from its very inception was blatant and unmistakable. Yet, one of the major denominations in American Christendom had ordained Jim Jones and had accepted Peoples Temple into affiliation. Indeed, a staff report issued in 1973 to that denomination (Disciples of Christ) held Peoples Temple up as an example:

> Peoples Temple is an interracial, vibrant, exciting congregation, called into being by God through its Pastor, Jim Jones, with a unique sense of the servant role of the church ... One gets the impression of being in the midst of the human race at its best; a community of people whose primary concern is to love and to serve.
>
> —Jerry McHarg
> Associate Regional Pastor
> Southern California
> April 6, 1973

Yet, Ron Javers, a reporter who survived a vicious attack upon a U.S. Congressman and accompanying press corps by Peoples Temple assassins in November, 1978, made this sobering observation:

> Jonestown is every evil that everybody thought—and worse. We knew that before the shooting started.
> —San Francisco Chronicle
> November 20, 1978

What was wrong? Why did the famous Peoples Temple go sour?

HISTORY OF JIM JONES AND THE PEOPLES TEMPLE

Early Years

People who knew Jim Jones as a child indicate that even when quite young he had both a desire and a charismatic ability to manipulate other youngsters. They tell stories of his playing church with other youngsters and beating them with a stick to keep them in line. But what did "playing church" mean? What, indeed, did it mean that Jones showed an interest in religion and flitted from church to church? Was Jim Jones a Christian believer as a young child?

It really does not appear so. Though Jones was introduced to Christian concepts through a neighbor lady, his mother, Lynetta, seems to have been the most dominant influence in his life. According to a former associate minister of Jones, mother Lynnetta never was a professing believer and raised her son to be an agnostic—and she lived with him till her death in 1977.

Jones's father, several years older than his wife, does not seem to have been very prominent in the rearing of his son. The parents separated when the boy was in his early teens, and the elder Jones died alone in a hotel room in their small Indiana hometown of Lynn. Lynetta dreamed of great things for her son and primed him to do big things in the world.

In high school Jim Jones met the second most important woman in his life: Marceline Boswell. She was a nurse at a nearby hospital where he worked part time. Marceline is said to have had a pronounced interest in people with problems. Between them, much time was spent discussing the problems of poor and downtrodden people. Years later, after Jim and Marceline were married, she reportedly said that Jim's hero in those days was Mao Tse-Tung, the new ruler of China.

Off to College

Following graduation from high school, Jones enrolled in Indiana University with lofty visions of becoming a doctor. A fellow student of those university days observed, "Jones believed himself then to be a Messiah."[1]

Young Jim was an embarrassment to student associates at IU as he expounded for hours on his religious and social theories. In fact, he did not get on at all well at the university, and soon he and Marceline were living in Indianapolis. His career plans changed: He decided he now wanted to become a faith healer.

Astonishing as it may seem, this decision was not made on the basis of any faith in God whatsoever. In a 1977 *New York Times* interview, Marceline Jones said that her husband "had not been lured to the ministry by deep religious faith, but because it served his goal of achieving social change through

Marxism"[2]—a political motif that was to stay with him until the very end. Interestingly enough, he does not seem to have confided his motivation to his congregation in the very early days.

Denomination-Hopping

When Jones entered Butler University in 1950, he listed his religion as Unitarian. Perhaps that unorthodox confession had a great deal to do with his stormy religious career over the next few years. One of his first jobs was with a Methodist church in Indianapolis. Ross Case, a former associate, recalls that this position ended in a blow-up, probably over the inclusion of the names of the Father, Son, and Holy Spirit in Baptism: Jones wouldn't use them. The Methodist superintendent revoked his license to preach and notified the draft board.

Jones was soon preaching in a small Pentecostal church, but trouble developed there as well, causing that relationship to fold rather quickly. In 1953, at the age of twenty-two, Jones, declaring that racism prevented him from effectively ministering to the poor and to minorities in any of the established churches, stormed off to start his own church.

Over the next few years, while still in Indianapolis, Jones's congregation, first called the Community Unity Church[3] and then Peoples Temple, grew numerically. Doctrinally, it was anything but orthodox. Ross Case says Peoples Temple was started as a "oneness" church—meaning unitarian. Jones plainly did not believe in the Holy Trinity.

But he was a "charismatic" leader; he possessed a magnetism by which he drew people to himself. With great fanfare he opened Peoples Temple to all races, making a distinct effort to especially bring in poor people. As time went on and his resources grew, he opened and widely publicized a free clothing store, free restaurant, and free grocery. He and Marceline also opened the first of a series of nursing homes.

To gain respectability in the religious world, Jones began to court another denomination: The Christian Church (Disciples of Christ). The Disciples of Christ allow considerable breadth in doctrine and practice—and each congregation is independent, choosing its own pastor and nominating him for ordination. With such recognition in view, Jones was proceeding deliberately, and by 1960 he succeeded in getting Peoples Temple listed by the Disciples of Christ as a member congregation. That relationship still existed on the day of the Jonestown massacre.

Father Divine and Jim Jones

In the early and mid-1950s, Jones began to develop some changes in style. Certain flamboyant "messiahs" of the day, particularly Father Divine and Daddy Grace, fascinated him. As he later told Case, he envied the devotion, adoration, and absolute loyalty given them by their flocks. He purposefully altered his style to reflect theirs.

It will be revealing, then, to detail a few facts about Father Divine, Jones's primary model. This will help us to understand some of his later practices.

1. Father Divine was God to his followers.
2. He required his disciples to be totally loyal to him.
3. His followers had to cast out all "mortal feelings";
   a. Parents and children had to forget each other.
   b. Husbands and wives were not to think about each other.
   c. Sexual relations between husbands and wives had to cease.
4. He provided free and inexpensive meals to thousands daily—and widely publicized the fact.
5. He claimed miraculous healings.
6. He had a passion for his view of social justice and feigned his cause to be peace and the brotherhood of man.
7. He forbade his disciples to use tobacco or intoxicants.
8. He pioneered having black and white people live together in racially harmonious households.
9. He took credit for killing people without touching them.
10. He somehow acquired wide real estate holdings from his followers.
11. He had his disciples set up businesses, take only enough for bare necessities, and give the rest to him.
12. He packed people into houses so he could realize a large profit, even though charging each of them little.

13. He spoke on the evils of insurance policies. His followers cashed them in and gave him the proceeds.
14. He called sex a "dirty thing," yet taught his followers that he was the legitimate object of sexual desire.
15. He claimed the power of miraculous healing; his followers carried pictures of him for healing.[4]

Impossible as it may seem that anyone would choose to imitate such obviously devious practices, Jones did just that. He did not fail to capitalize on any of the methods of Father Divine. Jones discovered early that many people are easily duped by grandiose spurious messianic claims, and he did not hesitate to play his game to the hilt.

Thus, as time went on, Jones developed his "healing techniques," coming up with an elaborate scheme for fake cancer cures that called for the use of chicken entrails and the assistance of aides. And, oh yes, he began to instruct his followers to call him "Father" and Marceline "Mother."

Though many people have believed that Jones proclaimed a biblical religion, it was obvious even in the years before 1960 that such was not even vaguely the case. On at least one occasion in those early days, he held up a Bible, threw it on the floor, and stomped on it, shouting, "People are worshiping this thing too much when they should be worshiping me!" That's hardly biblical. The scene was to be repeated, with variations, many times over the years.

The Magic Mix: Religion and Politics

By the early 1960s, Jones's attention turned to political matters. In 1961, Indianapolis Mayor Boswell appointed him Human Relations Commissioner. It was not long before political leaders noticed that he could deliver blocs of votes through his followers.

Also in 1961, the Disciples of Christ began underwriting some of his social service projects, and it was at that time Ross Case joined him as an associate minister. That year Jim and Marceline had their first and only natural son who was later joined by six black, white, and oriental adopted brothers and sisters.

In those days, Ross Case recalls, Jones also began to get into spiritualism. Later, faked seances were to be a common activity. Associates also recall that Jones was now obsessed with sex. He confided that he felt dirty and guilty about having sexual relations with his wife. On the other hand, the word was around that Marceline was upset because Jim was having affairs with women in the congregation. He was indeed doing so, and this was but the beginning of his use of sex as one means to control his followers.

Ego-centered control was also evident in the interrogation committee Jones established in the Peoples Temple. He said it was for the good of all, but not everybody agreed. Some people claimed this committee of trusted aides was established to deal with anyone who criticized Jones. In actual fact, it worked that way.

Evidence of Jones's growing paranoia also appeared in 1961 when he feigned to have a vision of Indianapolis in a thermonuclear holocaust. He conducted a scouting mission to Brazil and sent others to scout rural areas of Mendoceno County, California—two areas Jones said would be safe in a thermonuclear war.

Meanwhile, back home in Indiana, some Disciples of Christ leaders were beginning to be a bit bothered by Jones's claim to be a healer, his claim to be God, and certain other practices. In addition, civil authorities were becoming suspicious of the considerable number of real estate transfers from members of Peoples Temple to Jones himself and the Jim-Lu-Mar Corporation, controlled by him, his wife, and his mother. Nevertheless, the denomination made no move to discipline him, and the civil authorities took no action. The Disciples ordained him to the ministry in February, 1964.

Westward Ho

The heat was on. In 1965, Jones told his congregation that in addition to the fact that Indianapolis would be destroyed by a thermonuclear war that would start on July 15, 1967, the city was too racist for him to carry on effectively. They must, he said, move to a safe place—and that would be Redwood Valley, near Ukiah, California. Estimates vary on how many people actually moved, but the number is somewhere around 150.

Once again, the politically astute Jones began establishing

himself in the surrounding community. He taught school and made friends with politicians. The Temple set up several nursing homes, and Marceline became a state nursing home inspector. Peoples Temple members began to take in wayward children from the San Francisco area. Jones was made foreman of the County Grand Jury. And Peoples Temple was incorporated in the state of California.

Still preaching absolute devotion to himself, conducting elaborate fake healings, and raving for hours about sex, Jones gained few additional adherents. But his popularity and influence in the community were growing, and in late 1968 Deputy District Attorney Timothy Stoen joined the Temple. This added respectability, attracted the attention of others, and caused the Temple to prosper. Local people joined. People from the San Francisco Bay area interested in social causes began to make the trek to Ukiah.

Expansion

Jones began to expand his operation, preaching in San Francisco and other nearby cities. Then, Father Divine died, and Jones, claiming to have received his mantle, made a trip to Philadelphia and persuaded a contingent of the dead god's disciples to return with him. They and others were packed together into small living quarters, and the Temple flourished. Curiously, more and more people gave Jones all their money and all their real estate.

Now the pace of activity quickened dramatically. Jones purchased an auditorium in San Francisco, then one in Los Angeles. A fleet of thirteen Greyhound-type buses would pack Temple members in like cattle on Friday evening in Redwood Valley, travel to San Francisco for a marathon five or six-hour meeting there, pack up again and leave immediately for another such meeting in Los Angeles, and finally roll back into Redwood Valley early Monday morning. This was done so that Jones could give the impression of huge local followings.

Bad Press

There were cracks in the wall. In 1972, Lester Kinsolving wrote a series of articles on Jones and the Peoples Temple for the *San Francisco Examiner*. He challenged Jones's claims to have raised more than forty people from the dead—and exposed the fact that armed guards dominated the Temple parking lot. Only two installments were printed and "the rest were dropped by the *Examiner* after the Temple threatened to sue the newspaper."[5]

Jones did not allow the political activities of the Temple to lag. Mass rallies for social and radical causes were typically graced by several bus-loads of Temple members. Jones moved to San Francisco. By the early 1970s the church claimed 20,000 members in California—probably a gross exaggeration. Local elections in San Francisco were being affected by the tightly organized Temple voters. Jones began to publish *Peoples Forum,* a paper largely devoted to promotion of political causes. The writing was invariably stilted socialist rhetoric.

Sometime during this peak period, Jones also began to make the first arrangements for an "agricultural colony" in Guyana. Still, his greatest hopes for success rested in the United States. He confided to aides that he hoped to become president. On a more immediate front, after hundreds of Peoples Temple members worked to get out the vote, George Moscone won the 1975 mayoral election in San Francisco. Jones was made chairman of the Housing Authority in the city. He and the Temple were basking in praise everywhere. Politicians invited him to all events and wrote glowing letters about his work.

But all was not well. On August 1, 1977, *New West* magazine printed an article critical of the Temple—and of its leader. From former members who had dropped out came fantastic stories of bondage, fear, sexual misconduct, and duplicity. A few political figures began to be suspicious, and some cursory investigations were begun. But the biggest impact of this unfavorable publicity was upon Jones himself.

Guyana: Paradise Extremely Lost

By 1973 Jones had already made plans to move his whole operation to Guyana. What he intended, he said, was to build a model socialist society, a place where all peoples of all races could live and work together in perfect harmony. Now, his paranoia fed by the new criticism, he set his schedule ahead and moved there himself. The name of the utopian colony was, of course, Jonestown.

Many visitors to Jonestown were impressed. San Francisco

attorney Charles Garry said, "I have seen paradise."[6] But not everyone was so favorably impressed. In May, 1978, a group of fifty-seven relatives of Peoples Temple members petitioned Secretary of State Cyrus Vance to do something to save their relatives, who, they claimed, were living under tremendous oppression and in danger of their very lives.

The State Department assured them they could find nothing wrong. Later—too late—we were to learn that life in Jonestown was far from paradise. Work days were eleven to twelve hours in blazing sun and drenching humidity, with guards constantly on watch. Living quarters were so tightly packed that there was no privacy, even for married couples, who slept on separate bunks, separated from others only by a hanging blanket. Rice and gravy was the staple food, with beans also occasionally served. Nightly meetings were followed by Jones's interminable harangues over loudspeakers, often till three in the morning. Communication with relatives was tightly controlled, and letters were monitored. Infractions of the rules brought tortures even for children, who were sometimes lowered into a well till they were coughing and choking. A helpless dread hung over the colony.

Congressman Ryan: The Final Days

The end came so suddenly. United States Congressman Leo Ryan pressured Jones into a visit by him and an accompanying news crew. Coming with them were attorneys Charles Garry and Mark Lane to represent Jim Jones's interests. When the visitors arrived, the delicate balance of control in the camp was broken. In the midst of faked happiness and staged productions, the ragged edge of reality reared its head. The guests were staggered by the evil underlying the facade of "utopia." A few people decided to leave with the visitors, and Jones's paranoia was catapulted to mammoth proportions.

By the time the delegation from the States had departed for the airfield a few miles away, Jones had made up his mind to act. An assassination crew was dispatched to the airfield, but it failed to complete its task. The congressman and some of the newsmen were killed, but others escaped. The stage was now set. Jones called his congregation together to carry out the final act, which had been rehearsed as long ago as 1973 in San

Francisco: liquidation under the guise of mass suicide. Garry and Lane managed to escape. The last two Jonestown residents they saw were two armed men. Charles Garry described the encounter: "They told us," he said, his eyes reddened and his voice breaking, " 'We are going to die for revolutionary protest as an expression against racism and facism.' "[7]

Was Jones's flock obedient unto death? Most died. But according to the Guyana government's top pathologist, few died voluntarily. But voluntarily or not, they died—911 of them, in the greatest single perverted religious tragedy of our time. Dr. C. Leslie Mootoo[8] estimated that more than 700 of the 911 who died were murdered. It would seem that Jim Jones died trying to make come true for himself a 1953 prophecy about one of his idols: "If Father Divine were to die, mass suicides among the Negroes in his movement could certainly result."[9]

JIM JONES'S THEOLOGY

Jones had two distinct theologies: one for the observing public and quite another for his followers. Neither stood very still. Nevertheless, it is possible to provide snapshots of what he believed and taught over the years. We will see some progression or evolution, as well as just plain old pragmatism: If it contributes to control of people, use it.

A Unitarian Humanist

As already indicated, when Jones entered Butler University he identified himself as a Unitarian. His one-time associate, Ross Case, told us that when Peoples Temple was started a few years later, it was as a "oneness" church. The two terms mean generally the same thing, so we must consider what it means to be "unitarian."

Unitarians are those who consider God to be *one* person, in contrast to Trinitarians, who believe in God as *three* persons. To go so far as to call himself unitarian, Jones had to have some degree of understanding of the subject. His later pronouncements indicate he was probably experimenting with the ramifications of this theological position, which generally also included a belief in Jesus as human only and not divine.

267

One rather revealing incident relative to Jones's theology—and to his character—occurred in connection with his view on the virgin birth of Christ. In August, 1961, he called Case and told him he no longer believed in that doctrine. Later, he announced his view to the church and asked how many were with him. Only one person in the whole congregation held up his hand. The next day Jones reported that God had showed him he really did believe in the virgin birth after all.

Jones's Battle With the Bible

Jones's problem in the late fifties and early sixties was that he was having to re-educate his congregation theologically, particularly with regard to the Bible. Most of the people were out of church backgrounds and considered themselves Bible believers. The Temple had applied to and been accepted by the Disciples of Christ, a denomination which, broad as its theological views are, does generally regard the Bible as authoritative. The slogan "No creed but Christ, no doctrine but the Bible" is often repeated among the Disciples.

The minister of Peoples Temple, however, did not subscribe to such an axiom. He proceeded to systematically pick apart the Bible, a practice continued all the way to the end. Ex-members recall him going into tirades about the Bible, yelling and screaming that it was full of lies, tearing out pages, spitting on it, and stomping on it.

Jones's True God: Himself

From the beginning, the major emphasis at the Temple had been upon social service under the leadership and direction of Jim Jones. But beginning in 1959 or so, a subtle shift began to take place. For the public, the message was still service to mankind, the "humanistic ethics," as Jones so often called them, of Jesus Christ. For the congregation, however, his gospel included worship of Jim Jones. That was the heart of what the theological re-education was all about.

Soon Jones was calling himself the reincarnation of Jesus Christ. Then, as if that were not enough, he said he was the reincarnation of Jesus, Buddha, the Bab (prophet of Baha 'i), Lenin, and God Almighty. He also told his congregation, "The spirit of Father Divine has come upon me." Songs of adulation of Jones, modeled after those sung by Father Divine's disciples, were given to the congregation:

> I gotta tell it.
> I gotta tell it.
> I gotta tell it.
> I gotta tell ya how Jim Jones changed my life.
> I gotta tell it.
> I gotta tell it.
> I gotta tell ya how Jim Jones changed my life.
> Once I was burdened
> And filled with misery.
> Along came this prophet,
> And he delivered me.
> I gotta tell it.

(Song repeated by Birdy Marable, December 6, 1978)

The "Temple Theater"

Many aspects of the build-up of the "divinity" of Jones were anything but subtle. In Redwood Valley an absolutely unbelievable, but carefully staged, charade was once produced in the Temple parking lot. Hollywood would be jealous. Two shots rang out that day and startled members saw Jones fall to the ground, clutching his chest. Amidst screaming, moaning, and crying, aides carried his bloody body into his house. The frightened congregation was herded into the Temple to be protected from further attack. Suddenly, there appeared in their midst Jim Jones, weak but alive. Holding aloft a glass case containing his shirt with two blood-stained holes in it, he proclaimed that he had resurrected himself from the dead, reached into his body, and removed two bullets, leaving not even a scar. From that point on everyone was to call him Father, in the sense of God.

There were other such staged dramatics. On one occasion, as Jones was telling the congregation that he was the reincarnation of Christ, he held up his hands, saying, "See them bleed!" Sure enough, they appeared to be bleeding, though a former aide said the "blood" was from capsules he had hidden in his fists. At another time, he dropped pills into containers of water to make it appear he had turned it into wine.

Then there was the time the Temple ran out of chicken at a big dinner. Jones went into the kitchen and supposedly materialized chicken in the ovens. We got the report, however, from one man who said he saw people bringing cartons of Kentucky Fried Chicken in the back door.

There are still greater lengths to which Jones would go to be worshiped! In the services, he would cry out, "I am God! I am God!" Former Jones's devotee, Yulanda Crawford, in a notarized affidavit, says, "On numerous occasions I was in the congregation when he told us 'I am God' and 'there is no other God, and religion is the opium of the people.' " Others report that he said he was the actual God who made heaven and earth. He once flew into a rage when two women sang "Amazing Grace." On that occasion he said, "I'm the only God you'll ever see."

Reincarnation

Along with all this emphasis on his supposed personal diety, he had many people believing in reincarnation in general—that if they died, they would be reincarnated and come back. Several interviewees mentioned this as a possible factor in the mass suicide. This reincarnation hope was a major attraction for many followers. One woman who made it to Jonestown and back told us she personally did not believe Jim Jones was God. In fact, she never did and still does not believe in God at all, but she did believe in reincarnation, and she did believe Jones when he said he was the reincarnation of Jesus Christ.

But Jones seemed to have something for everyone. We talked with ex-Temple members who never did believe Jones's claim to be God, or his ideas about reincarnation. For them his appeal was elsewhere. "He said he was God; but I didn't believe it and didn't care." What this woman believed, she said, was Jones's criticisms of the Bible. She said his remarks didn't bother her because she wasn't a religious person at the time and thought the Bible was just another book. She was one of the people who was there for the cause of socialism, and Jones's anti-Bible propaganda seemed supportive of such a program.

A Religious Socialism

The mixture of religion and socialism at the Temple was curious. For years Jones required all Peoples Temple members to read a book called *Introduction to Socialism.* Some people say he wished to supplant the Bible with it. Among former members, we found several who had simply tolerated the religious aspect of the program. It was their opinion Jones used religion to get to the masses, as he himself often said, and that he used Baptism to pull in religious people.

The line for public consumption, on the other hand, may be seen in the heading of a Peoples Temple propaganda leaflet: "Peoples Temple . . . Brotherhood is our religion." Then, in the body of the leaflet, "Pastor Jim Jones has taught us that being our brother's keeper is the highest form of religion." Similarly, in an advertisement on spiritual healing, "We see our role primarily as practicing the humanistic ethics of Christ's teaching in Matthew 25." Also, "We believe that service to others is the highest indication of devotion and worship to deity, as well as a genuinely effective deterrent to despotism and tyranny from any side that threatens our free society."

Further, from *Peoples Forum,* July, 1976,

> Spokespersons for the church explained that Peoples Temple is a religious human service ministry which is demonstrating that people from all racial, religious, and socioeconomic backgrounds can put differences aside and unite on common ground to work for brotherhood, equality, and the general good of humanity.

Just to prove that they can put religious differences aside:

> Heavyweight Champ Muhammad Ali is a member of the Nation of Islam, with whom Peoples Temple has built a very close relationship since the adoption of their present policy of inclusiveness of all races and religions, and their denunciation of militancy and violence.[10]

A Master of Redefinition

The purely naturalistic dimension of the Peoples Temple's public religion is further demonstrated in these extracts:

271

Peoples Forum speaks from the Judeo-Christian viewpoint. We hold that Jesus Christ is the Savior whose teachings offer a key to the greatest evolvement in human consciousness.

As we have said, the judgment of Jesus Christ upon the church is based on ethical humanism.

. . . He spoke of Heaven as an ideal to be attained here on earth.

. . . Hell on the other hand is poverty, war, racism, and all forms of human deprivation.

In the long run, whether we are atheist or Christian, our salvation will be accomplished not on the basis of what we profess, but on what good we do, one for another.[11]

On occasion, Peoples Temple publications gave hints concerning how God should be viewed:

Our theology comes out of the same roots of our involvement with the people. We don't even try to define God beyond a statement of our belief in the humanistic teachings of Jesus Christ and the Judeo-Christian ethic that 'God is Love.' Thus, we naturally resent any attempt to put Peoples Temple, as well as other churches and socially concerned groups who share this same concern, in the bag of fanatical religious sects who believe they have the only answer to human morality and a corner on the market of divinity.[12]

In the same issue, we are told that "Christians cannot judge atheists as evil or diabolical." Here, as in several other issues, dialogues between "the atheist" and "the Christian" are pretended in which "the atheist" always makes telling points against Christianity and "the Christian" always concedes some important point. For example,

. . . it is the spirit rather than the letter of the Bible that inspires us. We cannot dispute that it contains errors and even atrocities. But one can also find in the Bible, especially in the ethical humanistic teachings of Jesus Christ, great lessons and truths that are among the highest ever known to man. . . . The point is . . . and even many Christians have missed the essence . . . that GOD IS LOVE. God (Love, Good) is in us.[13]

Color Him Anti-Christian

Anyone who does more than a cursory reading of the *Peoples*

Forum will discover that its editorial policy was not just the presentation of a humanistic religion, but, indeed, a deliberate and active attack upon orthodox Christianity. This is well demonstrated in an article endorsing the views of a group of British theologians who had jointly written a book denying the divinity of Jesus Christ. Following the endorsement, the *Forum's* own view is set forth:

> The important thing is not whether Jesus was divine, born of a virgin or ascended from the grave after death. What *is* important is that he was an exemplary human being. And it is not whether one confesses his divinity that makes one a follower, but the extent to which one is willing to emulate the example he set as a human being—one who dared to love others and love justice more than life itself.
>
> In a sense, it is the same kind of religious dogmatism that is confronting these soul-searching theologians that confronted and eventually crucified Jesus in his own time. In John 10:33–34, Jesus was represented as saying:
> 'Many good works have I shown you from my Father: for which of these works do you stone me?' Then they answered him, saying, 'For a good work we stone thee not; but for blasphemy; and because that thou, being a man makest thyself God.' Jesus answered them, 'Is it not written in your law, I said, Ye are Gods?'
> Far from claiming divinity here, he is elevating the concept of man. Many who dispute the tenet of divinity are saying the same thing: the refinement and virtue incarnated in this teacher are attainable and perfectable in all men and women. 'Let this mind be in you, which was also in Christ Jesus: Who, being in the form of God, thought it not robbery to be equal with God' (Philippians 2:5–6).[14]

Three overiding points stand out in the clever mishmash of Jim Jones's theology: deification of himself, anti-Christianity, and Marxism. As one reporter put it, "In Jones' cultish socialism, the spiritual and political were joined."[15] It was not, however, true, as someone else wrote, that, "... the religious content of his message was fundamentalist, born-again Christianity."[16] Nothing could be further from the truth! In actuality, Jones used every tool he could find in his attempt to build his own idealization of a socialist society in which he would be the Almighty Ruler, the sole leader and controller.

Perhaps Clare Janaro, who arrived in Guyana to join the colony a day after the final event, was not far wrong in saying, "I know now Jim Jones was not Jesus Christ, but the devil himself and he led me down the path where I'm at today."[17]

JIM JONES'S METHOD OF OPERATION

In Guyana as in San Francisco, Los Angeles, Redwood Valley, and Indianapolis, appearances did not mirror reality.[18]

Actually, with Jim Jones, appearances and reality seldom matched. Everything he did publicly had cold calculation behind it. When he was kind and gentle with a poor and aged woman from a minority group, he was motivated by the value his actions had in building his power base. When he screamed indignantly at social injustice, the same goal was in view. Oh, there is no doubt that Jones grew worse as the years progressed. But there is clear evidence that his aim was to head up a new utopia from the day he first opened the doors of Peoples Temple in Indianapolis.

E Pluribus Jones

Jones's activities were so many and so diverse over the years that they defy being described as forming a tight, well thought out, strategic network. He experimented, and many of his projects failed. Several of his endeavors were contradictory. Some of his programs and policies were designed for the long run, and some were hurried into effect for the control of the people immediately under his seemingly ubiquitous thumb. Part of what became stock in his bag of tricks evolved over the years. Nevertheless, as we examine what he did, we must keep in mind the dream he pictured from the beginning: a socialist utopia presided over by Jim Jones.

The Temple did have a basic core whose allegiance to Jones stretched way back to the 1950s in Indianapolis. They were not necessarily his top confidantes, but they were there—and they were useful to him throughout the whole development of his program right to the day of the mass murder-suicide. Why did they stay with Jones? What kind of power could command such allegiance for so long a time? What long-term tools did Jones employ over the years to recruit and maintain such a devoted following?

An Appearance of Compassion

When I say "appearance of compassion," it need not be denied that, being human, Jones actually had a measure of concern for the people with whom he worked. Nevertheless, his pattern plainly demonstrates that this was not his primary motivation. He worked long hours for his way of social better-ment. He adopted seven children of assorted races and back-grounds. His manner and tone were kindly as he talked with people who felt some kind of need. People felt he actually cared for them *personally,* and his promises were for peace and well-being. In both Indiana and California, he established nursing homes to which he proudly pointed as evidence of his love for elderly people. Older people in particular were drawn by Jones's professed humanitarianism.

At face value these efforts were good, but things aren't always what they appear to be. Dorothia Hindman once visited her mother in one of Jones's nursing homes in Indianapolis: "My mother was tied to a chair and eight old women were sleeping in one room. No wonder neighbors heard women screaming at night," she said.[19] Underlying Jones's beneficial endeavors was not a genuine concern for the poor and downtrodden. Rather, it was a genuine concern to lift up Jim Jones and his ego-centered program. Therefore, those touched by his "good programs" were more often than not hurt by them in the long run.

Faith Healing

We interviewed one former member who had been with Jones for twenty years. Her reason for staying so long? "He healed me of cancer." She had seen much that was evil and had finally left him, but she still believed in that miracle. No, she didn't believe God had healed her. In fact, she didn't believe in God at all and never had, but she had stuck with Jones all those years since the 1950s, because "He healed me of cancer."

You may say, "That's an extreme case," and I feel the same

way. But the fact is, Jim Jones had a lot of followers who were convinced of his power to heal. That was a major tool in his building such a following. How did he do it?

Early in his "ministry" Jones learned there are a lot of sick people out there who are desperate for a cure. Undoubtedly, he attended the sessions of other "faith healers," for his methodology reveals an imitation of many standard practices. Jones knew every trick in the book and unhesitatingly used them all. He knew, for example, that many illnesses are psychosomatic or disappear without treatment. He used that fact in his cures, and also as an answer to his critics. As a result of a controversy over the possibility of fraud in his Indianapolis days, Jones learned to hedge. Thus, a statement in *Peoples Forum*, April, 1976, reads:

> As it is understood that only a medical physician or psychiatrist can determine accurately whether the source of the physical problem is physiological or psychosomatic, there is no attempt to say what the physical problem could be.

But that wasn't nearly enough. There had to be spectacular cures. Trusted aides provided information on who was in the audience with various pains, stomach aches, and the like—and on which ones were there because they believed in faith healing. These were specifically picked out by Jones, who "miraculously" identified them and their ailments, and then "miraculously" healed them.[20]

Then there was the "healing of cancers," developed to a high science over the years. This very successful deception, originally developed in Indianapolis, was a great favorite of Jones. A 1972 leaflet advertising his healing meetings claims that "tumorous masses" were passed in every service. Fulfilling such astounding predictions required the careful "ripening" of chicken livers, gizzards, and other entrails. An unsuspecting person, perhaps an elderly lady with an unspecified stomach ache, would be picked out of the audience. Jones would identify a cancer, produce a cure, and send his victim off to the women's room with, say, his wife Marceline. Marceline would have the chicken entrails wrapped in a napkin, placed in a plastic bag, and tucked in her purse. The victim would sit on the stool and Marceline would hold the plastic bag to "catch" the "mass" and by sleight of hand, come up with the "cancer." Then, as she escorted the victim back into the auditorium, the "cancer" would be waved victoriously aloft—then wisked away before anyone got a close look.

Still, there had to be more spectacular cures. Certain trusted aides, particularly women who were skilled actresses, were carefully made up to resemble crippled elderly people. Thus, in the middle of the service, an "old woman" in a wheel chair would be wheeled to the front and would shakily beg Jones to heal her broken body. Of course, he obliged, and she jumped from her chair, ran up and down the aisles, and quickly disappeared. Jones never failed. And, amazingly, even some of the people who participated in fake healings still believed Jones could heal. They just thought theirs was faked to keep the ball rolling while Jones saved his energy!

Then, once the knowledge of Jones's great powers was safely implanted in their minds by these healing demonstrations, people were sold pictures of Jones to keep them safe while driving, to protect them from fire, and to heal them. Birdie Marable, a former member, tells of having the task of carrying these through the congregation on trays, "like a cigarette girl." Oh yes, healing oil and prayer cloths were sold—even through the mail!

Revelations and Resurrections

But that was not at all the end of the miraculous. Jones's spies obtained personal information from the homes of people who were to be especially impressed. In a meeting Jones would point out those people and get "revelations" about them. Also, Temple members who worked in the post office, in hospitals, and in other places where information was available were to supply it upon request. One woman tells the story of how a Temple member visited her the day before a meeting to which she was invited. Jones had a "revelation" about her at the meeting. The pattern was repeated several times before she discovered just how the Temple member was gaining access to private information. In the short hallway to her bathroom was a tiny alcove in which lay a small packet containing addresses and personal correspondence. By watching one day, she discovered that her visitor, who just happened to need to use the bathroom each time, picked up the packet on the way in and replaced it on the way back. This particular "talent" had other uses as well. Jones kept some people in bondage by his claim that he knew everything they said and did.

To make the miraculous complete, however, something else had to be added: the power over life and death. Former members tell the story of the night Jones singled out a particular woman and said, "You lied to me. Drop dead." And she fell to the floor. In the back a man rose and said, "I don't believe that. It's a fake." And Jones said, "You drop dead." And he fell to the floor. There were others as well. But before the evening was over, Jones, pretending to argue with himself and allowing the audience to persuade him, brought them "back to life." Each, in turn, knelt before him, thanking him abjectly for his grace.[21]

Somehow or other, rumors got around that Jones had resurrected more than forty people from the dead. More control: He can kill you if you misbehave, and he can resurrect you if you die.

Organization of the Kingdom: Jones and the Planning Commission

Former members and associates are not altogether consistent when they tell about what the organizational situation was within the Temple. Quite obviously, Jones didn't lay all his cards openly on the table, so there was some confusion in the minds of all, but more so for those who were not close to him.

Outwardly, the basic organization under him was a planning commission or council of a hundred or so, and then the congregation. But things weren't that simple. Above the planning commission, there was apparently an inner circle of twenty or so—mostly white women, according to one source.[22] Also, it seems there was a small elite group of secretaries and counselors (more appropriately called spies) within the planning commission. Jones also spoke of his "angels," who, he said, would take care of defectors. Exactly who they were, he didn't say (though members were sure they knew), and what they would do he didn't say (though the threat was obviously death).

Sandy Parks: "They told me something would happen to one of my daughters, and the fear of that held me."

Obviously, there was not much in the way of cooperative government. Jones did not let his right hand know what the left was doing. Further, in all likelihood there was some degree of fluidity in the elite groups and some were taken into confidence on one matter and others on another. The organization revolved around Jones himself, and he used whatever organizational tools he felt would most effectively take him to his goal.

WHAT MADE PEOPLE STAY?

An obvious question is: In the midst of all this centralization on Jones—his total dominance of the group—why did people stay? Did they stay because they wanted to? Did they believe in what he was doing? Or, were they afraid to leave?

Of course, everyone had to be held by something. Over the long run only a few would stay completely voluntarily. There were those who really did believe. But there is overwhelming evidence that many stayed for other reasons, such as fear and guilt. However, they stayed. There had to be ways for Jones to be assured of each person's loyalty. This was particularly true of those who had leadership roles or who had access to sensitive matters. Jones had his ways and he used them. Four major means of control were practiced.

1) The Devil in Mr. Jones: Sexual Bondage

We don't know much about Jones's sexual behavior in the early period of the movement in Indianapolis, except that he was guilty of adultery in those days. That was also the time he was beginning to call sex "dirty." In 1960, he was definitely mimicking Father Divine in such matters as separating some husbands and wives and discouraging sexual relations between them.

By the time of the move to Redwood Valley, Jones seemed to be obsessed with sex—so much so that some people who left the Temple (Birdie Marable, for one) said he had a sex demon. At

279

first it was more apparent in the planning commission than anywhere else. But people who attended adult education classes taught by Jones in the Ukiah schools in the mid-1960s said that sex talk was common there. Among Jones's closest aides, however, it was more than talk. The women in the upper echelons were frequently called upon for sex with Jones. As a matter of fact, in that elite group it was well-known that you had to have sexual relations with Jones in order to be trusted.

Nor was it only the women who were called upon. The "pastor" of the Peoples Temple did not practice sexual discrimination. He also had sex with men—and had them photographed engaging in perversions with him.

Then began those days when Temple meetings for the entire membership (only people with validated I.D. cards were allowed in) consisted of three and four hours of sexual raving by Jones—with a little Marxism thrown in. Jones told husbands and wives they should not have sex and that he was the only man fit to engage in sex with women. All other men were latent homosexuals. As a matter of fact, all women were latent lesbians. Jones said he was constantly exhausted from the sexual demands of the women of the congregation, for whom he was the only acceptable partner. Shades of Father Divine!

In Temple meetings people were sometimes forced to strip naked before everyone. Jones also ordered sexual perversion before the people. Sandy Parks told us she had seen it but would not talk about it because it was so horrible. Others were less reticent. Accounts of oral sex and public copulation have been reported by people who were present.

Certain women were singled out by Jones as his favorite partners, but no one was exempt. Thus, many men and women in the Temple were gripped by guilt over illicit sexual activities.

Fear of being exposed with respect to sexual activities with Jones was one of his primary tools of securing loyalty, loyalty through threat. That fear coupled with guilt over the sin itself kept many from leaving long after they had become disenchanted with the movement. The sexual bondage grew as the years went by, and so did the leader's sexual misbehavior. At the end in Guyana, so we are told, he openly kept a mistress— and she died in his bed.

What Jones's wife, Marceline, thought about his promiscuity at this point is not known, but she was with the Temple until the end.

2) Interrogation, Catharsis, and Punishment

Way back in the Indianapolis days, Jones established an interrogation committee.[23] That was after he had visited Father Divine's operation in Philadelphia and had seen how advantageous and effective it was for a committee of fervent loyalists to deal with opposition to the leader. Former members tell us one could say anything against Jesus, God, or the Bible; but any criticism of Jones was blasphemy. People brought before that committee would be grilled for hours about plots and sins against Jones. This committee, however, was only the beginning of things of this nature.

The concept grew. In Redwood Valley, Jones instituted "catharsis" sessions for the planning commission. Catharsis is supposed to mean a cleansing or purification through purging. But there was nothing cleansing about these catharsis sessions. Putrification would be a better description! People unleased their pent-up emotions all right, but the poor victim was devastated, and all were dirtied by the filth pouring out of their mouths.

You see, Jones's catharsis sessions started with the selection of someone Jones wished to humiliate. That person was put "on the floor" in front of the entire group. Then everyone, including and especially family members, was to find something to blast him with. "Isn't it true you wish to sleep with so and so's wife? Describe your fantasies concerning her. When did you last sleep with a woman? Describe the circumstances. Isn't it true you like men more than women?" And on and on for five and six hours at a stretch. The person *had* to "confess." At least three things were accomplished by this sort of thing. First, the person was indeed humiliated. Further, the "confession" provided something additional to hold over the victim's head. Finally, people's hostile feelings toward Jones (not allowed) could be poured out against someone else. No one dared relax in those meetings. All were watched. Anyone who failed to participate or who acted distracted might be next in

281

line for the same treatment. A special session might even be called in the middle of the night. You never knew. Planning commission members often got no more than two to five hours of sleep, and there were times when these marathon meetings went on all night. One former member said, "Jones made people zombies by these catharsis sessions." After five or six hours of such treatment, the victims were grateful just to be released. Their battered psyches and senses would not soon recover, and they would long remember the pointed fingers, contorted faces, and angry voices of their close associates as they shouted all kinds of accusations. Wounded, ashamed, and afraid, the "purified" ones had no place to hide and no one to turn to—except "Father," who now "trusted and loved" them more than ever.

Then there was "discipline." In the early years in Redwood Valley, children were spanked before the congregation if their grades were not up to snuff, and older members of the Temple were reprimanded in public for their failures. But things gradually changed as Jones began to make more use of discipline and punishment to control people. Particularly irritating to him was the matter of desertion of Temple members and those who associated with deserters.

A young woman, whose family later left the Temple, told us how she came to be beaten publicly. A young teen-ager at the time, she made the mistake of hugging a close friend in the parking lot. Innocent? Not if that close friend had just left the Temple! Jones immediately called her to the front of the auditorium and had her struck seventy-five times with a large board. Her father, who along with the rest of the family had to watch helplessly, put it bluntly, "Her butt looked like hamburger."

Soon, it was not just children and youth who were being beaten. Birdie Marable, who was a member when the beatings were at their worst, thinks the beating of older people started in 1972. She recalls having seen two old ladies in their sixties and seventies beaten. Jones apparently took particular delight in degrading people. Ross Case told us the story of a dignified old lady called Mother LeTourneau. Jones called her before the congregation and made her repeat obscenities and swear words over and over.

The beatings got worse. In the San Francisco Temple, Jones

had a boxing ring set up. The offender, usually a child at first, but later adults as well, was led to the front and his or her sins were enumerated. Then a larger, stronger person, sometimes more than one, came into the ring and pummeled the hapless victim to a pulp. Oh yes, after every punishment the victim had to struggle to the platform and speak into a microphone held out by Jones, "Thank you, Father."

Later, punishment for children became more vicious. They were led from the auditorium and given electrical shocks with a cattle prod. All the way back they screamed, "Thank you, Father," over and over again. Jones had established punishment as a means of control by fear. Sandy Parks, who left in 1974, said, "I would have left sooner but for fear." Jones threatened death and he threatened beatings, and it was known that some defectors had died.

3) Money

Jones was always intent upon the accumulation of wealth. Offerings were not enough, nor was the biblical tithe. Jones wanted everything. Even in Indianapolis he had shown an ability to acquire the property of his disciples. Esther Mueller gave Jones $25,000 and the profits from the sale of her furniture. Later, she told her son, "He just wanted money and power. His hands were too good for work."[24]

The old people who were packed like sardines into nursing homes and given minimal care in the early days were also victims of Jones's callous schemes for collecting money. Their Social Security checks were turned over to him, and they were carefully milked of any cash or property they might possess.

As a matter of fact, nursing homes became a standard source of income for Jones. In Redwood Valley, one of the first things he did was open a nursing home. He jammed people in and used every imaginable means at his disposal to cut corners. Taking care of old people was a very profitable business. In Guyana, when Congressman Ryan and the news crew entered Jonestown, they found a twenty by forty foot barracks in which there were sixty or more bunks—double and triple tiered. And guess who was housed there? Old women, all very frightened and all claiming in sad, timid voices that they were very happy.[25] Undoubtedly, their Social Security checks were among the hundreds found at Jonestown.

From the nursing homes (and the dormitories he had seen in Father Divine's "heaven") Jones undoubtedly got the idea for what he called "communes." At first it was planning commission members whom he pressured to live communally, but his communal scheme soon spread far beyond them. He sent family members to separate dwelling places—the husband to one place, the wife to another, and the children somewhere else. Communal living, of course, accomplished more than one goal: It produced more money by lowering housing costs, and it gave Jones infinitely greater control over people's lives. Commented former follower Lena McCown on what it was like to live in those quarters, "People who lived in places run by the Temple were housed up like cattle."

Quite evidently, there was a consistent pattern that his demands on people followed. Former member Wanda Johnson says that she, her husband, and her sons were so enraptured by Jones's idea of Marxist Christianity that they gave the Temple their house, land, savings, and cars. Then, they were moved into separate overcrowded dormitories and given two dollars a week each for a living allowance.[26] Her report squares with those given by many other people.

Al and Jeannie Mills told us their experience was slightly different. Back in the early 1970s when they were members, they were told they were to be sent on a mission to help poor people. That meant, of course, they should sign over their property to the Temple so it could be cared for. They did, but the missionary assignment never materialized. Nevertheless, the Temple took over the properties, and the Mills were afraid to complain. They were not placed in dormitories but in a house where they were given thirteen Temple children to care for—with minimal funds.

These special living situations made it possible for the Temple to take the entire paychecks of those placed there. How profitable was it? Jackie Swinney, a former member who was one of those who moved from Indianapolis to California back in 1965, says, "We (the Temple) were clearing $8,000 to $10,000 per month when we were just in Redwood Valley."[27] Swinney's job? Commune finances.

Property was commonly extorted from members, leaving them with nothing. They were routinely ordered to sign blank deeds. Large numbers of real estate transfers involving Peoples Temple were recorded in both Mendocino County and San Francisco in recent years. Many pieces of property were sold by Temple officials for members who had moved to Guyana. Millions of dollars worth of property were involved—all of it going into the coffers of Jim Jones's cult.

Nothing owned personally by Temple members was exempt from being taken. If you didn't have money to give, you were pressured to give your "extra" clothes, your rings, your watches, anything you didn't "need." Then special stores were set up to sell the items collected. The pressure was also on to make pies, cakes, and cookies, which were sold on the street, or perhaps to work at one of the Temple's regular fund-raising pancake breakfasts.

Life insurance? Who needs it? After all, Jim Jones will take care of you. Birdie Marable told us that old people in particular were pressured to cash in their insurance policies and sign the proceeds over to the Temple. Injured in an automobile accident? Let the Temple attorneys sue. They will handle things for you, and there will be more money for the cause.

There were offerings, of course. Jones would take multiple offerings and lie about what had come in during the first ones so people would feel obligated to give more. And what about those trays of Jones's pictures carried around during the meetings? The sales from that enterprise brought in hundreds of dollars each week. Keeping people poor keeps people easier to control: Jones knew it and practiced it. People couldn't afford to leave. Their homes, savings, cars, and whatever else could be turned to cash was gone. To leave meant to start all over, and not just anyone can do that, particularly older people. In the name of a Marxist society, Jones had stripped his members financially and controlled them in part by holding their whole economical existence in his hands.

Jones did, of course, raise money from sources besides the members themselves. The youth groups were organized for street begging. Each youth was given a collection can and placed on a busy street corner. Each was given a quota—larger if you were under discipline.

Oh yes, we must not forget Jones's mass mailing techniques. Mailing lists were obtained, the appeal methods of other "faith healers" studied, and monthly mailings prepared. A former member once in charge of this activity told us that the minimum received was $300 a day, with an $800 average.

Every aspect of Temple life was designed to turn a profit, part of Jones's control-through-economics program. He collected millions of dollars and actually used only a small proportion of it. Members were often reduced to begging for subsistence, but foreign bank accounts grew. Following the Jonestown massacre, accounts containing tens of millions of dollars were discovered, but some money may never be located.

4) Control by Blackmail

Over and over again, former members reported that Jones made everybody write out and sign confessions to some crime or other. If they hadn't committed any, they were told to make up something. These were put in the Temple files along with the signed blank deeds and other false and libelous material. Tim Stoen, former assistant district attorney in Ukiah and once one of Jones's top aides, tells the story of how Jones talked him into signing a statement that his new-born son had been sired by Jones, by agreement of Stoen and his wife. Jones said signing the statement was an act of faith, the sort of thing absolutely necessary: "We can't build God's kingdom on earth unless we trust one another."[28] Stoen's wife later left the Temple alone, convinced the thing was evil. Stoen himself went to Guyana, but returned to the United States in 1977. At that point, he, too, left the Temple, but typical of Jones's practice of requiring a hold on anyone who left Guyana, the child had been kept in Jonestown. When the Stoens tried to get the child back, Jones released a copy of the document signed by Stoen and claimed the child was his. The issue was still unresolved when six-year-old John Stoen died in the Jonestown massacre.

A similar ploy was obviously behind the reaction of the Temple in May, 1978, to an attempt by a group of concerned relatives to get government help. A Temple news release calls the concerned relatives ". . . a politically motivated conspiracy using former members of Peoples Temple who have worked within our organization as agent provocateurs." Continuing the attack, the release further alleged,

The statement of "Concerned Relatives" was signed by a sordid crew of individuals who, among other things, have tried blackmail; have embezzled from Peoples Temple while infiltrating it; have been engaged in the manufacture of ammunition and have advocated ridiculous mad schemes of violence in order to achieve revolutionary "ends" in the classic manner of agent provocateurs. Included in the group are people who have used and trafficked in drugs; some who have molested children, including their own, such as Maria Katsaris [who] just publicly exposed her father; who have operated credit card rackets, forged checks, stolen money from the treasury in the amount of thousands of dollars; who have actually abused and treated black youngsters as house slaves; who have engaged in welfare fraud and who have exhibited in series of [sic] highly unstable personal patterns in their private lives, e.g., sadism. [29]

All this was given as if they actually had evidence that the concerned relatives had committed the crimes listed. Of course they did: from forced, false, presigned confessions! And Maria Katsaris, who supposedly denounced her father for molesting her as a child, was apparently Jones's mistress at the very end. Indeed, after the massacre, she was found dead in his bed.[30]

As we see, Jones had certainly built a fantastic complex of means to keep people in bondage. If nothing else worked, the threat of death was there. Many who wanted to leave the Temple heard him say, "If you do, my angels [translate: assassins] will take care of you." There were enough unexplained deaths to make that threat serious.

JONES'S PUBLIC IMAGE

There is much more that could be said about the evil methods by which Jones maintained control inside the Temple. But we have seen enough. Let us examine his public image and the means by which he maintained it.

George Hunter, editor of the *Ukiah Daily Journal,* reflecting upon his years of experience with Jones, said: "He was an extremely persuasive man who had a different faith and a different message for everyone he dealt with. He was able to hook in with each one in an individual way."[31] That was probably one of the most seductive qualities about Jim Jones. He could make people believe that what they believed and thought was what he believed and thought. He didn't mind any kind of deception in such matters as long as it suited his purpose.

Public Temple Services

The fare served to the public differed considerably from what went on behind locked doors in the sessions to which only card-carrying members were admitted. Public services might start with an African-style dance group or a Temple singing group. Then there would be singing—no, not Christian hymns, but almost always "We Shall Overcome" and often "Born Free" and other songs borrowed from the civil rights movement. They would inevitably progress, though, to repetitious, hypnotic, singing of songs to and about Jones, such as:

> I know he's God, Almighty God,
> I know he's God, Almighty God,
> I know he's God,
> I know he's God,
> I know he's God Almighty, God Almighty, God Almighty, God.

Finally, Jones would come out, perhaps to introduce a guest such as Angela Davis or some other well-known figure in the world of social causes. Next, he would be up, perhaps to answer questions in a low-key manner, and then he would progress to some spectacular "healing," which would climax the meeting.

Such "services" attracted many people to the Temple who had no interest in God, but who loved the apparent warmth and fellowship of the gathering, or who were looking for a place to engage in social work, or who were desperately hoping for a cure for some real or imagined illness. The wily Jones always adjusted the emphasis in any given service to the kind of audience he had.

Causes and Demonstrations

Because Jim Jones's supreme goal was a socialist utopia with him as its leader, he obviously desired to recruit people who also envisioned such a utopia. To aid his recruiting program, he needed a reputation for supporting popular social causes in order to project the proper image. Of course, on the inside of his movement, he already had a start toward that image in his nursing homes, "communes," "homes for wayward children," and free meals programs. But Jim Jones was never content to be away from the political limelight outside of the movement. Besides, he was power-hungry.

Election Campaigns

Throughout his career, Jones demonstrated a knack for getting appointed to public office. He proved that back in Indianapolis. In the early 1970s, however, he embarked upon a systematic program to give the appearance of wholehearted support of the popular causes. He devised a means of doing this without spending much money or committing his financial resources extensively. This new program did involve, however, extensive use of the huge people resources he had built up.

Masses of Peoples Temple members were strategically sent out to demonstrate for causes, appear at political rallies, and work to elect government officials. In San Francisco, as early as 1971, the emphasis and man-power was put behind mostly liberal causes and Democratic political candidates. But as late as 1972 in Redwood Valley, support shifted to Republican Party candidates and Richard Nixon. The effect was significant. People on the outside became alarmed at the power Peoples Temple possessed politically. To quiet such fears, Jones assured the public in 1973: "If some are threatened by the size of Pastor Jones's congregation, such fears should be allayed, because our large number is never used as a political force."[32] Obviously, these soothing words of Jones were quite unfounded.

A wide variety of people and causes did benefit from the use of that large number as a political force: Indian activist Dennis Banks, several candidates for political office in the San Francisco area, and various civil rights causes. So prominent did Jones and the Temple become at election time that State Assemblyman Willie Brown is reported to have said: "In a tight race like the ones that George (Moscone) or Freitas or Hongisto had, forget it without Jones."[33] But Jones did not care so much about the candidates and the issues. He was an opportunist, so he threw his weight behind those he thought were winners and could therefore help him most.

Everything was grandstanded. In February, 1974, the Peoples Temple issued a news release saying that Jones, in a private letter to Randolph Hearst, had offered to surrender himself and four officials of the church to the Symbionese Liberation Army in exchange for Patty Hearst and the safe conduct out of this country for SLA members. Naturally, the contents of the "private letter" were released. Only in that way could the desired publicity be obtained.

Jones typically gave few interviews, and the Peoples Temple generally was shy about admitting unannounced visitors. "Make an appointment" was the standard announcement to those who wished to visit. The reasons were always very plausible: "We do not wish to have our people disturbed by surprise visits." But one-time adherents say that visitors were deceived. Tours for politicians were deliberately staged. Church members were the actors, dressing in specified clothing and acting out roles. Guests were then shown, for example, supposedly rehabilitated heroin addicts. Even services and meetings were staged for visitors, who would be the butt of Jones's humor after they left.

One of Jones's most brazen efforts was his program to get the permanent loyalty of the press. After the 1972 fiasco in which a reporter, Lester Kinsolving, had actually dared to print material critical of Jones and the Temple, Jones sought ways to ingratiate himself to the press at large. The summer, 1973, issue of *The Temple Reporter* carries a long article on freedom of the press. That same issue contains an excerpt from the *Congressional Record* for June, 1973, in which a congressman records with great fanfare the fact that Peoples Temple had given $4,400 to twelve newspapers, a newsmagazine, and a television station. As you can see, Jones had made a little money go a long way. He had spread $4,400 among twelve recipients. That was not very much for each one. But for *years* afterwards, Jones's publications boasted of these "significant" grants.

His big opportunity with the press came, however, when four Fresno *Bee* newsmen were jailed for refusing to reveal confidential sources. Peoples Temple publications reeked with rhetoric over the injustice of it all. Jones bussed 600 members to demonstrate on one occasion, and when the hearing time came, he had 1,000 on hand. Of course, it was noticed and commended. There is a picture in one issue of *Peoples Forum* showing Washington columnist Jack Anderson "extending his thanks and appreciation to Reverend Jones." Newspapers everywhere picked up the story, and there were letters of commendation, including one from San Francisco Mayor Moscone. And speaking of those letters . . .

Letter-Writing Campaigns

Peoples Temple had a permanent letter-writing committee of ten to twenty persons. Their job was to see to it that on issues of concern to Jones there was a constant stream of letters from his followers to the appropriate public figures. When Jones spoke at a political rally, the politicians involved received a flood of letters. When Jones was on a radio or television station, hundreds of letters rolled in. Every issue imaginable was cause for a letter-writing campaign.

In addition to the letters sent by the committee itself (often in the names of nonexistent people), Temple members were expected to write—sometimes as many as one hundred letters in a week. They were given instructions containing basic content, wrote their letters, and brought them in for clearance. These letters were then mailed from various cities in assorted states.

Though the letters were expected to have an impact on the issues involved, one of the major purposes behind the letter-writing program was to get letters back from prominent people—particularly letters in praise and support of Jones and the Temple. When such letters did arrive, they were carefully filed. Jones's various publications proudly and monotonously quoted from letters he had somehow obtained from government officials and others. When times of crisis came, special news releases, composed largely of selections from such letters came out of the Temple. Of course, the *Peoples Forum* regularly printed quotes from these letters.

The Peoples Forum

In 1976, Jones began publishing his own newspaper. *Peoples Forum* advertised a circulation of 600,000, but it is doubtful the press run was ever one-tenth that many. In the pages of the paper there were always feature articles on various liberal and radical causes. Pictures of Jones in the company of prominent political figures always appeared. Often there was a religious column, clearly designed to cut down orthodox Christianity and cast doubt upon the Scriptures.

From *Peoples Forum* you would gather that "the cause" was human dignity for all people. Jones kept people scared there was imminent danger of the loss of all vestiges of freedom in our society. He predicted an impending fascist takeover and anti-black race war, and at the end in Guyana he was trying to convince his disciples it had already happened in the United States. Disillusioned former followers of Jones said, however, that the cause was just a front—a means of capturing people to be brought under his control. One young women who had been in Peoples Temple with her parents from 1969 to 1976 told us, "Jones made you believe there was a cause, but there was none."

Jones and the Disciples of Christ

From the time he first managed affiliation with the Disciples of Christ denomination, Jones played up the connection. The sign outside each of his "church" buildings always read "Peoples Temple Christian Church (Disciples of Christ)." Those same words appeared on publications, news releases, and the stationery of the Temple. Whenever it was convenient, he ran news articles about the denomination in the *Peoples Forum*.

There were times when it was very convenient to refer to the Disciples. Jones was not careful about accuracy. In a 1977 fund-appeal mailing for the Guyana project, he referred to "the Regional Bishop of the nationwide Disciples of Christ denomination (to which Peoples Temple belongs), Reverend Gerald McHarg." The Disciples, of course, do not have bishops and do not believe in them. The same leaflet says, "Peoples Temple is part of the nationwide Disciples of Christ denomination. The denomination requires strict and meticulous accounting of its member church's finances." Nothing could be further from the truth! The Disciples believe firmly in congregational autonomy, and there definitely is no such requirement, nor any means to accomplish it. Further, at that very moment, Jones was hiding money in banks all over the world and making no accounting to anyone. In this matter, as in so many others, he was simply using the unaware Disciples of Christ in his program of massive deception.

Naturally, Jones kept in his files appropriate quotes from Disciples officials to throw in on appropriate occasions. The January, 1977, edition of *Peoples Forum* quotes Dr. Karl Irvin, Jr., president of the Northern California-Nevada Region of Christian Churches as saying:

> The ministry of Jesus Christ, which is the action of God in the midst of the world, has been more clearly revealed by the Peoples Temple than any other member church of the Disciples of Christ denomination. That's an awesome thing and I just praise God for you.

Obviously, Dr. Irvin did not know the facts when he wrote that statement.

The Disciples were not the only ones in Christendom who liked what they saw in Peoples Temple. In 1977, after suspicion had fallen upon Jones and Peoples Temple, they put out, "in response to a sensational smear campaign," a collection of quotes, including the following:

> Rev. Jones has contributed spiritually to the San Francisco Council of Churches Board of Directors since becoming a member.— Donneter E. Lane, Executive Director, San Francisco Council of Churches.

> Peoples Temple offers a tremendous witness to the Gospel of liberation and justice within our community.—Rev. Norman E. Leach, Program Administrator, San Francisco Council of Churches.

REFUTATION OF JIM JONES AND PEOPLES TEMPLE

It is true that he came from a religious background, but what he did and how he thought have no relationship to the views and teachings of any legitimate form of historic Christianity.

We have witnessed a false messiah who used the cloak of religion to cover a confused mind filled with a mixture of pseudo-religion, political ambition, sensual lust, financial dishonesty, and, apparently, even murder. None of this has anything to do with true faith in God.—Billy Graham, *The New York Times*, December 5, 1978.

A Defacto Rebuttal: 20–20 Hindsight

Why bother to write a refutation of Jim Jones and the Peoples Temple? After all, he is dead and his work has wilted. Isn't an attack on them sort of like flogging a dead horse? Now that it's all over, why not just forget about it and go on with life?

The problem is that many people wish to consider the final outcome, the death of more than 900 people, as the result of an aberration, a twisting, which came about at the end of Jim Jones's life. They believe that, basically, he accomplished a lot of good and that many poor and minority people were helped by him and the Temple. Therefore, we should mourn his passing as that of a true servant of God.

There are others, who certainly would not go that far, who recognize Jones and his work as evil, but who say, "How could we have known? Aren't good works a sign of godliness or righteousness? Didn't Christ say, '. . .that they may see your good works and give glory to your Father who is in heaven' [Matt. 5:16]? Wouldn't it be arrogant to go around saying that certain good works are ungodly while others are godly?"

Creed Determines Conduct

We must rid ourselves once and for all of the attitude that what you believe is less important than what you do! It is often expressed in such terms as "life is more important than doctrine." Lately, many belittle insistence on proper doctrine as irrelevant because ". . . the letter killeth but the Spirit giveth life" (2 Cor. 3:6; KJV). The implication in that naive statement is that "life" is something apart from what you believe. We must reject such allegations as patent fallacy.

Christ summarized the Law as "Thou shalt love the Lord thy God with all thy heart, and with all thy soul, and with all thy mind. This is the first and great commandment. And the second is like unto it, Thou shalt love thy neighbor as thyself" (Matt. 22:37–39; KJV). Central to all else is love of God. But to love Him, we must know who God is, for we are obviously not called upon to love and worship a nebulous "higher being." We

294

are to worship Him both in spirit and in truth. As we have indicated elsewhere in this book, the Scriptures point to God as Father, Son, and Holy Spirit—three persons in one undivided nature. That is why the Apostles' Creed, dating back to the earliest days of the Church, dwells upon the God in whom we believe:

> I believe in God the Father Almighty, Maker of heaven and earth, and in Jesus Christ His only Son our Lord, Who was conceived by the Holy Ghost, born of the Virgin Mary, suffered under Pontius Pilate, was crucified, dead and buried. He descended into hell. The third day, He rose again from the dead. He ascended into Heaven and sitteth at the right hand of God the Father Almighty. From thence He shall come to judge the quick and the dead. I believe in the Holy Ghost, the Holy Catholic Church, the communion of saints, the forgiveness of sins, the resurrection of the body and the life everlasting. Amen.

Before the one, holy, catholic, and apostolic Church was divided into East and West (and later into the fragments that exist today), it held seven councils that were recognized as ecumenical by both East and West. Remarkably, *every one* of those councils was called to deal with some heresy that had arisen concerning the nature of God or of the incarnation of the Son. In everyone of them, the delegates, believing they were led by the Holy Spirit, searched the Scriptures to be certain the ultimate decree of the council would reflect that which had always been believed by the Church of Jesus Christ. To these heroes of the faith, what we believe was so important they gave it the highest priority. Their conclusions form the core of the faith of all of believing Christendom today—even that of those who profess to have no creed.

Is what we believe unimportant: On the contrary, what we believe, particularly about God and the Incarnation, is *so* important that I even dare to say the works done by those who hold heretical views on these matters are evil, regardless of the fact that people benefit from them. Consider Jim Jones and the Peoples Temple. In view of what we have learned about his theology, it seems significant that no one we know about who followed him claimed to have done so because they saw the Father, Son, and Holy Spirit worshiped or the Lord loved with heart, soul, mind, and strength. They all followed for the healing, the miracles, or the social programs.

It does not seem superfluous to point out that Jesus said,

> Many will say to Me on that day, Lord, Lord, have we not prophesied in thy name? and in thy name have cast out devils? and in thy name done many wonderful works? And then will I profess unto them, I never knew you depart from me, ye that work iniquity. (Matt. 7:22,23; KJV)

Claims of miracles done in the name of the Lord mean nothing—much less pretended miracles done in the name of the pretender.

But though the falseness of the "miracles" done by Jones is now most discernible because of his exposure, there are other charlatans around pretending to do miracles in the name of the Lord. We must heed the warnings of Jesus. In whom do these miracle-workers profess to believe? Do they respect the Scriptures and the Church? Do they hold to the faith of Christendom as it has been passed down to us through the centuries? These are among the questions the Church must ask and answer. Otherwise we leave our people defenseless before the chicanery of evil men and women looking for personal gain. Yes, the body of Christ has the right, duty, and obligation to investigate thoroughly every claimant and to denounce those found false.

A Religion of Brotherhood

A song Jones expropriated from Father Divine epitomizes the core of his and his Temple's theology:

> Brotherhood is our religion.
> For democracy we stand.
> We love everybody,
> We need every hand.
> It's based on the constitution,
> And certainly God's command.
> These are the rights we adore:
> Liberty, equality, fraternity for all—
> These are the rights we adore.

Brotherhood is *not* the Christian religion. There is brother-hood (yea, and sisterhood) *in* Christianity, but it is based on our new birth by the Holy Spirit into the body of Christ. Love of God comes first and, through it, love to "those of the household of faith," and finally to those outside. Now, there is a nice cozy ring to the phrase, "Brotherhood is our religion." But what does it really mean? It means there is no god but man. That is atheism, not Christianity. Whatever religion Jim Jones may have espoused was in no way, shape, or form Christianity. It was its antithesis. Therefore, we would have to say that at best, Peoples Temple had a religion of atheistic humanism.

But underneath, things were even worse in Peoples Temple. Jim Jones claimed to be the reincarnation of every historical figure whose name, he thought, would impress his congregation. He capped this off with the claim to be God Almighty, a most exalted claim, worthy of his father, the devil (Isa. 14:13,14). This arrogant claim was not unknown outside the Temple; indeed, we interviewed several people who were aware of it.

Discipline and the Disciples

But in spite of all this, Peoples Temple not only belonged to the Disciples of Christ, it was cited approvingly by them in that denomination for its works. As a matter of fact, all indications are that the Disciples were proud of being allied to Peoples Temple all the way up to the Guyana massacre. Later, they were told in a letter from their General Minister and President,

> . . . we should not attempt to minimize our relationship to both the minister and the congregation involved in this horror, but should take the opportunity to explain in public who we really are and what we stand for in terms of diversity and freedom within unity.[34]

What do the Disciples of Christ stand for? In a basic presentation, James C. Suggs says,

> Beyond the fundamental affirmation that "Jesus is the Christ, the Son of the living God, and . . . (my) personal Savior," doctrinal diversity is normal in the Christian Church. Thanks to the liberty

we cherish, Disciples can be found at the extremes of both the conservative right and the liberal left of Christian thought.[35]

Since their inception, the Disciples have held that all that is necessary or appropriate to define the faith is that simple statement about Christ. Indeed, they argue that it is going further that divides Christendom. Well, they are wrong. The ancient creeds of Christendom divide all right: They divide the Church from non-Christendom! They divide the Church from the likes of Jim Jones. The early Church discovered that certain definitions had to be made to exclude heresy. Dare we diminish these definitions? In the case of Peoples Temple, apparently not even the Disciples' inadequate simple formula was applied.

Perhaps the problem is that the Disciples are among the most vulnerable of groups in Christendom to being ripped off by a man like Jones. A picture of the difficulties they face is given in their news release following the massacre:

> The Disciples' *Design for the Christian Church,* the document under which the church operates, describes procedures only for congregations withdrawing at their own initiative. . . .

> The Disciples of Christ have no procedure for judging a congregation unfit and removing it from the denominational yearbook . . . .

> Under our church polity, it is neither possible, nor has it been desirable, to conduct investigations of the activities or ministries of local congregations. We have stood firmly for a variety of styles and approaches to Christian mission and ministry . . . .

In the case at hand *we have seen the devastation that can result when the Church is unable or unwilling to discipline.* All of us have been splattered with filth as a result of the connection of the Peoples Temple to Christendom. It is time, therefore, to say to the Disciples: "Stop, Disciples of Christ denomination! That's enough! Come back to the ancient ecumenical statements of faith, the basic creeds of Christendom. Swallow your pride and admit you were wrong in denying their necessity. Claim the creeds, institute ecclesiastical discipline, and let's get on with the building up of the one, holy, catholic, and apostolic Church."

The Issues for Christendom

But our cry must reach far beyond the walls of the Disciples of Christ denomination. It needs to penetrate to the heart of all modern Christendom. The Jonestown tragedy cannot be blamed simply on the Disciples. Part of the blame must be shouldered by all of us in confessing Christendom, either for not blowing the whistle on Jones or for tolerating the condition in Christendom that allows such perversions to hide under the banner of the Church.

There are several vital points at issue. One is *doctrinal*. All the information necessary to condemn Jim Jones as a heretic has been easily accessible for years. Unfortunately, the Disciples of Christ, and indeed Christendom at large, are dotted with heretics who are unchecked and undisciplined.

Another issue is *morality*. Jones was openly immoral, publicly and unrepentantly claiming to be the father of an illegitimate child. Those who benignly separate "life" from "doctrine" could at least have called his morality into account. Perhaps there is generally a closer watch on morals than there was in this case, but Christendom at large is experiencing an increasing laxness in such matters. The prophets of old, the Scriptures, the ancient Church, the Reformers, all cried out against both the practice of sin and indifference to it.

But the major problem, the greatest issue of all, is *the state of the Church,* of Christendom. One thing this particular tragedy reveals is the terrible condition to which Christ's body has fallen in these days. This odious and wicked cult did not rise up in a corner! People knew about it—including church officials. The stench was apparent way back in Indianapolis. An evil aroma hung like a cloud around Jim Jones's head when the Disciples accepted the Temple as a member congregation in 1960. The odor was extremely strong when they approved his ordination in 1964—so much so that even the very liberal John Harms, who served on the examination committee, was uneasy. It didn't make any difference, though, for Jones was quickly approved and ordained "because he seemed to be groping for a more rational approach to religion, and because he was an effective leader of the poor and oppressed."[36]

After Jones moved to Redwood Valley, however, things

grew even worse. Far more was publicly known there about the devious and ascending spirit of Mr. Jones. He was now more open in proclaiming his deity. Songs of praise were sung to him. He proclaimed himself the reincarnation of every great historical figure who fit with his schemes of self-exaltation. At least one American Baptist pastor knew that Jones was reveling in being called Jesus Christ by his followers.[37]

In San Francisco, the Reverend Hannibal Williams, president of the San Francisco Interdenominational Alliance, knew things were amiss. He tried to stop Jones's takeover of other churches' congregations. He only succeeded in getting threats on his life. Later, Pastor Williams was to say: "There's all this talk about how he was doing a lot of good and then he became berserk in the jungle. You know that's not so."[38]

Here was this arrogant, unrepentant, sexual pervert, proclaiming himself to be God, calling Jesus a bastard and Mary a whore;[39] and local Christendom sat idly by. Nay, through the Disciples of Christ, we were wallowing in the reflected glory of his "good works."

What Could Have Been Done?

There are many, and not just in the Church either, who are wondering today about possible answers to that question. Cults and heresies don't usually produce such a visible tragedy as Jonestown, so we generally are able to shrug them off and go our way. This one, however, shocked the sensibilities of our temporally oriented and death-fearing society. So we wonder what could have been done.

One necessity is a return to the common faith—orthodoxy. But many in Christendom, both conservative and liberal, do not like that idea one little bit. We discovered this dislike when the first edition of *Mindbenders* came under attack for its heavy emphasis on the orthodox faith. Most of those who opposed that emphasis call themselves orthodox.

In conservative Protestantism in particular there are many people who think that each person's having an open Bible is enough to maintain orthodoxy—that if we all believe the Bible, we will automatically come up with the same faith. In the same vein, many liberals believe each person should determine for himself or herself the appropriate core of belief and in turn respect and accept the beliefs of others as valid for them.

These views, and their several variations, make it impossible for modern Christendom either to hold a common faith or to have a faith in common with those who have gone before us. The cold hard fact is that the conservative and liberal extremes in this case are *not* opposite at all. Both espouse the same identical cause. They are merely different manifestations of rational humanism. They implicitly deny the possibility of the Church being a God-governed society, taught and guided by the Holy Spirit either now or in the past.

There *is* a basic set of doctrines on which all Christendom should, indeed *must,* come to agreement. It is represented in part in the doctrinal statements of the seven ecumenical councils held before the Church divided into East and West.[40] In addition, there is the Apostles' Creed, the content of which Christendom has accepted from the beginning. Further, an exploration into the history of doctrines will show there are indeed many other points of ecumenical doctrine, such as justification by faith, the new birth, inspiration of the Scriptures, Baptism, and the Lord's Supper. If we agree on these foundations of the faith and jointly reject those who contradict them, we will find ourselves with a platform from which we can exclude heretics such as Jim Jones.

We may not prevent Jones's kind from existing, but we could sound the warning loud and clear. Hundreds, yes thousands, could be spared the tragedy of associating with them.

Secondly, we must return to discipline and care for each other. We must begin to actively consider *all* Christendom as the one, holy, catholic, and apostolic Church. That means caring enough to attack apostasy wherever we find it in our ranks, and there is plenty of it there. It means denominations and independents, and whatever else we call ourselves, must be willing to watchfully enter into each other's affairs—to actively accept the role of being our brother's keeper.

Here is what it means: Christian leaders will need to be alert and cooperative enough for one to say to another, "so-and-so who is aligned with you is teaching such-and-such heresy. Here is my evidence. If you need help in correcting him, I will be available. If you must excommunicate him, we will stand behind your discipline."

Such cooperation is not too much to expect in our day, is it? All that is required is Christian leadership so committed to the Lord, His gospel, and His Church that money, position, and security are no threat. All that is required is a wholehearted and unreserved commitment to the reunion of the one, holy, catholic, and apostolic Church.

Too much to ask in these days of ultimate fragmentation and diversity of doctrine? No. One Jonestown massacre should be enough to get our attention.

In the fourth century, all looked lost for the Church. For decades, Arian heretics held almost all the major bishoprics. Their influence was far more broad and united than that of the heretics and cultists that flourish in our day. It seemed that this destructive heresy had once and for all diluted the doctrine of Christ. But no, faithful leaders were willing to die, to be exiled, to fight. Many suffered great indignities and great loss, and some did die. But they followed the Lord, they stuck to the gospel, and the Church was rescued from ruin.

May it be so even today.

A BRIEF PROFILE OF
JIM JONES AND THE PEOPLES TEMPLE

1. History
   —From the beginning, Jones held a non-Christian stance describing himself in college as a Unitarian.
   —By 1960, the Peoples Temple was listed as a member congregation by the Disciples of Christ, and in 1964 Jones was ordained to the ministry by that denomination.
   —Father Divine heavily influenced Jones.
   —Jones built a name for himself through political and social involvement wherever he went.
   —Jones's activities began in Indianapolis in the early 1950s

and took him, in the mid-sixties, to Ukiah, California, then on to San Francisco, and finally to Guyana.

—Death came for Jones and over 900 followers in a murder-suicide massacre in late 1978 in Guyana.

2. Beliefs
   —A spattering of unitarianism, ethical humanism, reincarnation, and Marxism.
   —Jones denied the deity of Christ, the Trinity, the authority and inspiration of the Holy Scriptures.
   —Jones claimed to be the reincarnated Jesus Christ, and the Almighty God.
   —The overriding goal of Jones's religion was to establish a utopian socialist society over which he would reign and be worshiped.

3. Method of Operation
   —Jones established public credibility for himself and his work through political and community involvement.
   —Tactics to gain and convince devotees included false healings, revelations, and miracles.
   —Jones himself ran the Peoples Temple operations, supported by his hand-picked planning commission.
   —Members were kept in tow by Jones through sexual bondage, humiliation, physical beatings, taking away members' money and homes, blackmail and threat of death upon desertion.
   —The official publication of the Temple was begun in 1976 and called *The Peoples Forum,* which often ran photos of Jones with public figures.
   —Officially, Jones and the Peoples Temple operated under the Disciples of Christ denomination.

4. Refutation
   —The sole object of worship in the Church is never another human being, but always the Triune God.
   —In the Christian faith, *both* doctrine and life-style are vital. True faith produces true conduct. The Church does not recognize as Christian those who appear to have one without the other. Jones, by the way, had neither.

—The bottom line of historic Christianity is never the brotherhood of man, but always Jesus Christ as Lord over His people.

PEOPLES TEMPLE—FOOTNOTES

1. Kenneth E. Lemons, quoted in the *Ukiah Daily Journal,* November 27, 1978.
2. *The Tennessean,* Nashville, December 3, 1978.
3. I'm not absolutely certain this was the Temple's first name. It is said to be so in Marshall Kilduff and Ron Jones, *The Suicide Cult* (New York: Bantam Books, 1978), p. 160. An Indianapolis source, however, says it was called the Christian Assembly Church. No matter, it was to be Peoples Temple.
4. For more details, see Sara Harris, *Father Divine, Holy Husband,* (New York: Doubleday and Company, 1953).
5. Santa Rosa *Press-Democrat,* December 3, 1978.
6. San Francisco *Sun-Reporter,* November 10, 1977.
7. As reported by correspondent Wallace Turner, in *The New York Times,* November 23, 1978.
8. *Santa Barbara News-Press,* December 17, 1978.
9. Sara Harris, *Father Divine: Holy Husband,* pp. 319–320.
10. *Peoples Forum,* April, 1976.
11. *Peoples Forum,* October, 1976.
12. *Peoples Forum,* December, 1976.
13. *Peoples Forum,* November, 1977.
14. *Peoples Forum,* August, 1977.
15. *Time,* December 4, 1978.
16. Lacy Fosburg, *The New York Times,* November 23, 1978.
17. *Redding Record Searchlight,* November 25, 1978.
18. Tim Reiterman, *San Francisco Examiner,* November 21, 1978.
19. Associated Press article by Sid Moody and Victor Graham, printed in *Santa Barbara News Press,* November 26, 1978.
20. Marshall Kilduff and Ron Javers, *The Suicide Cult* (New York: Bantam Books, 1978). Also confirmed by information given to us by Ross Case, the McCowns, and the Parks family.
21. Story related to us by Birdie Marable, former Peoples Temple member.
22. Marshall Kilduff and Ron Javers, *The Suicide Cult,* pp. 60–61.
23. Described by Thomas Dickson, former associate minister in Peoples Temple, to Eunice MeLayea, *San Francisco Chronicle,* November 22, 1978.
24. Associated Press article by Sid Moody and Victoria Graham, printed in the *Santa Barbara News-Press,* November 26, 1978.
25. Marshall Kilduff and Ron Javers, *The Suicide Cult,* p. 158.

26. Article by Les Gedbetter, *The New York Times,* November 21, 1978.
27. *San Francisco Chronicle,* August 19, 1977.
28. *San Francisco Sunday Examiner and Chronicle,* February 26, 1978.
29. From *Open Statement by Members of Peoples Temple in Jonestown, Guyana, South America,* released May 10, 1978, pp. 1–2.
30. *San Francisco Examiner,* November 21, 1978.
31. Reported by Lacy Fosburg in *The New York Times,* November 23, 1978.
32. *The Temple Reporter,* Summer, 1973, p. 6.
33. Reported by Marshall Kilduff and Phil Tracy, "Inside Peoples Temple," *New West,* August 1, 1977, p. 30.
34. Letter from Kenneth L. Teegarden, General Minister and President, Disciples of Christ, November 28, 1978.
35. James C. Suggs, *This We Believe* (St. Louis: The Bethany Press), p. 5.
36. *Christianity Today,* December 15, 1978, p. 39.
37. *Ibid.*
38. Jeanie Kasindorf, "The Seduction Temple of San Francisco," *New West,* December 18, 1978, p. 53.
39. Interview with former Temple members George and Lena McCown.
40. These councils are: I Nicea, A.D. 325; I Constantinople, A.D. 381; Ephesus, A.D. 431; Chalcedon, A.D. 451; II Constantinople, A.D. 553; III Constantinople, A.D. 680; II Nicea, A.D. 737.

PART IV

The Church
Takes on the Cults

The Church
Takes on the Cults

It would be impossible to conclude a book of this nature without a specific word concerning what the Church of Jesus Christ is all about. We have exposed the counterfeit cults; let us consider briefly how the community of God's people function before Him, among themselves, and in the world.

To do this, we will consider four incredibly important areas which make the true Church absolutely unique—especially when compared with the error of the modern cults:

1. *We are ruled by an absolutely unmatched Savior-King* who died for His people, is Lord today, and who will rule ultimately all of creation forever.
2. *We have an unparalleled offering* from God supplied by Him, repeated to Him, and actively involving all His people.
3. *We are a Spirit-led Priesthood,* bringing salt and light to even the alienated world.
4. *We experience God's will,* empowered by His Spirit, delivered from "dead works," motivated by His grace and leadership. Through our union with the glorified human nature of Jesus Christ, we have come into communion with God.

In saying all this, there is something which must be honestly admitted before we consider these truths. That is, much of what we call the Church has failed—often miserably—in carrying out its role before God, itself, and the world. Though it is still loved and even protected by the Lord, it has moved an embarrassingly great distance away from its original foundations. And while there are countless splendid exceptions to these allegations, they do for the most part stand true in wide circles of Christendom—Protestant, Roman Catholic, and the Eastern Church. No doubt this apostasy has been a contributing factor to the spiraling sizes of these modern cults with their faulty saviors and practices.

Protestant leaders herald the Reformation and the great truths it reestablished. Most all churchmen would agree that justification by faith in Christ and a renewed emphasis on the Holy Scriptures were gained. Thank God they were. But there were other areas still left to recover.

We have never fully regained worship. Authority in the Church has not been reclaimed. And whatever happened to our oneness as a body? A sense of community is still missing.

So as we the Church of the Living God take on the cults, let us remember there is much work the Spirit of God seeks to do in our own midst. It is happening in places; there are outposts of His kingdom thriving before Him. But as we challenge the cults we are simultaneously issuing a call to our own people, saying, "Where we're off base, it's time to ask God for strength to sweep out our own houses, lest we fall to the same criterion by which we judge!"

I. AN UNMATCHED SAVIOR

The unique thing about Christianity is *Christ!* There has never been another in all of heaven and earth to rival Him. The Scriptures say:

> He is the image of the invisible God, the first-born of all creation; for in Him all things were created, in heaven and on earth, visible and invisible . . . all things were created through him and for him (Col. 1:15,16).

Which of the seven false systems we have considered would boast a founder even remotely comparable to the Lord Jesus Christ? To those cults who insist He is their founder we say: "Split from that false prophet who is constantly ripping you off and come back home to the rule of the Lord Jesus in *His* Church."

Among the lovely creeds of the historic faith, one of the oldest, *The Apostles Creed,* "says it all" of the Son of God:

Conceived by the Holy Ghost, born of the Virgin Mary, suffered under Pontius Pilate, was crucified, died, and buried; He descended into hell; the third day He arose from the dead; He ascended into heaven and sitteth on the right hand of God the Father Almighty; from thence He shall come to judge the quick and the dead . . .

In this creed are three cardinal truths about our Savior, Jesus Christ, which are unmatched in all of history.

First, He died for His people. While men like Sun Myung Moon and Maharaj Ji get rich quick off their people, Jesus Christ died for His. While Witness Lee instructs his followers to crush their own souls by dying on their own crosses, Jesus Christ has *taken our place in death* Himself. King David saw this prophetically down through the centuries when he said of His Shepherd, "He restoreth my soul."

There is a song currently being sung in the churches which goes:

> He paid a debt He did not owe,
> I owed a debt I could not pay,
> I needed someone to wash my sins away,
> And now I sing a brand new song
> "Amazing Grace" the whole day long
> Christ Jesus paid the debt that I could never pay.

When Jesus Christ died on the cross, and later presented His sacrifice to the Father on the mercy seat of heaven, the debt was paid for the sins of all men. And in coming to Him as our Lord, we receive the forgiveness of our sins. Apart from Jesus Christ, there is no freedom from sin.

Secondly, Jesus Christ is alive and well at the right hand of God—that place of righteous authority in all of heaven and earth. The resurrection of Jesus Christ is unique, because those who began all the other religions of men are still in their graves. And numerous other "masters" and "lords" are rushing headlong into death to join them. The people of God have a Savior who allows them to yell "Victory" at death. The sting and fear of death is gone because Jesus Christ rose and in doing so whipped the enemy of death.

311

Thirdly, the Lordship of Jesus Christ will one day expand from His current headship over the Church in heaven and on earth, to reach out to rule the entire universe. He's coming back! And His kingdom shall have no end. That, my friend, is something to remember.

When I was young, sometimes all the boys in the neighborhood would form two opposing sides for a war. Often, two "leaders" were appointed who would choose the sides. It was important to get on the side which would win—and this could usually be determined in advance by evaluating the personnel on both sides.

After all the dust settles here on earth, I want to be on the side which wins. You may like a certain guru, the private opinion of a so-called teacher, or the new truth of a current prophet. But as for me, I'll take the Lordship of Christ as He is now ruling in the historic Church. After all, He's delivered on everything else He promised. And He promised us He'd be there in the end, too.

II. AN UNPARALLELED OFFERING

A concept of the Church which has suffered great loss is its function as a priesthood before both God and the world.

Israel, as a nation of priests, brought burnt offerings and peace offerings. Those burnt offerings qualified them to be in the Lord's presence. The peace offering of thanksgiving defined the essence of worship. The worshipers came to the Lord to give Him thanks and praise. One can hardly read the Psalms and other portions of Scripture involving worship without realizing that thanksgiving and praise were at the heart of Israel's worship:

Let us come into his presence with thanksgiving . . .
O come, let us worship and bow down,
let us kneel before the Lord, our Maker. (Ps. 95:2,6)!

Ascribe to the Lord the glory due his name;
bring an offering, and come into his courts!
Worship the Lord in holy array . . . (Ps. 96:8,9).

And when David had finished offering the burnt offerings and the
peace offerings, he blessed the people in the name of the Lord . . .
"Oh give thanks to the Lord. . . .
bring an offering, and come before him!
Worship the Lord in holy array. . . ."
Then all the people said, "Amen," and praised the Lord.
(1 Chron. 16:2,8,29,36).

Once in the Lord's presence, Israel praised the Lord for who
He was and thanked Him for all He had done for them.

A Kingdom of Priests

Israel was a kingdom of priests under the Old Covenant.
The Church, over which Jesus Christ is High Priest, is a kingdom of priests under the New Covenant. The same concepts
and terminology are used for both. The apostle Peter described the New Covenant priesthood as "holy" and "royal."

And like living stones be yourselves built into a spiritual house, to
be a holy priesthood, to offer spiritual sacrifices acceptable to God
through Jesus Christ (1 Pet. 2:5).

But you are a chosen race, a royal priesthood, a holy nation, God's
own people, that you may declare the wonderful deeds of him who
called you out of darkness into his marvelous light (1 Pet. 2:9).

That is a description of worship. A priesthood must have
acceptable sacrifices to offer God. The priesthood cannot enter
the Lord's presence for worship empty-handed. Because of
the Lord Jesus Christ, the Church comes to the very presence
of God Himself.

But you have come to Mount Zion and to the city of the living God,
the heavenly Jerusalem, and to innumerable angels in festal
gathering, and to the assembly of the first-born who are enrolled in
heaven, and to a judge who is God of all, and to the spirits of just
men made perfect, and to Jesus, the mediator of a new covenant,
and to the sprinkled blood, that speaks more graciously than the
blood of Abel (Heb. 12:22-24).

Remembrance, Plus

The New Covenant priesthood, the Church, has essentially one offering to bring to God, and connected to this one are two others.

If we are to understand the meaning of our one offering, we must grasp the concept of *anamnesis*. This is the Greek word used by the Lord when He established the Eucharist (also known as the Communion and the Lord's Supper). *Anamnesis* has usually been translated into English as "remembrance."

> For I received from the Lord what I also delivered to you, that the Lord Jesus on the night when he was betrayed took bread, and when he had given thanks, he broke it, and said,
> "This is my body which is for you. Do this in remembrance [*Anamnesis*] of me."
> In the same way also the cup, after supper, saying,
> "This cup is the new covenant in my blood. Do this, as often as you drink it, in remembrance [*anamnesis*] of me."
> For as often as you eat this bread and drink the cup, you proclaim the Lord's death until he comes (1 Cor. 11:23-26).

The word *anamnesis* cannot be adequately translated by any one English word, and "remembrance" falls short of the mark. *Remembrance* denotes the calling to mind of an historical event. When this happens our minds fix on something that is already done and finished. No present or future reality is involved—only the past. In the Greek language the basic word for "remembrance" was *mneme*.

It happens that the word *anamnesis* was philosophically distinguished from *mneme* by carrying with it the idea of a re-living, a re-presenting, and an active participation in a past event.

The Lord's Supper involves an active participation of the priesthood in the Lord's incarnation, life, death, burial, resurrection, ascension, reign, and the hope of His return to establish His kingdom in its fullest sense. *Anamnesis*, then, involves the past, the present, and the future. At that table, we are there, reaping all the benefits of all that He has done, is doing, and will do!

Anamnesis not only means an active participation in a present *re-living* of those events. A *re-presenting* is also involved. Remember we said the Church, the New Covenant priesthood, could not come to the Lord's presence for worship without an offering. *This offering is the Lord Jesus Christ Himself.* He is the only offering which will provide access to the Holy of Holies for the Church. More precisely, the offering is His body and blood. He said ". . . this is my body . . ." and ". . . this is my blood . . ." (Mark 14:22,24).

The Eucharist

So often through the centuries, puzzled people have asked, "How can the bread and the wine of the Eucharist be the body and the blood of the Lord?"

Philosophical speculations on this question are harmful and useless. The Lord does not ask His Church to understand *how*, but to *believe*. We can safely leave the *how* to Him. The ancient Fathers of the Church exclaimed in relation to the Lord's Supper, "O, Great Mystery!"

In the Eucharist, the Church re-presents the Lord's body and blood to the Father. That re-presentation allows her access into the Holy of Holies for worship. Let's be careful about something. By "re-present" we do not mean "re-sacrifice." That would be crucifying the Son of God afresh. The Lord was crucified only once, at a specific point in time. By "re-present" we mean re-presenting that once-for-all sacrifice of Jesus Christ to the Father. It is His sacrifice of Himself which qualifies us for worship.

Present Yourselves

> I appeal to you therefore, brethren, by the mercies of God, to present your bodies as a living and holy sacrifice, holy and acceptable to God, which is your spiritual worship (Rom. 12:1).

The people of the Church are to present themselves as a holy sacrifice, acceptable to God. We can only be acceptable in connection with the body and blood of the Lord Jesus Christ.

When the worshipers under the Old Covenant offered their sacrifices, they placed their hands on the heads of the animals offered. Thus, they identified themselves with their offerings. Both the offering and the offerer were accepted by God. So we are acceptable because we are identified with the Lord Jesus in His offering.

The apostle Paul points out that some wonderful things result from this type of worship. Our minds are transformed so we can know the will of God. Spiritual gifts in all their variety begin to function in the Church. Love and good deeds begin to show themselves.

Praise

Having re-presented the body and blood of the Lord, and having presented themselves, the people of the Church are ready to make a third kind of offering. The essence of New Covenant worship is the same as that of the Old, namely, thanksgiving and praise. (Why has the Church used the name "Eucharist" more than any other to designate the Lord's Supper? Because that word means, literally, "thanksgiving." Thanksgiving lies at the very heart of Christian worship.)

The priesthood meets at the throne of God to thank and praise Him for who He is and for what He has done for them!

> Through Him then let us continually offer up a sacrifice of praise to God, that is, the fruit of lips that acknowledge his name (Heb. 13:15).

So it is that when the priesthood is at the Lord's Table, they are meeting with God around His throne and praising Him by giving thanks.

What is praise? Some people seem to think it means going around saying, "Praise the Lord." That is fine, but sometimes it gets to be a habit, an empty cliché.

Our praise and thanksgiving should center on the specifics of who He is and what He has done for us. That will make us a grateful people. A Church which does that can be a congregation of people thankful about all areas of their lives. *Worship is saying "thank you."*

In stark contrast to the praise and thanksgiving of God's people, consider Romans, chapter one. It repeatedly speaks of those unbelievers God gave over to all the evil, degrading things they could think up to do. Why would He do that? *Because they wouldn't honor Him or give Him thanks.*

Here is a fact to be remembered: human beings really hurt themselves when they don't honor and thank God. The Church, the priesthood of God, is supposed to remedy this condition by being a thankful people. We must never fall into an attitude that we have earned everything we have. Our very existence depends upon the grace and goodness of God! Mankind could not exist, for example, if the Lord did not *actively* provide air to breathe.

We must reject the godless view of deism which teaches that God created the universe, then left it to run on its own. Ideas like that cause people to ignore God and live thanklessly. The priesthood must learn to look for, and thank God for, the benefits in creation. Such thanksgivings, added to praise for the benefits given through the incarnation of the Son, make for a very thankful people!

What of the cults we have examined? They do not worship the true and living God, and they are not a thankful people! They think they have earned what they have because they have supposedly kept their rules and regulations which were laid down by self-appointed leaders. Think about it.

When an employee receives his weekly paycheck, he recognizes he has earned the money. If he says "thank you" to his employer, it is merely a gesture of courtesy. A cult may praise its god, but the people feel they have piled up points and earned the reward. The praise is just a gesture. Having no gratitude for the unmerited grace and goodness of God, they have no real thanks to give.

Eating the Sacrifice

Under the Old Covenant, the worshipers ate the peace offering of thanksgiving.

> And the flesh of the sacrifice of his peace offerings for thanksgiving shall be eaten on the day of his offering; he shall not leave any of it until the morning (Lev. 7:15).

Notice: the sacrifice wasn't completed till it was eaten! Today, when the priesthood of the New Covenant worships, we too eat the sacrifice. Why is the Eucharist called "the Supper" and "Communion?" Because eating is involved: we are dining with the great King, eating the sacrifice which He has provided.

Our Lord Jesus said:

> Truly, truly, I say to you, unless you eat the flesh of the Son of man and drink his blood, you have no life in you; he who eats my flesh and drinks my blood has eternal life, and I will raise him up at the last day. For my flesh is food indeed, and my blood is drink indeed. He who eats my flesh and drinks my blood abides in me, and I in him (John 6:53-56).

The mainstream, historic Church has consistently held He was speaking here of the Eucharist. The bread and wine of the Communion is the body and blood of the Lord. And God said to partake of it.

Some cults do eat a sacrifice. Hare Krishna devotees think they are eating Krishna everytime they eat sacrificed food. But this sacrifice is not like the Eucharist. It has nothing to do with a sacrifice provided by God. It is all a sacrifice provided by the worshipers. There is nothing of the Christian Eucharist (other than perhaps a memory) in Hare Krishna sacrifice.

Some cults with a Christian background occasionally observe the Table of the Church. But they see the bread and wine only as symbols, and their observance is just an empty, lifeless ceremony. No, these cults cannot have communion and fellowship with the Lord. They are empty and their religion is dead. Jude's description fits them well:

> . . . waterless clouds, carried along by winds; fruitless trees in late autumn, twice dead, uprooted; wild waves of the sea, casting up the foam of their own shame . . . (Jude 12,13).

III. A SPIRIT-LED MINISTRY

The Church is a priesthood, offering true sacrifices to God at His throne. In that worship He feeds His people, and their lives are changed. They go from worship prepared to live as His people in the world. When our worship is real, filled with praise and thanksgiving around the Table, we're prepared to act and minister like His people.

What's our role? *Mediation.* We are to mediate, to act as God's representatives on behalf of the world.

In His "Sermon on the Mount," the Lord told His people,

You are the salt of the earth; but if salt has lost its taste, how shall its saltness be restored? It is no longer good for anything, except to be thrown out and trodden under foot by men. You are the light of the world. A city set on a hill cannot be hid. Nor do men light a lamp and put it under a bushel, but on a stand, and it gives light to all in the house. Let your light shine before men, that they may see your good works and give glory to your Father who is in Heaven (Matt. 5:13-16).

That describes our responsibility to mediate between God and the world. Two words give the key: "salt" and "light." We could make many applications from those two words. The Lord made just two: How salt gives taste and how light gives sight.

Salt

How are we to be salt to the world? Our moral behavior is to stand out, for one thing. Deep down inside, everybody knows what good moral behavior is. Such basic things as love, kindness, patience, self-control, justice, and integrity come to mind. God has these qualities. He makes them available to His priesthood to be shown to the world.

Don't take this wrong. Godliness is not self-righteousness. That's counterfeit. Because of God's grace, the priesthood is able to show the genuine article. As the Apostle Peter said,

His divine power has granted to us all things that pertain to life and godliness . . . (2 Pet. 1:3).

and

Maintain good conduct among the Gentiles . . . (1 Pet. 2:12).

When the priesthood accepts the grace of God to live godly lives, the world around becomes a better place to live.

It makes sense. Most people like salt on their food because it tastes better. Without salt, food tastes flat. In the same way, a world without the salt of godly lives is flat, unsavory, and hard to take. Such a society becomes obnoxious and repulsive.

When such qualities as love, justice, and integrity begin to disappear from a neighborhood, people begin to get on each other's nerves. They lose interest in the people next door and become apathetic. Isolationism sets in. Coldness becomes the order of the day. Soon the neighborhood turns into a society of strangers. Self interest and ego trips take over.

The love of money grows, and people get ripped off by excessive profit-taking. The little people, especially widows and orphans, get hurt the most. Government leaders get into shady deals and immoral relationships. In short, it turns into a dog-eat-dog society. Is it any wonder such a society becomes nauseating even to itself?

And what about God? How does He look at this state of affairs? He is especially angry with those who in their arrogance and ungodliness put down the truth. Why? Because He cares.

A situation like this calls for mediation . . . for salt. On the one hand we have a sick society; on the other, a holy God. But if God in His holiness is angry, He also cares. So He has provided a mediator to be *in* the mess, but not *of* it.

That mediator is His priesthood, the Church. At its head is the Lord Jesus Christ, the great High Priest. Joining Him are the many members of His body, His people. Only they can salt society and turn away God's anger. When the priesthood is salty in society (showing love, kindness, and integrity), aliens are far more apt to be reconciled to God through His Son.

You see, God's love and care are not vague. His love has "arms" that touch the world; they're called the Church. His kindness is to be experienced by the world through the Church. Thus, it is something tangible which leads people to repentance. Those people who reject God's kindness by remaining stubborn and hard-hearted are storing up anger against themselves.

The world needs to see godliness in action. That's why the Lord warned His priesthood against losing its salt. There's no way the world can be salted by a priesthood that has lost its salt. Unfortunately, the Church today isn't very salty. We've been too much captured by the spirit of the age. Instead of salting the world, we're knuckling under and adopting its philosophy and behavior. We've blended in, and righteousness and justice have gone by the boards.

Real live love and justice have been replaced by Madison Avenue evangelistic techniques and ineffective, impersonal social programs. In a saltless Church, spiritual con artists abound—in the pulpit, over the radio, and on TV—getting rich and/or powerful off the people of God. Relationships among Christians have become cosmetic, lacking commitment and loyalty. The world mocks.

A Church in that condition is tasteless even to itself. It certainly cannot mediate between God and the world. There is a warning in the history of Israel. That nation was called to be a kingdom of priests, but they failed to such an extent that,

> The name of God is blasphemed among the Gentiles because of you. (Rom. 2:24).

Israel lost its salt and the Church is close to doing the same.

Can the cults we have examined mediate salt to the world? Can they show godliness to the world? No, they cannot! Many, such as Sun Myung Moon and Guru Maharaj Ji, are wealthy. They have become rich off their religion and are getting richer. Maharaj Ji has a teenaged craze for expensive cars. Moon is living with his second or third wife, having divorced at least one. Does that show moral stability and godliness? They have the mentality of the rich, and are therefore not poor in spirit.

Maharishi Mahesh Yogi travels around making converts, then leaves them to make it on their own. That certainly doesn't square with the instructions the Lord gave to Peter when He told him to care for the sheep. It's more like a wolf which enters a sheepfold in order to get himself some lamb chops!

The Way, International, while professing to be Christian, denies the Trinity. The Local Church redefines it. Since godliness comes from the Father, Son, and Holy Spirit, how can they salt society with the very qualities of the God they deny?

Light

The Church is to be not only *salt,* but *light* to the world. Without light, people do not know where to go. It's better by far to have light than darkness when we enter a room filled with tables, chairs, and other objects which can make shin bones sore.

And the light of the world is also good to have around. Light is another aspect of God's nature. ". . . God is light, and in him is no darkness at all" (1 John 1:5).

We were designed to function in God's light. Outside of it we don't do too well. What has happened is that the world has stepped outside of God's light and is trying to make it in the dark. God loves the world and wants it to see by His light. He has named the Church as the go-between for this light. Jesus said, "You are the light of the world."

We said love was tangible, and so is light. Light, of course, can be seen. The question is, *how* will God's light be seen? "Let your light so shine before men, that they may see your good works and give glory to your Father who is in heaven" (Matt. 5:16). Of course! The priesthood, the church, mediates God's light to the world, through good works.

How?

Evangelism? That *alone* will never show God's light to the world. Spirit-led evangelism is a good work, but there's lots more to be done. When the Lord talked about light, He said the Church should be easy to see:

> A city set on a hill cannot be hid. Nor do men light a lamp and put it under a bushel, but on a stand; and it gives light to all who are in the house (Matt. 5:14-15).

The priesthood must be something visible to the people who live around it. The Church doesn't withdraw, and it doesn't just come out to say "come and join us." The Church must be visible to our neighbors, the people who live the closest to us geographically. Neighbors will see a lot of light in a short time if we care. A Church whose members care is a visible, locatable priesthood.

But how do the people of a church decide what good works

322

to do? There are lots of good things you could do, far more than any of us could manage. How do we decide?

IV. WE EXPERIENCE GOD'S WILL

We find out what God wants. We worship Him right in His presence, and we learn from Him what we should do. *The Holy Spirit tells us.*

> For we are his workmanship, created in Christ Jesus for good works, which God prepared beforehand, that we should walk in them (Eph. 2:10).

The priesthood isn't supposed to just arbitrarily choose the good works it will do. We do the ones God has shown us to do.

> For God is at work in you, both to will and to work for his good pleasure (Phil. 2:13).

Dead Works

You've heard the term "dead works?" Those are the ones done on the basis of habit rather than by active leadership of the Lord in the Church. When we do what He tells us, we benefit. As a family, the priesthood had better take care of its own. If we don't, how can we mediate light to the world?

Suppose a family let it be known that it believed in God, but didn't take care of its own members. Its old people were left to die alone. Its children ran wild in the streets. There's no way the neighbors would agree they *really* believed in God.

It's the same way with the Church family. A Church that doesn't take care of its own people will be mocked by the world. On the other hand, a priesthood that does take care of its own gives light to the world.

Also, the world gets direct benefits from a priesthood which listens to the Holy Spirit. The neighbors receive good deeds. No church is fully hearing from God if it *just* takes care of its own. Hearing, it will reach out to the people who live around it. Remember, the second half of God's royal law is summed up in the statement, ". . . You shall love your neighbor as yourself . . ." (James 2:8).

That's right! Love reaches out to neighbors. Active love is a characteristic of a healthy priesthood. That action causes people to glorify our Father who is in heaven.

Think back through the cults we have examined. Do they demonstrate the good works that come from the Father in heaven? They can't, because they don't have access to Him to find out what He wants done! The works they do are the results of the various arbitrary rules and regulations they've set up. These works are dead. Look them over to see if you can find any works that cause people to glorify our heavenly Father.

Jesus Christ and Good Deeds

During His stay on earth, our Lord was salt and light. He listened to His Father. His moral behavior could not be challenged. He once asked a hostile crowd, "Which of you convicts Me of sin?" (John 8:46).

At another time, when He was brought to trial and questioned about what He taught, He said:

> . . . I have spoken openly to the world; I have always taught in synagogues and in the temple, where all Jews come together; I have said nothing secretly. Why do you ask me? Ask those who have heard me, what I said to them; they know what I said (John 18:20-21).

The Lord had no doctrines to hide. He spoke openly to the world. The truth doesn't need to slip around in the dark for fear it will be known. Every cult we've examined has things reserved only for the elite to know.

The apostle Peter said the Lord went about doing good. Everybody could see that He believed what He said. The apostle John said the Lord did so many works he didn't think the world could hold all the books that could be written about them. He salted and lightened the world.

So, the priesthood is to be salt and light to the world. Salt and light equal godliness and good works. The world will see and feel the impact, and become more palatable both to God and to itself.

The apostle Peter was present and heard the Lord give those instructions about salt and light. Later he wrote a letter on the subject. He emphasized the *action* of salt and light.

> But you are a chosen race, a royal priesthood, a holy nation, God's own people, *that you may declare the wonderful deeds of Him who called you out of darkness into his marvelous light* [italics mine]. Once you were no people but now you are God's people; once you had not received mercy but now you have received mercy (1 Pet. 2:9-10).

> Maintain good conduct among the Gentiles, so that in case they speak against you as wrongdoers, they may see your good deeds and glorify God on the day of visitation (1 Pet. 2:12).

Motivated by Grace

What causes the priesthood to behave rightly? Why does the Church act a certain way towards the world? The answer is important, because it helps save the priesthood from falling into legalism.

The behavior of legalists is motivated by the keeping of rules and regulations. Their rules tell them what to do and what not to do. Such behavior becomes very impersonal, because rules are impersonal. Soon all the spirit disappears and the conduct becomes self-righteous and stiff. A person under such a burden easily becomes nasty and mean.

The nation of Israel is the all-time classic example of why behavior motivated by rules and regulations won't work. Their 1,500-year history between the giving of the Ten Commandments at Sinai and the coming of Jesus Christ in the flesh clinches the argument against legalism. Don't get me wrong. I'm not saying something is wrong with the Ten Commandments. The problem lies in the fact that human nature is unable to fulfill the moral demands of those commandments. All through its history, Israel demonstrated that weakness.

The New Covenant priesthood, the Church, is told to profit from Israel's history. We are *not* to take rules as our motivation for behavior. Hypocrisy would be the result. We have seen that in the case of the seven cults. It is possible to modify behavior by controlling the mind, but inside sits the same miserable, sinful human nature which fails to make it with God.

What, then, is the proper motivation for the priesthood's behavior? The Church is an eschatological community of aliens and strangers living in a mostly unbelieving world. (The word "eschatological" refers to ultimate destiny.)

We are a people with a future in which our present is all wrapped up. The priests of this community called "the Church" have been delivered from the power of sin. We have been sprinkled with the Lord's blood and have been born again to a living hope through His resurrection from the dead. We are aliens and strangers because our inheritance is in another world. That other world is the eternal kingdom of God, represented here for now by the Church. Our hope is set on that world, and that hope will be realized at the return of Jesus Christ from heaven.

That's important background for learning proper motivation for "good behavior." *We do what is right because we have been brought into a living relationship with God the Father through God the Son.* We can have an obedience which is personal and living because we have a Holy Father. He loves us, we love Him, and we listen to what He tells us. If we grasp that, we've got the proper motivation. It's behaving properly because we want the world to see what our Father and Lord are like. That's the only kind of motivation which will cause the world to glorify the Father.

No, the motivation to holy behavior for the Church is not impersonal rules. The Church certainly must recognize and appreciate the validity and ideals contained in the Law of God. But the people of the Church have a living relationship with the Father, Son, and Holy Spirit.

Christian love does not love in order to be loved. Ordinarily, love is conditional—I'll love you if you'll love me. But Christians love the people outside the Church as well as their brothers and sisters. That is what the Lord said! Be a friendly people.

What is a Church? What is the nature of this priestly body, this priesthood? It is *not* a group of unrelated Christians each doing his own thing. The important thing for the members of the Church to see is that they belong together and are interrelated with each other. They're a community of God living in the community of the world. A genuine community living in the midst of a pseudo one. The Church can't mediate unless its people are knit together into an effective unit.

A Serving Leadership

But how are people going to be knit together? It doesn't just automatically happen because there are several Christians around. No, what is needed is a gracious, serving leadership with authority. The people of God in a church cannot hold together without an authority from God that is both over and under them.

> Obey your leaders and submit to them; for they are keeping watch over your souls, as men who will have to give an account. Let them do this joyfully, and not sadly, for that would be of no advantage to you (Heb. 13:17).

> But we beseech you, brethren, to respect those who labor among you and are over you in the Lord and admonish you, and to esteem them very highly in love because of their work (1 Thess. 5:12-13).

You just can't escape the need for leadership with authority. Look at the family. Children need the authority of gracious and loving parents. How else are they going to grow up in peace and stability? Children doing as they please, whenever they please, don't treat each other well. They don't treat outsiders well. They disgrace the family. The same thing is true for the Church.

How It All Adds Up

The Church is a priesthood involved in divine action in the world. Its action is God's action. God established His priesthood in order to serve Him in the world. We have a Savior, and thus have an acceptable offering, a Spirit-led worshiping community, and can know and do God's will through His revealed Scripture and the positive direction of His Holy Spirit.

No, it is not individual priests acting independently. It is a functioning community of priests. This community must be visible to the world. When it functions, it will be seen preaching the gospel, studying the Scripture, and actively providing the minority of mercy. Out of free hearts who serve the Lord gladly come love, joy, and peace.

No cult can provide anything like it!

Bibliography

1. A. C. Bhaktivedanta Swami Prabhupada. *Krishna Consciousness: The Topmost Yoga System.* Los Angeles: ISKCON Books, 1970.
2. A. C. Bhaktivedanta Swami Prabhupada. *The Nectar Of Devotion.* New York: The Bhaktivedanta Book Trust, 1970.
3. Athanasius. *The Orations Against The Arians,* translated in *The Ancient and Modern Library of Theological Literature.* London: Griffith Farran & Co. (No date or editor given.)
4. Baxter, Ernie. "The Multi-Million Dollar Religion Ripoff," *Argosy.* August, 1974.
5. Cameron, Charles, Editor. *Who Is Guru Maharaj Ji?* New York: Bantam, 1973.
6. Campbell, Anthony. *Seven States of Consciousness: A Vision of Possibilities Suggested by the Teachings of Maharishi Yogi.* New York: Harper and Row, 1974.
7. *Christianity in Crisis.* Washington, D.C.: Holy Spirit Association for the Unification of World Christianity, 1973.
8. Davis, Rex and Richardson, James T. *A More Honest and Objective Look at the Children of God,* a paper presented at the Society for the Scientific Study of Religion, annual meeting, Milwaukee, Wisconsin. October, 1975.
9. *Divine Principle.* Washington, D.C.: Holy Spirit Association for the Unification of World Christianity, 1973.
10. Enroth, Ericson, and Peters. *The Jesus People.* Grand Rapids, Mich.: Eerdman's, 1972.
11. Hilary. *The Trinity.* (Edited by Stephen McKenna. *The Fathers Of The Church,* Volume 25.) Washington, D.C.: The Catholic University of America Press, 1954. (Reprinted with corrections, 1968.)
12. Irenaeus. *Adversus Haereses,* IV, xiv, i. Edited by Henry

Bettenson. *The Early Christian Fathers*. London: Oxford University Press, 1956.

13. Justin Martyr. *The First Apology*, ii. Edited by Cyril Richardson. *Early Church Fathers*. New York: Macmillan, 1970.

14. Kelley, Ken. "Blissed out with the Perfect Master," *Ramparts*. July, 1973.

15. Lee, Sang Hun. *Unification Thought*. Washington, D.C.: Holy Spirit Association for the Unification of World Christianity, 1973.

16. Lee. *The Practical Expression of the Church*. Los Angeles: Stream Publishers, 1970.

17. Lee. *The Economy of God*. Los Angeles: Stream Publishers, 1968.

18. Lee. *The All-Inclusive Spirit of Christ*. Los Angeles: Stream Publishers, 1969.

19. Lee. *The Four Major Steps of Christ*. Los Angeles: Stream Publishers, 1969.

20. Lee. *The Knowledge of Life*. Los Angeles: Stream Publishers, 1973.

21. Lee. *How To Meet*. Los Angeles: Stream Publishers, 1970.

22. Lee. *The Parts of Man*. Los Angeles: Stream Publishers, (no date given).

23. Lee. *Christ Versus Religion*. Los Angeles: Stream Publishers, 1971.

24. Lee. *The Vision of God's Building*. Los Angeles: Stream Publishers, 1972.

25. Lee. *The Clear Scriptural Revelation Concerning the Triune God*. Anaheim, Calif.: Living Stream Ministry, (no date given).

26. Lee. *False Accusations Exposed and Refuted in the Light of the Scriptures*. Anaheim, Calif.: Living Stream Ministry, (no date given).

27. Lee. *The Baptism in the Holy Spirit*. Los Angeles: Stream Publishers, 1969.

28. Lefkowitz, Lewis J. a study by the Office of the New York Attorney General, Sept. 10, 1974.

29. Levine, Faye. *The Strange World of the Hare Krishnas*. Greenwich, Conn.: Fawcett, 1974.

30. Maharishi Mahesh Yogi. *The Science of Being and Art of Living*. London: George Allen and Unwin Limited, 1963.

31. Maharishi Mahesh Yogi. *On the Bhagavad-Gita: A New Translation and Commentary.* Chap. 1-6. Baltimore: Penguin Books, 1967.

32. McWilliams, Peter. *The TM Program : A Basic Handbook.* Greenwich, Conn.: Fawcett Books, 1976.

33. Schaff, Philip and Wace, Henry. Editors. *A Select Library Of Nicene And Post-Nicene Fathers Of The Christian Church,* Volumes IV and XIV. Reprinted by Wm. B. Eerdman's Publishing Co., Grand Rapids, Mich. (Photolithoprinted by Cushing-Malloy, Inc., Ann Arbor, Mich.), 1971 and 1974.

34. Schaff, Philip. *Creeds Of Christendom,* Volume III. New York: Harper & Brothers, Franklin Square, 1877.

35. *Time Magazine.* "Children of Doom." Feb. 18, 1974.

36. Wierwille, Victor Paul. *The Bible Tells Me So.* New Knoxville, Ohio: American Christian Press, 1971.

37. Wierwille, Victor Paul. *Jesus Christ is Not God.* New Knoxville, Ohio: American Christian Press, 1971.

38. Wierwille, Victor Paul. *The New Dynamic Church.* New Knoxville, Ohio: American Christian Press, 1971.

39. Wierwille, Victor Paul. *Power for Abundant Living.* New Knoxville, Ohio: American Christian Press, 1971.

40. Wierwille, Victor Paul. *Receiving The Holy Spirit Today.* New Knoxville, Ohio: American Christian Press, 1972.